Praise for
Griftopia

"A relentlessly disturbing, penetrating exploration of the root causes of the trauma that upended economic security in millions of American homes . . . a polemic, a full-scale indictment of Wall Street and Washington . . . Taibbi has written a necessary and engaging corrective to the noxious idea that the tragedy of recent years was an inevitable byproduct of the market system."

—*The New York Times Book Review*

"Taibbi chronicles the corruption of the political process with indignation and dark humor. The takeaway? Be angry, but blame the right culprits."

—*Time*

"A major book."

—*The New York Observer*

"Matt Taibbi is, by some margin, the best polemical journalist in America . . . Taibbi's scorching takedown has likely deprived Goldman's partners of hundreds of millions of dollars in net worth."

—*Bookforum*

"Taibbi builds an account of bailout America around a broad indictment of the way the political class and the investor class intersect and sometimes collude. . . . An illuminating account of . . . behind-the-scenes negotiations."

—*The Nation*

"[*Griftopia*] could still cement Taibbi's stature as one of Wall Street's most vocal populist critics. Last year, shortly after the article came out, Goldman observed that vampire squids are 'very small and harmless to humans.' If the firm thought that would be the end of it, the arrival of *Griftopia* shows it's time to think again." —*Barron's*

"After the financial catastrophes that nearly brought this country to its knees in 2008, the American [public] deserved some clarity, an explanation that could be understood. It still does. With *Griftopia*, [Taibbi sifts] through every popped bubble and unraveled Ponzi scheme to find more complex tales of thievery." —*The Onion* A.V. Club

"Few targets, regardless of their political persuasion, escape Taibbi's poisoned darts." —*Bloomberg Businessweek*

"*Griftopia* will educate, inform and entertain people who follow the news obsessively and those who only check in from time to time. It's a most impressive effort." —Seattlepi.com

"Taibbi eviscerates Wall Street for what he considers frauds perpetrated on the American people over the last ten years. Delving into complicated financial history and lingo, Taibbi deftly lays the subject bare, rendering heretofore-dense subject matter simple without being simplistic. . . . An important and worthy read." —*Publishers Weekly*

GRIFTOPIA

GRIFTOPIA

*A Story of
Bankers, Politicians,
and the Most
Audacious Power
Grab in American
History*

MATT TAIBBI

SPIEGEL & GRAU TRADE PAPERBACKS
New York • 2011

2011 Spiegel & Grau Trade Paperback Edition

Published in the United States by Spiegel & Grau, an imprint of The Random
House Publishing Group, a division of Random House, Inc., New York.

SPIEGEL & GRAU and Design is a registered trademark of Random House, Inc.

Originally published in hardcover and in slightly different form in the United States
by Spiegel & Grau, an imprint of The Random House Publishing Group, a division
of Random House Inc., in 2010.

Library of Congress Cataloging-in-Publication Data
Taibbi, Matt.
Griftopia / Matt Taibbi.
p. cm.
ISBN 978-0-385-52996-9
eBook ISBN 978-0-385-52997-6
1. Political corruption—United States. 2. Deception—Political aspects—
United States. 3. Despotism—United States. 4. United States—Politics
and government—2009– 5. United States—Politics and
government—2001–2009. I. Title.
JK2249.T35 2010
973.932—dc22
2010015067

Printed in the United States of America

www.spiegelandgrau.com

2 4 6 8 9 7 5 3

Book design by Susan Turner

To my wife, Jeanne

CONTENTS

GRIFTOPIA

I

The Grifter Archipelago; or, Why the Tea Party Doesn't Matter

"MR. CHAIRMAN, DELEGATES, and fellow citizens . . ."

The roar of the crowd is deafening. Arms akimbo as the crowd pushes and shoves in violent excitement, I manage to scribble in my notebook: *Place going . . . absolutely apeshit!*

It's September 3, 2008. I'm at the Xcel Center in St. Paul, Minnesota, listening to the acceptance speech by the new Republican vice-presidential nominee, Sarah Palin. The speech is the emotional climax of the entire 2008 presidential campaign, a campaign marked by bouts of rage and incoherent tribalism on both sides of the aisle. After eighteen long months covering this dreary business, the whole campaign appears in my mind's eye as one long, protracted scratch-fight over Internet-fueled nonsense.

Like most reporters, I've had to expend all the energy I have just keeping track of who compared whom to Bob Dole, whose minister got caught griping about America on tape, who sent a picture of whom in African ceremonial garb to Matt Drudge . . . and because of this I've made it all the way to this historic Palin speech tonight not having the faintest idea that within two weeks from this evening, the American economy will implode in the worst financial disaster since the Great Depression.

Like most Americans, I don't know a damn thing about high finance. The rumblings of financial doom have been sounding for months now—the first half of 2008 had already seen the death of Bear Stearns, one of America's top five investment banks, and a second, Lehman Brothers, had lost 73 percent of its value in the first six months of the year and was less than two weeks away from a bankruptcy that would trigger the worldwide crisis. Within the same two-week time frame, a third top-five investment bank, Merrill Lynch, would sink to the bottom alongside Lehman Brothers thanks to a hole blown in its side by years of reckless gambling debts; Merrill would be swallowed up in a shady state-aided backroom shotgun wedding to Bank of America that would never become anything like a major issue in this presidential race. The root cause of all these disasters was the unraveling of a massive Ponzi scheme centered around the American real estate market, a huge bubble of investment fraud that floated the American economy for the better part of a decade. This is a pretty big story, but at the moment I know nothing about it. Take it as a powerful indictment of American journalism that I'm far from alone in this among the campaign press corps charged with covering the 2008 election. None of us understands this stuff. We're all way too busy watching to make sure X candidate keeps his hand over his heart during the Pledge of Allegiance, and Y candidate goes to church as often as he says he does, and so on.

Just looking at Palin up on the podium doesn't impress me. She looks like a chief flight attendant on a Piedmont flight from Winston-Salem to Cleveland, with only the bag of almonds and the polyester kerchief missing from the picture. With the Junior Anti-Sex League rimless glasses and a half updo with a Bumpit she comes across like she's wearing a cheap Halloween getup McCain's vice-presidential search party bought in a bag at Walgreens after midnight—four-piece costume, Pissed-Off White Suburban Female, $19.99 plus tax.

Just going by the crude sportswriter-think that can get any campaign journalist through a whole presidential race from start to finish if he feels like winging it, my initial conclusion here is that John McCain is desperate and he's taking one last heave at the end zone by serving up this overmatched electoral gimmick in a ploy for . . . what? Women? Extra-horny older married men? Frequent Piedmont fliers?

I'm not sure what the endgame is, but just going by the McCain campaign's hilariously maladroit strategic performance so far, it can't be very sophisticated. So I figure I'll catch a little of this cookie-cutter political stump act, snatch a few quotes for my magazine piece, then head to the exits and grab a cheesesteak on the way back to the hotel. But will my car still be there when I get out? That's where my head is, as Sarah Palin begins her speech.

Then I start listening.

She starts off reading her credentials. She's got the kid and nephew in uniform—check. Troop of milk-fed patriotic kiddies with Hallmark Channel names (a Bristol, a Willow, *and* a Piper, a rare Martin Mull–caliber whiteness trifecta)—check. Mute macho husband on a snow machine—check. This is all standard-issue campaign decoration so far, but then she starts in with this thing about Harry Truman:

> My parents are here tonight, and I am so proud to be the daughter of Chuck and Sally Heath. Long ago, a young farmer and haberdasher from Missouri followed an unlikely path to the vice presidency.
>
> A writer observed: "We grow good people in our small towns, with honesty, sincerity, and dignity." I know just the kind of people that writer had in mind when he praised Harry Truman.
>
> I grew up with those people.
>
> They are the ones who do some of the hardest work in America, who grow our food, run our factories, and fight our wars.
>
> They love their country, in good times and bad, and they're always proud of America. I had the privilege of living most of my life in a small town.

I'm on the floor for the speech—stuck in the middle of a bunch of delegates from, I believe, Colorado—and at the line "They are the ones who do some of the hardest work," the section explodes in cheers.

I look back up at Palin and she has a bit of a confident grin on her face now. Not quite a smirk, that would be unfair to say, but she's oozing confidence after delivering these loaded lines. From now through the end of her speech there will be a definite edge to her voice.

Before I have any chance of noticing it she's moved beyond the speaking part of the program and is suddenly, effortlessly, deep into the signaling process, a place most politicians only reach with great effort, and clumsily, if at all. But Palin is the opposite of clumsy: she's in the dog-whistle portion of the speech and doing triple lutzes and backflips.

She starts talking about her experience as mayor of Wasilla, Alaska:

> I guess a small-town mayor is sort of like a "community organizer,"
> except that you have actual responsibilities. I might add that in
> small towns, we don't quite know what to make of a candidate who
> lavishes praise on working people when they are listening and then
> talks about how bitterly they cling to their religion and guns when
> those people aren't listening.
>
> We tend to prefer candidates who don't talk about us one way
> in Scranton and another way in San Francisco.

The TV talking heads here will surely focus on the insult to Barack Obama and will miss the far more important part of this speech—the fact that Palin has moved from talking about small-town folks as *They* a few seconds ago to *We* now—*We* don't know what to make of this, *We* prefer this. It doesn't take a whole lot of thought to figure out who this *We* is. Certainly, to those listening, if you're part of this *We,* you know. If you're not part of it, as I'm not, you know even more.

Sarah Palin's *We* is a very unusual character to make an appearance in a national presidential campaign, where candidates almost to the last tend to scrupulously avoid any hint that they are not talking to all Americans. Inclusiveness, telegenic warmth, and inoffensiveness are the usual currency of national-campaign candidates. Say as little as possible, hope some of the undecideds like your teeth better than the other guy's—that's usually the way this business works.

But Palin, boldly, has tossed all that aside: she is making an impassioned bunker speech to a highly self-aware *We* that defines itself by the enemies surrounding it, enemies Palin is now haughtily rattling off one by one in this increasingly brazen and inspired address.

She's already gone after the "experts" and "pollsters and pundits" who dismissed McCain, the "community organizer" Obama, even the city of San Francisco (*We* are more likely to live in Scranton), but the more important bit came with the line about how people in small towns are the ones who "do some of the hardest work." The cheer at that line was one of recognition, because what Palin is clearly talking about there are the people this crowd thinks don't do "the hardest work," don't fight our wars, don't love our country.

And *We* know who *They* are.

What Palin is doing is nothing new. It's a virtual copy of Dick Nixon's "forgotten Americans" gambit targeting the so-called silent majority—the poor and middle-class suburban (and especially southern) whites who had stayed on the sidelines during the sixties culture wars. That strategy won Nixon the election against Humphrey by stealing the South away from the Democrats and has been the cornerstone of Republican electoral planning ever since.

The strategy of stoking exurban white resentment against encroaching immigration, against the disappearance of old values, against pop-culture glitz, against government power, it all worked so well for the Republicans over the years that even Hillary Clinton borrowed it in her primary race against Obama.

Now Palin's *We* in St. Paul is, in substance, no different from anything that half a dozen politicians before her have come up with. But neither Nixon nor Hillary nor even Ronald Reagan—whose natural goofball cheerfulness blunted his ability to whip up divisive mobs—had ever executed this message with the political skill and magnetism of this suddenly metamorphosed Piedmont flight attendant at the Xcel Center lectern.

Being in the building with Palin that night is a transformative and oddly unsettling experience. It's a little like having live cave-level access for the ripping-the-heart-out-with-the-bare-hands scene in *Indiana Jones and the Temple of Doom*. A scary-as-hell situation: thousands of pudgy Midwestern conservatives worshipping at the Altar of the Economic Producer, led by a charismatic arch-priestess letting loose a grade-A war cry. The clear subtext of Palin's speech is this: other politicians only talk about fighting these assholes, I actually will.

Palin is talking to voters whose country is despised internationally, no longer an industrial manufacturing power, fast becoming an economic vassal to the Chinese and the Saudis, and just a week away from an almost-total financial collapse. Nobody here is likely to genuinely believe a speech that promises better things.

But cultural civil war, you have *that* no matter how broke you are. And if you want that, I, Sarah Palin, can give it to you. It's a powerful, galvanizing speech, but the strange thing about it is its seeming lack of electoral calculation. It's a transparent attempt to massmarket militancy and frustration, consolidate the group identity of an aggrieved demographic, and work that crowd up into a lather. This represents a further degrading of the already degraded electoral process. Now, not only are the long-term results of elections irrelevant, but for a new set of players like Palin, the outcome of the election itself is irrelevant. This speech wasn't designed to win a general election, it was designed to introduce a new celebrity, a make-believe servant of the people so phony that later in her new career she will not even bother to hold an elective office.

The speech was a tremendous success. On my way out of the building I'm stuck behind a pair of delegates who are joyously rehashing Palin's money quotes:

> BUTT-HEAD: You know what they say the difference is between a hockey mom and a pit bull?
> BEAVIS: Yeah.
> BUTT-HEAD: No, I mean, you remember?
> BEAVIS: Oh, yeah!
> BUTT-HEAD: She's like, "Lipstick!"
> BEAVIS: Yeah, lipstick! (*both explode in laughter*)

I reach out and tap one of them on the shoulder.

"Hey," I say. "Can I ask you two what you think Sarah Palin will actually accomplish, if she gets elected?"

Beavis stares at me. "I think she's gonna take America back," he says.

Getting this kind of answer on campaign jaunts is like asking someone why they like Pepsi and having them answer, "Because I believe it's the choice of a new generation."

"Yeah, okay," I say. "But what actual policies do you want her to enact, or what laws do you think she's going to pass?"

They both frown and glance down at my press pass, and I realize instantly the game is up. I'm not part of the *We*. Butt-Head steps forward in a defensive posture, shielding his buddy from the liberal-media *Ausländer*.

"Wait a minute," he says. "Who do you work for, exactly?"

Here's the big difference between America and the third world: in America, our leaders put on a hell of a show for us voters, while in the third world, the bulk of the population gets squat. In the third world, most people know where they stand and don't have any illusions about it.

Maybe they get a parade every now and then, get to wave at shock troops carrying order colors in an eyes-right salute. Or maybe, if they're lucky, the leader will spring for a piece of mainstream entertainment—he'll host a heavyweight title fight at the local Palace of Beheading. Something that puts the country on the map, cheers the national mood, distracts folks from their status as barefoot scrapers of the bottom of the international capitalist barrel.

But mostly your third-world schmuck gets the shaft. He gets to live in dusty, unpaved dumps, eat expired food, scratch and claw his way to an old enough age to reproduce, and then die unnecessarily of industrial accidents, malnutrition, or some long-forgotten disease of antiquity. Meanwhile, drawing upon the collective whole-life economic output of this worthy fellow and 47 million of his fellow citizens, the leader and about eighteen of his luckiest friends get to live in villas in Ibiza or the south of France, with enough money for a couple of impressive-looking ocean cruisers and a dozen sports cars.

We get more than that in America. We get a beautifully choreographed eighteen-month entertainment put on once every four years, a beast called the presidential election that engrosses the population to the point of obsession. This ongoing drama allows everyone to subsume their hopes and dreams for the future into one all-out, all-or-nothing battle for the White House, a big alabaster symbol of power we see on television a lot. Who wins and who loses this contest is a matter of utmost importance to a hell of a lot of people in this country.

But *why* it's so important to them is one of the great unexplored mysteries of our time. It's a mystery rooted in the central, horrifying truth about our national politics.

Which is this: none of it really matters to us. The presidential election is a drama that we Americans have learned to wholly consume as entertainment, divorced completely from any expectations about concrete changes in our own lives. For the vast majority of people who follow national elections in this country, the payoff they're looking for when they campaign for this or that political figure is that warm and fuzzy feeling you get when the home team wins the big game. Or, more important, when a hated rival loses. Their stake in the electoral game isn't a citizen's interest, but a rooting interest.

Voters who throw their emotional weight into elections they know deep down inside won't produce real change in their lives are also indulging in a kind of fantasy. That's why voters still dream of politicians whose primary goal is to effectively govern and maintain a thriving first world society with great international ambitions. What voters don't realize, or don't want to realize, is that that dream was abandoned long ago by this country's leaders, who know the more prosaic reality and are looking beyond the fantasy, into the future, at an America plummeted into third world status.

These leaders are like the drug lords who ruled America's ghettos in the crack age, men (and some women) interested in just two things: staying in power, and hoovering up enough of what's left of the cash on their blocks to drive around in an Escalade or a 633i for however long they have left. Our leaders know we're turning into a giant ghetto and they are taking every last hubcap they can get their hands on before the rest of us wake up and realize what's happened.

The engine for looting the old ghetto neighborhoods was the drug trade, which served two purposes with brutal efficiency. Narco-business was the mechanism for concentrating all the money on the block into that Escalade-hungry dealer's hands, while narco-chemistry was the mechanism for keeping the people on his block too weak and hopeless to do anything about it. The more dope you push into the neighborhood, the more weak, strung-out, and dominated the people who live there will be.

In the new American ghetto, the nightmare engine is bubble economics, a kind of high-tech casino scam that kills neighborhoods just like dope does, only the product is credit, not crack or heroin. It concentrates the money of the population in just a few hands with brutal efficiency, just like narco-business, and just as in narco-business the product itself, debt, steadily demoralizes the customer to the point where he's unable to prevent himself from being continually dominated.

In the ghetto, nobody gets real dreams. What they get are short-term rip-off versions of real dreams. You don't get real wealth, with a home, credit, a yard, money for your kids' college—you get a fake symbol of wealth, a gold chain, a Fendi bag, a tricked-out car you bought with cash. Nobody gets to be *really* rich for long, but you do get to be pretend rich, for a few days, weeks, maybe even a few months. It makes you feel better to wear that gold, but when real criminals drive by on the overpass, they laugh.

It's the same in our new ghetto. We don't get real political movements and real change; what we get, instead, are crass show-business manipulations whose followers' aspirations are every bit as laughable and desperate as the wealth dreams of the street hustler with his gold rope. What we get, in other words, are moderates who don't question the corporate consensus dressed up as revolutionary leaders, like Barack Obama, and wonderfully captive opposition diversions like the Tea Party—the latter a fake movement for real peasants that was born that night in St. Paul, when Sarah Palin addressed her *We*.

If American politics made any sense at all, we wouldn't have two giant political parties of roughly equal size perpetually fighting over the same 5–10 percent swatch of undecided voters, blues versus reds. Instead, the parties should be broken down into haves and have-nots—a couple of obnoxious bankers on the Upper East Side running for office against 280 million pissed-off credit card and mortgage customers. That's the more accurate demographic divide in a country in which the top 1 percent has seen its share of the nation's overall wealth jump from 34.6 percent before the crisis, in 2007, to over 37.1 percent in 2009. Moreover, the wealth of the average American plummeted during the crisis—the median American household net worth was $102,500 in 2007, and went down to $65,400 in 2009—while the top 1 percent saw its net worth hold relatively steady, dropping from $19.5 million to $16.5 million.

But we'll never see our political parties sensibly aligned according to these obvious economic divisions, mainly because it's so pathetically easy to set big groups of voters off angrily chasing their own tails in response to media-manufactured nonsense, with the Tea Party being a classic example of the phenomenon. If you want to understand why America is such a paradise for high-class thieves, just look at the way a manufactured movement like the Tea Party corrals and neutralizes public anger that otherwise should be sending pitchforks in the direction of downtown Manhattan.

There are two reasons why Tea Party voters will probably never get wise to the Ponzi-scheme reality of bubble economics. One has to do with the sales pitch of Tea Party rhetoric, which cleverly exploits Main Street frustrations over genuinely intrusive state and local governments that are constantly in the pockets of small businesses for fees and fines and permits.

The other reason is obvious: the bubble economy is hard as hell to understand. To even have a chance at grasping how it works, you need to commit large chunks of time to learning about things like securitization, credit default swaps, collateralized debt obligations, etc., stuff that's fiendishly complicated and that if ingested too quickly can feature a truly toxic boredom factor.

So long as this stuff is not widely understood by the public, the Grifter class is going to skate on almost anything it does—because the tendency of most voters, in particular conservative voters, is to assume that Wall Street makes its money engaging in normal capitalist business and that any attempt to restrain that sector of the economy is thinly disguised socialism.

That's why it's so brilliant for the Tea Party to put forward as its leaders some of the most egregiously stupid morons on our great green earth. By rallying behind dingbats like Palin and Michele Bachmann— the Minnesota congresswoman who thought the movie *Aladdin* promoted witchcraft and insisted global warming wasn't a threat because "carbon dioxide is natural"—the Tea Party has made anti-intellectualism itself a rallying cry. The Tea Party is arguing against the very idea that it's even necessary to ask the kinds of questions you need to ask to grasp bubble economics.

Bachmann is the perfect symbol of the *Dumb and Dumber* approach to high finance. She makes a great show of saying things that would get a kindergartner busted to the special ed bus—shrieking, for instance, that AmeriCorps was a plot to force children into liberal "reeducation camps" (Bachmann's own son, incidentally, was a teacher in an AmeriCorps program), or claiming that the U.S. economy was "100 percent private" before Barack Obama's election (she would later say Obama in his first year and a half managed to seize control of "51 percent of the American economy").

When the Chinese proposed replacing the dollar as the international reserve currency, Bachmann apparently thought this meant that the dollar itself was going to be replaced, that Americans would be shelling out yuan to buy six-packs of Sprite in the local 7-Eleven. So to combat this dire threat she sponsored a bill that would "bar the dollar from being replaced by any foreign currency." When reporters like me besieged Bachmann's office with calls to ask if the congresswoman, a former tax attorney, understood the difference between *currency* and *reserve currency,* and to ask generally what the hell she was talking about, her spokeswoman, Debbee Keller, was forced to issue a statement clarifying that "she's talking about the United States . . . The legislation would ensure that the dollar would remain the currency of the United States."

A Democratic staffer I know in the House called me up after he caught wind of Bachmann's currency bill. "We get a lot of yokels in here, small-town lawyers who've never been east of Indiana and so on, but Michele Bachmann . . . We've just never seen anything quite like her before."

Bachmann has a lot of critics, but they miss the genius of her political act. Even as she spends every day publicly flubbing political SAT questions, she's always dead-on when it comes to her basic message, which is that government is always the problem and there are no issues the country has that can't be worked out with basic common sense (there's a reason why many Tea Party groups are called "Common Sense Patriots" and rally behind "common sense campaigns").

Common sense sounds great, but if you're too lazy to penetrate the mysteries of carbon dioxide—if you haven't mastered the whole concept of *breathing* by the time you're old enough to serve in the U.S. Congress—you're not going to get the credit default swap, the synthetic collateralized debt obligation, the interest rate swap. And understanding these instruments and how they were used (or misused) is the difference between perceiving how Wall Street made its money in the last decades as normal capitalist business and seeing the truth of what it often was instead, which was simple fraud and crime. It's not an accident that Bachmann emerged in the summer of 2010 (right as she was forming the House Tea Party Caucus) as one of the fiercest opponents of financial regulatory reform; her primary complaint with the deeply flawed reform bill sponsored by Senator Chris Dodd and Congressman Barney Frank was that it would "end free checking accounts."

Our world isn't about ideology anymore. It's about complexity. We live in a complex bureaucratic state with complex laws and complex business practices, and the few organizations with the corporate willpower to master these complexities will inevitably own the political power. On the other hand, movements like the Tea Party more than anything else reflect a widespread longing for simpler times and simple solutions—just throw the U.S. Constitution at the whole mess and everything will be jake. For immigration, build a big fence. Abolish the Federal Reserve, the Department of Commerce, the Department of Education. At times the overt longing for simple answers that you get from Tea Party leaders is so earnest and touching, it almost makes you forget how insane most of them are.

"It's not in the enumerated powers of the U. S. Constitution," says Bill Parson, a Tea Party–friendly Republican Senate candidate in Nevada who was gracious enough to take me around the state in the spring of 2010. I'd asked him about his attitude toward certain proposed financial regulations, like a mandate that derivatives such as credit default swaps be traded and cleared on open exchanges, just like stocks.

Parson is a big, burly ex-marine with an affable disposition who, like a lot of retired military types, never learned that a flattop starts looking weird on men after the age of fifty or so. He and his campaign manager, a witty and sharp-tongued older woman named Karel Smith who works as a blackjack dealer, are my tour guides on a trip around the Nevada Republican primary race, which features multiple Tea Party candidates, including eventual nominee Sharron Angle.

My whole purpose in going to Nevada was to try to find someone in any of the races who had any interest at all in talking about the financial crisis. Everyone wanted to talk about health care and immigration, but the instant I even mentioned Wall Street I got blank stares at best (at one voter rally in suburban Vegas I had a guy literally spit on the ground in anger, apparently thinking I was trying to trick him, when I asked him his opinion on what caused AIG's collapse). Parson, meanwhile, seemed obsessed with a whole host of intramural conservative issues that make absolutely no sense to me whatsoever—at one point he spent nearly an hour trying to explain to me the difference between people who call themselves conservative and people who *are* conservative. "You have people who say, 'Well, I really think we ought to help people, but I'm a conservative,'" he says. "So it's like, you can't find anything in their statement that shows they're a conservative. Do you see the distinction?"

I nod, trying to smile: helping people is bad, right? I'm really trying to like Parson—he's been incredibly hospitable to me, even though he knows I work for the hated *Rolling Stone* magazine, but half the time I can barely follow the things he's saying. I keep trying to bring him back to the economy, but he keeps countering with his belief that we need to abolish the Departments of Energy and Labor, to say nothing of financial regulators like the Securities and Exchange Commission and the Commodity Futures Trading Commission. The DOE and the DOL, he says, aren't in the Constitution.

"But neither is toothpaste, or antibiotics," I say. "I mean, they wrote the Constitution a long time ago. It's missing a few things. This is a whole realm of financial crime that was not even conceived of back then. How do you police the stuff that's not in the Constitution?"

Parson frowns and looks ahead at the road—we're driving through the Nevada desert at night. Then he turns slightly and gives me a *This one goes to eleven* look. "Well," he says, "I just keep getting back to what *is* in the enumerated powers of the Constitution . . ."

Parson's entire theory of the economy is the same simple idea that Bachmann and all the other Tea Partiers believe in: that the economy is self-correcting, provided that commerce and government are fully separated. The fact that this is objectively impossible, that the private economy is now and always will be hopelessly interconnected not only with mountains of domestic regulations (a great many of which, as we'll see, were created specifically at the behest of financial corporations that use them to gain and/or maintain market advantage) but with the regulations of other countries is totally lost on the Tea Paty, which still wants to believe in the pure capitalist ideal.

Bachmann spelled this out explicitly in an amazing series of comments arguing against global integration, which showed that she believed the American economy can somehow be walled off from impure outsiders, the way parts of California are walled off from Mexico by a big fence. "I don't want the United States to be in a global economy," she said, "where our economic future is bound to that of Zimbabwe."

The fact that a goofball like Michele Bachmann has a few dumb ideas doesn't mean much, in the scheme of things. What is meaningful is the fact that this belief in total deregulation and pure capitalism is still the political mainstream not just in the Tea Party, not even just among Republicans, but pretty much everywhere on the American political spectrum to the right of Bernie Sanders. Getting ordinary Americans to emotionally identify in this way with the political wishes of their bankers and credit card lenders and mortgagers is no small feat, but it happens—with a little help.

I'm going to say something radical about the Tea Partiers. They're not all crazy. They're not even always wrong.

What they are, and they don't realize it, is an anachronism. They're fighting a 1960s battle in a world run by twenty-first-century crooks. They've been encouraged to launch costly new offensives in already-lost cultural wars, and against a big-government hegemony of a kind that in reality hasn't existed—or perhaps better to say, hasn't really mattered—for decades. In the meantime an advanced new symbiosis of government and private bubble-economy interests goes undetected as it grows to exponential size and robs them blind.

The Tea Party is not a single homogenous entity. It's really many things at once. When I went out to Nevada, I found a broad spectrum of people under the same banner—from dyed-in-the-wool Ron Paul libertarians who believe in repealing drug laws and oppose the Iraq and Afghan wars, to disaffected George Bush/mainstream Republicans reinventing themselves as anti-spending fanatics, to fundamentalist Christians buzzed by the movement's reactionary anger and looking to latch on to the "values" portion of the Tea Party message, to black-helicopter types and gun crazies volunteering to organize the bunkers and whip up the canned food collection in advance of the inevitable Tea Party revolution.

So in one sense it's a mistake to cast the Tea Party as anything like a unified, cohesive movement. On the other hand, virtually all the Tea Partiers (with the possible exception of the Ron Paul types, who tend to be genuine dissidents who've been living on the political margins for ages) have one thing in common: they've been encouraged to militancy by the very people they should be aiming their pitchforks at. A loose definition of the Tea Party might be fifteen million pissed-off white people sent chasing after Mexicans on Medicaid by the small handful of banks and investment companies who advertise on Fox and CNBC.

The formal beginning of the Tea Party was a classic top-down media con. It took off after a February 20, 2009, rant on CNBC by a shameless TV douchewad named Rick Santelli, who is today considered a pre-prophet for the Tea Party movement, a sort of financial John the Baptist who was dunking CNBC-viewer heads in middle-class resentment before the real revolution began.

Of course, CNBC is more or less openly a propaganda organ for rapacious Wall Street banks, funded by ad revenue from the financial services industry. That this fact seems to have escaped the attention of the Tea Partiers who made Santelli an Internet hero is not surprising; one of the key psychological characteristics of the Tea Party is its oxymoronic love of authority figures coupled with a narcissistic celebration of its own "revolutionary" defiance. It's this psychic weakness that allows this segment of the population to be manipulated by the likes of Sarah Palin and Glenn Beck. The advantage is that their willingness to take orders has allowed them to organize effectively (try getting one hundred progressives at a meeting focused on *anything*). The downside is, they see absolutely nothing weird in launching a revolution based upon the ravings of a guy who's basically a half-baked PR stooge shoveling propaganda coal for bloodsucking transnational behemoths like JPMorgan Chase and Goldman Sachs.

Rick Santelli's February 20 rant came in response to an announcement by the administration of new president Barack Obama that it would be green-lighting the "Homeowner Affordability and Stability Plan," a $75 billion plan to help families facing foreclosure to stay in their homes.

Now, $75 billion was a tenth of the size of the TARP, the bank bailout program put forward by Bush Treasury secretary Hank Paulson that directly injected capital onto the balance sheets of failing Wall Street companies. And $75 billion was more like a hundredth, or perhaps one two-hundredth, the size of the *overall* bailout of Wall Street, which included not just the TARP but a variety of Fed bailout programs, including the rescues of AIG and Bear Stearns and massive no-interest loans given to banks via the discount window and other avenues.

The Tea Partiers deny it today, but they were mostly quiet during all of those other bailout efforts. Certainly no movement formed to oppose them. The same largely right-wing forces that would stir up the Tea Party movement were quiet when the Fed gave billions to JPMorgan to buy Bear Stearns. Despite their natural loathing for all things French/European, they were even quiet when foreign companies like the French bank Société Générale were given billions of their dollars through the AIG bailout. Their heroine Sarah Palin enthusiastically supported the TARP and, electorally, didn't suffer for it in the slightest.

No, it wasn't until a bailout program a tiny fraction of the size of the total bailout was put forward by a new president—a black Democratic president—that the Tea Party really exploded. The galvanizing issue here was not so much the giving away of taxpayer money, which had been given away by the *trillions* just months earlier, but the fact that the wrong people were receiving it.

After all, the target of the Obama program was not Sarah Palin's *We,* not the people who "do some of the hardest work," but, disproportionately, poor minorities. Santelli used language similar to Palin's when he launched into his televised rant on the floor of the Chicago Board of Trade.

"Why don't you put up a website to have people vote on the Internet as a referendum to see if we really want to subsidize the losers' mortgages!" he barked, addressing Barack Obama. "Or would we like to at least buy cars and buy houses in foreclosure and give them to people that might have a chance to actually prosper down the road, and reward people that could *carry the water instead of drink the water?*"

That was the money shot. After that iconic line, a random trader from the CBOT sitting next to Santelli piped in.

"That's a novel idea!" he said, sarcastically.

It's important to understand the context here. The Chicago Board of Trade is where commodities like futures in soybeans, corn, and other agricultural products are traded. The tie-clad white folks Santelli was addressing had played a major role in bidding up the commodities bubble of the summer of 2008, when prices of commodities—food, oil, natural gas—soared everywhere, despite minimal changes in supply or demand.

Just a year before Santelli's rant, in fact, riots had broken out in countries all over the world, including India, Haiti, and Mexico, thanks to the soaring costs of foods like bread and rice—and the big banks themselves even admitted at the time that the cause for this was a speculative bubble. "The markets seem to me to have a bubble-like quality," Jim O'Neill, chief economist for Goldman Sachs, had said during the food bubble. And Goldman would know, since its commodities index is the most heavily traded in the world and it is the bank that stands to gain the most from a commodities bubble.

Santelli was addressing a group of gamblers whose decision to bid

up a speculative bubble had played a role in a man-made financial disaster causing people around the world to literally starve.

And *these* were the people picked to play the role of fed-up "America" in the TV canvas behind Santelli during his "spontaneous" rant.
When CNBC anchor Joe Kernen quipped that Santelli's audience of
commodities traders was like "putty in your hands," Santelli balked.

"They're not like putty in our hands," he shouted. "This is America!"

Turning around, he added: "How many of you people want to pay
for your neighbor's mortgage that has an extra bathroom and can't pay
their bills? Raise your hand."

At this rhetorical question, "America" booed loudly. They were
tired of "carrying water" for all those lazy black people!

"President Obama," Santelli raved on. "Are you listening?"

Santelli went on to marshal forces for the first Tea Party. Here's how
it went:

SANTELLI: You know, Cuba used to have mansions and a
relatively decent economy. They moved from the individual to the
collective. Now they're driving '54 Chevys, maybe the last great
car to come out of Detroit.

KERNEN: They're driving them on water, too, which is a little
strange to watch.

SANTELLI: There you go.

KERNEN: Hey Rick, how about the notion that, Wilbur pointed
out, you can go down to two percent on the mortgage . . .

SANTELLI: You could go down to minus two percent. They can't
afford the house.

KERNEN: . . . and still have forty percent, and still have forty
percent not be able to do it. So why are they in the house? Why
are we trying to keep them in the house?

SANTELLI: I know Mr. Summers is a great economist, but boy, I'd
love the answer to that one.

REBECCA QUICK: Wow. Wilbur, you get people fired up.

SANTELLI: We're thinking of having a Chicago Tea Party in July.
All you capitalists that want to show up to Lake Michigan, I'm
gonna start organizing.

From there the crowd exploded in cheers. That clip became an instant Internet sensation, and the Tea Party was born. The dominant meme of the resulting Tea Parties was the anger of the "water carriers" over having to pay for the "water drinkers," which morphed naturally into hysteria about the new Democratic administration's "socialism" and "Marxism."

The Tea Party would take up other causes, most notably health care, but the root idea of all of it is contained in this Santelli business.

Again, you have to think about the context of the Santelli rant. Bush and Obama together, in a policy effort that was virtually identical under both administrations, had approved a bailout program of historic, monstrous proportions—an outlay of upwards of $13 to $14 trillion at this writing. That money was doled out according to the trickle-down concept of rescuing the bad investments of bank speculators who had gambled on the housing bubble.

The banks that had been bailed out by Bush and Obama had engaged in behavior that was beyond insane. In 2004 the five biggest investment banks in the country (at the time, Merrill Lynch, Goldman, Morgan Stanley, Lehman Brothers, and Bear Stearns) had gone to then–SEC chairman William Donaldson and personally lobbied to remove restrictions on borrowing so that they could bet even more of whatever other people's money they happened to be holding on bullshit investments like mortgage-backed securities.

They were making so much straight cash betting on the burgeoning housing bubble that it was no longer enough to be able to bet twelve dollars for every dollar they actually had, the maximum that was then allowed under a thing called the net capital rule.

So people like Hank Paulson (at the time, head of Goldman Sachs) got Donaldson to nix the rule, which allowed every single one of those banks to jack up their debt-to-equity ratio above 20:1. In the case of Merrill Lynch, it got as high as 40:1.

This was gambling, pure and simple, and it got rewarded with the most gargantuan bailout in history. It was irresponsibility on a scale far beyond anything any individual homeowner could even conceive of. The only problem was, it was invisible. When the economy tanked, the public knew it should be upset about something, that somebody had been irresponsible. But who?

What the Santelli rant did was provide those already pissed-off viewers a place to focus their anger *away* from the financial services industry, and away from the genuinely bipartisan effort to subsidize Wall Street. Santelli's rant fostered the illusion that the crisis was caused by poor people, which in this county usually conjures a vision of minorities, no matter how many poor white people there are, borrowing for too much house. It was classic race politics—the plantation owner keeping the seemingly inevitable pitchfork out of his abdomen by pitting poor whites against poor blacks. And it worked, big-time.

It's February 27, 2010, Elmsford, New York, a very small town in Westchester County, just north of New York City. The date is the one-year anniversary of the first Tea Parties, which had been launched a week after the original Santelli rant.

Here in Westchester, the local chapter—the White Plains Tea Party—is getting together for drinks and angst at a modest Italian restaurant called the Alaroma Ristorante, just outside the center of town.

My original plan here was to show up and openly announce myself as a reporter for *Rolling Stone,* but the instant I walk into this sad-looking, seemingly windowless third-class Italian joint, speckled with red-white-and-blue crepe paper and angry middle-aged white faces, I change my mind.

I feel like everyone here can smell my incorrect opinions. If this were a Terminator movie there would be German shepherds at the door barking furiously at the scent of my liberal arts education and my recent contact with a DVD of *Ghost World.*

Along the walls the local Tea Party leaders have lined up copies of all your favorite conservative tomes, including Glenn Beck's *Arguing with Idiots* (the one where Beck appears, har har, to be wearing an East German uniform on the cover) and up-and-comer Mark Levin's *Liberty and Tyranny: A Conservative Manifesto.* I'm asked to sign some sort of petition against Chuck Schumer, and do, not mentioning to this very Catholic-looking crowd that my beef with Schumer dates back to his denouncing me for having written a column celebrating the death of the pope years ago.

The crowd is asked to gather in the main dining room for speeches and a movie. I stupidly sit in the front row, next to the TV—meaning that if I want to leave early, I'll have to get up and walk past at least two dozen sets of eyes. Once seated, I pick up a copy of the newspaper that's been handed out to each of us, a thing called the *Patriot*. The headline of the lead story reads:

BLACK HISTORY MONTH SHOULD BE ABOUT BLACK HISTORY

The author of this piece, a remarkable personage named Lloyd Marcus, identifies himself at the bottom of the page as follows:

Lloyd Marcus (black) Unhyphenated American, Singer/Songwriter, Entertainer, Author, Artist and Tea Party Patriot.

Marcus is the cultural mutant who wrote the song that's now considered the anthem of the Tea Party. If you haven't heard it, look it up—the lyrics rock. The opening salvo goes like this:

Mr. President, your stimulus is sure a bust. It's a socialistic scheme
The only thing it will do is kill the American dream
You wanna take from achievers, somehow you think that's fair
And redistribute to those folks who won't get out of their easy chair!

Bob Dylan, move on over! In any case, the Marcus piece in the *Patriot* rips off the page with a thrilling lede.

"I've often said jokingly," he writes, "that Black History Month should more accurately be called 'white people and America suck' month."

The argument is that Black History Month dwells too much on the downside of white America's relationship to its brothers of African heritage, slavery and torture and the like, and ignores the work of all the good white folk through the years who were nice to black people (did you know it was a white teacher who first suggested George Washington Carver study horticulture?).

According to Marcus, all this anti-white black history propaganda is undertaken with the darkly pragmatic agenda of guilting the power structure into offering up more of our hard-earned tax dollars for entitlement programs.

I look around. You'd have to be out of your fucking mind to write, as Marcus did, that Black History Month is a ploy to lever more entitlement money out of Congress, but the ho-hum nonresponse of the white crowd reading this bit of transparent insanity is, to me, even weirder.

There have been a great many critiques of the Tea Party movement, which is often described as a thinly disguised white power uprising, but to me these critiques miss the mark. To me the most notable characteristic of the Tea Party movement is its bizarre psychological profile. It's like a mass exercise in narcissistic personality disorder, so intensely focused on itself and its own hurt feelings that it can't even recognize the lunacy of a bunch of middle-class white people nodding in agreement at the idea that Black History Month doesn't do enough to celebrate nice white people.

As this meeting would go on to demonstrate, the Tea Party movement is not without some very legitimate grievances. But its origins—going back to Santelli's rant—are steeped in a gigantic exercise in delusional self-worship.

They are, if you listen to them, the only people in America who love their country, obey the law, and do any work at all. They're lonely martyrs to the lost national ethos of industriousness and self-reliance, whose only reward for their Herculean labors is the bleeding of their tax money for welfare programs—programs that of course will be consumed by ungrateful minorities who hate America and white people and love Islamic terrorists.

There's a definite emphasis on race and dog-whistle politics in their rhetoric, but the racism burns a lot less brightly than these almost unfathomable levels of self-pity and self-congratulation. It would be a lot easier to listen to what these people have to say if they would just stop whining about how underappreciated they are and insisting that they're the only people left in America who've read the Constitution. In fact, if you listen to them long enough, you almost *want* to strap them into chairs and make them watch as you redistribute their tax money directly into the arms of illegal immigrant dope addicts.

Which is too bad, because when they get past the pathetic self-regard and start to articulate their grievances, they are rooted in genuine anxieties about what's going on in this country. In the case of these Westchester County revolutionaries, the rallying cry was a lawsuit filed jointly by a liberal nonprofit group in New York City and the Department of Housing and Urban Development against the county. The suit alleged that Westchester falsified HUD grant applications, asking for federal grant money without conforming to federal affirmative action guidelines designed to push desegregation.

The county lost the suit and as a result was now going to be forced by the federal government to build seven hundred new subsidized low-income housing units in the area. Whereas subsidized housing in the county had historically been built closer to New York City, the new ruling would now place "affordable housing" in places like Elmsford whether Elmsford wanted it or not.

The first speaker is a fireman and former Republican candidate for county legislator named Tom Bock. Bock isn't a member of the Tea Party (when I talked to him later on he was careful to point that out) but he is sympathetic to a lot of what they're about. Asked to address the crowd, he launches into the local issue.

"We should never have settled this lawsuit," says Bock, a burly man in jeans and a cop's mustache. "I don't think Westchester County is racist. There may be people who are racist, but I don't think that anyone is going to say to anyone who can afford a house, you can't move here because you're black or Hispanic. Nobody's going to say you can't move into Westchester because of race.

"What they say," Bock goes on, "is you can't move into Westchester because of *money*."

The crowd cheers. The odd thing about Bock's speech is that, throughout the course of this lawsuit, nobody ever really accused the citizens of Westchester of being racist. There was never any grassroots protest against racism or segregation in the county. The entire controversy was dreamed up and resolved behind closed doors by lawyers,

mostly out-of-town lawyers. What they accused the *government* of
Westchester of was having an inadequate amount of zeal for submitting
the mountains of paperwork that goes hand in hand with antiquated,
Johnson-era affirmative action housing programs.

The Westchester housing settlement that resulted from that suit is
the kind of politics that would turn anyone into a Tea Partier—a classic example of dizzy left-wing meddling mixed with socially meaningless legal grifting that enriches opportunistic lawyers with an eye for
low-hanging fruit.

What happened: A nonprofit organization called the Anti-
Discrimination Center based out of New York City stumbled upon a
mandate in federal housing guidelines that required communities applying for federal housing money to conduct studies to see if their
populations were too racially segregated. They then latched on to
Westchester County, which apparently treated this mandate as a for-
mality in applying for federal grants—they hadn't bothered to conduct
any such studies—and launched a lawsuit.

How important this bureaucratic oversight was ("They forgot to
check a box, basically," was how one lawyer involved described it) is a
matter of debate, but the county was, undeniably, technically in violation. The Obama administration joined the center in the lawsuit, and
the county's lawyers, who understood they were busted, advised the
community that it had no choice but to walk the legal plank. They settled with the government.

So far, so good. But then things went off the rails. The resulting settlement was a classic example of nutty racial politics. It was white lawyers
suing white lawyers (the lead counsel for the Anti-Discrimination Center,
Craig Gurian, is a bald, bearded New Yorker who looks like a model for
a *Nation* house ad) so that low-income blacks and Hispanics living close
to New York City in places like Mount Vernon and Yonkers, none of
whom were ever involved in the suit in any way, could now be moved to
subsidized housing in faraway white bedroom suburbs like Mount Kisco
and Croton-on-Hudson.

Meanwhile, for so heroically pushing for all this aid to very
poor minorities, all the white lawyers involved got paid huge money.

The Anti-Discrimination Center got $7.5 million, outside counsel from a DC firm called Relman, Dane & Colfax got $2.5 million, and EpsteinBeckerGreen, the firm that defended Westchester County, got paid $3 million for its services. "There wasn't a single minority involved with the case," says one lawyer who worked on the suit.

Meanwhile, just $50 million was ultimately designated for new housing, and even that money might not all be spent, since it is dependent in part upon whether or not the county can find financing and developers to do the job.

"It could all not come off," says Stuart Gerson, one of the lawyers for Westchester County. "Everybody's approaching it in good faith, but you never know."

This Westchester case smells like a case of sociological ambulance chasing, with a bunch of lawyers surfing on the federal housing code to a pile of fees and then riding off into the sunset. It's not hard to see where the creeping paranoia that's such a distinctive feature of the Tea Party comes from. After Westchester County agreed to this settlement, it kept making moves that limited the rights of the local communities to have a say about where these subsidized housing units would be located.

For instance, it eventually passed a measure repealing the so-called right of first refusal. Previously, when the county wanted to place a housing unit in a place like Elmsford, what it would do is take a piece of county land and sell it to developers. Residents of the town of Elmsford, however, would in the past have always had a right to buy the property themselves.

"But they took that away," Bock explained to me later. "They keep chipping away."

Another example: In the past, when a town was mandated to build affordable housing with HUD money by the county, there had always been room to try to set aside that housing for local residents. Bock cited the example of a housing project in his home town of Greenburgh. The building was built on the site of what had been a two-story halfway house that had been a source of much local controversy owing to constant complaints about crime, crack vials on neighboring lawns, and so on. The building was ultimately torn down amid promises from the county that the new building would be used either as an old folks' home or as housing for municipal employees of the town.

But HUD ultimately balked at that plan. New rules were instituted that eliminated any local input into the process. Now, if municipal employees of a town like Greenburgh or Elmsford want to be placed in HUD housing in their town, they had to put their names into a lottery system with applicants from all over the state. "So now you don't have a say in who gets to live in these units either," Bock explains.

To the Tea Partiers, this is a simple case of taxation without representation. They look at the timeline of stories like this—first a federal settlement, then the right of first refusal removed, then local control over the application process terminated—and they imagine a grim endgame.

"I think this is all headed for eminent domain," says Bock, by phone, a month after the Tea Party meeting.

"So you think," I ask him, "that ultimately the government is just going to seize properties in towns like Elmsford willy-nilly and plant affordable housing units there?"

"Yes," he says.

Is that crazy? Sure, a little. But given what's happened in the last few years in Westchester, it's not *completely* crazy. It's not in the same ballpark of craziness, for instance, as thirteen million Tea Partiers believing the Obama health care plan—a massive giveaway to private profit-making corporations—is the first step in a long-range plan to eliminate the American free enterprise system and install a Trotskyite dictatorship. And the reason the former is less crazy than the latter is that they don't need to read 1,200-page legislative tomes to know the issue; all they have to do is look out the window and see their world changing in ways they can't control.

That's why the Tea Party has responded to the financial crisis with such confusion. Most of the Tea Partiers view national politics through the prism of what they have seen, personally, in their own communities: intrusive government and layer upon layer of regulatory red tape. When Bock talks about the process for building the new apartment units, for instance, he laughs.

"I always tell people, rule of thumb, once the project is approved, you're still two years away from the first shovel hitting the ground," he says. "It just takes that long to get all the permits and the paperwork done."

I ask him if experiences like that would color his opinion on, say, the deregulation of the financial services industry in the late nineties. "Absolutely," he says. When I bring up the repeal of the Glass-Steagall Act (which prevented the mergers of insurance, investment banking, and commercial banking companies) and the 2000 law that deregulated the derivatives industry, Bock demurs. I'm not sure he knows what I'm talking about, but then he plunges forward anyway. In his opinion, he says, the deregulation of Wall Street was the right move, but it was just implemented too quickly.

"I think it needed to be done more gradually," he says.

This is how you get middle-class Americans pushing deregulation for rich bankers. Your average working American looks around and sees evidence of government power over his life everywhere. He pays high taxes and can't sell a house or buy a car without paying all sorts of fees. If he owns a business, inspectors come to his workplace once a year to gouge him for something whether he's in compliance or not. If he wants to build a shed in his backyard, he needs a permit from some local thief in the city clerk's office.

And, who knows, he might live in a sleepy suburb like Greenburgh where the federal government has decided to install a halfway house and a bus route leading to it, so that newly released prisoners can have all their old accomplices come visit them from the city, leave condom wrappers on lawns and sidewalks, maybe commit the odd B and E or rape/murder.

This stuff happens. It's not paranoia. There are a lot of well-meaning laws that can be manipulated, or go wrong over time, or become captive to corrupt lawyers and bureaucrats who fight not to fix the targeted social problems, but to retain their budgetary turf. Tea Party grievances against these issues are entirely legitimate and shouldn't be dismissed. The problem is that they think the same dynamic they see locally or in their own lives—an overbearing, interventionist government that seeks to control, tax, and regulate everything it can get its hands on—operates the same everywhere.

There are really two Americas, one for the grifter class, and one for everybody else. In everybody-else land, the world of small businesses and wage-earning employees, the government is something to be avoided, an overwhelming, all-powerful entity whose attentions usually presage some kind of financial setback, if not complete ruin. In the grifter world, however, government is a slavish lapdog that the financial companies that will be the major players in this book use as a tool for *making* money.

The grifter class depends on these two positions getting confused in the minds of everybody else. They want the average American to believe that what government is to him, it is also to JPMorgan Chase and Goldman Sachs. To sustain this confusion, predatory banks launch expensive lobbying campaigns against even the mildest laws reining in their behavior and rely on carefully cultivated allies in that effort, like the Rick Santellis on networks like CNBC. In the narrative pushed by the Santellis, bankers are decent businessmen-citizens just trying to make an honest buck who are being chiseled by an overweening state, just like the small-town hardware-store owner forced to pay a fine for a crack in the sidewalk outside his shop.

At this writing, Tea Partiers in Tennessee have just launched protests against Republican senator Bob Corker for announcing his willingness to work with outgoing Democrat Chris Dodd on the Consumer Financial Protection Agency Act, a bill that is pitifully weak in its specifics but at least addresses some of the major causes of the financial crisis—including mandating a new resolution authority section that would help prevent companies from becoming too big to fail and would force banks to pay for their own bailouts in the future. The same Tea Partiers who initially rallied against bailouts of individual homeowners now find themselves protesting against new laws that would force irresponsible banks in the future to bail themselves out.

How was this accomplished? Well, you have CNBC's Larry Kudlow—a classic trickle-down capitalist from the cufflinks-and-coke-habit school that peaked in the 1980s—suddenly wrapping his usual Wall Street propaganda in Tea Party rhetoric. He angrily warns that this

new CFPA bill will result in a hated liberal viceroy—in this case, Elizabeth Warren, chair of the Congressional Oversight Panel for TARP and
one of the few honest people left in Washington—regulating small
businesses to death.

"The Fed itself apparently would have no say on CFPA rule-
making, which is sort of like giving Elizabeth Warren her own wing at
the central bank in order to make mischief. At a minimum, she'll need
grown-up supervision," Kudlow sneered on his blog. "Many smaller
community bankers and non-bank Main Street lenders—such as stores
with layaway plans, check-cashing companies, pay-day lenders, and
even car dealers—could be put out of business by Elizabeth Warren."

These are all lies, but they fly, maybe because they *are* lies,
and comforting in their way. The fact that an unapologetic fat cat like
Kudlow—one who talks and acts and dresses like a fat cat—can, when
convenient, throw on the mantle of a populist revolt and get away with
it reassures us that for all the talk about pitchforks and revolutions and
fighting back, the Tea Party movement remains in thrall to the authority of the rich and powerful. Which renders the so-called movement
completely meaningless.

The insurmountable hurdle for so-called populist movements is
having the nerve to attack the rich instead of the poor. Even after the
rich almost destroyed the entire global economy through their sheer
unrestrained greed and stupidity, we can't shake the peasant mentality
that says we should go easy on them, because the best hope for our collective prosperity is in them creating wealth for us all. That's the idea at
the core of trickle-down economics and the basis for American economic policy for a generation. The entire premise—that the way society works is for the productive rich to feed the needy poor and that any
attempt by the latter to punish the former for their excesses might in-
spire Atlas to shrug his way out of town and leave the rest of us on our
own to starve—should be insulting to people so proud to call themselves the "water carriers." But in a country where every Joe the
Plumber has been hoodwinked into thinking he's one clogged toilet
away from being rich himself, we're all invested in rigging the system
for the rich.

What's accelerated over the last few decades, however, is just how thoroughly the members of the grifter class have mastered their art. They've placed themselves at a nexus of political and economic connections that make them nearly impossible to police. And even if they could be policed, there are not and were not even laws on the books to deal with the kinds of things that went on at Goldman Sachs and other investment banks in the run-up to the financial crisis. What has taken place over the last generation is a highly complicated merger of crime and policy, of stealing and government. Far from taking care of the rest of us, the financial leaders of America and their political servants have seemingly reached the cynical conclusion that our society is not worth saving and have taken on a new mission that involves not creating wealth for all, but simply absconding with whatever wealth remains in our hollowed-out economy. They don't feed us, we feed them.

The same giant military-industrial complex that once dotted the horizon of the American states with smokestacks and telephone poles as far as the eye could see has now been expertly and painstakingly refitted for a monstrous new mission: sucking up whatever savings remains in the pockets of the actual people still living between the coasts, the little hidden nest eggs of the men and women who built the country and fought its wars, plus whatever pennies and nickels their aimless and doomed Gen-X offspring might have managed to accumulate in preparation for the gleaming future implicitly promised them, but already abandoned and rejected as unfeasible in reality by the people who run this country.

But our politics—even in the form of "grassroots" movements represented by Tea Partiers (who line up to support a narcissistic, money-grubbing hack like Palin) or MoveOn (who rallied their followers behind a corporation-engorging health care bill)—is silent about this. Instead, it grounds our new and disturbing state of affairs in familiar, forty-year-old narratives. The right is eternally fighting against Lyndon Johnson; the left, George Wallace. When the Republicans win elections, their voters think they've struck a blow against big government. And when a Democratic hero like Barack Obama wins, his supporters think they've won a great victory for tolerance and diversity. Even I thought that.

The reality is that neither of these narratives makes sense anymore.

The new America, instead, is fast becoming a vast ghetto in which all of us, conservatives and progressives, are being bled dry by a relatively tiny oligarchy of extremely clever financial criminals and their castrato henchmen in government, whose main job is to be good actors on TV and put on a good show. This invisible hive of high-class thieves stays in business because when we're not completely distracted and exhausted by our work and entertainments, we prefer not to ponder the dilemma of why gasoline went over four dollars a gallon, why our pension funds just lost 20 percent of their value, or why when we do the right thing by saving money, we keep being punished by interest rates that hover near zero, while banks that have been the opposite of prudent get rewarded with free billions. In reality political power is simply taken from most of us by a grubby kind of fiat, in little fractions of a percent here and there each and every day, through a thousand separate transactions that take place in fine print and in the margins of a vast social mechanism that most of us are simply not conscious of.

This stuff is difficult to unravel, often fiendishly so. But those invisible processes, those unseen labyrinths of the Grifter Archipelago that are indifferent to party affiliation, are our real politics. Which makes sense, if you think about it. It should always have been obvious that a country as rich and powerful as America should be governed by an immensely complex, labyrinthine political system, one that requires almost unspeakable cunning and wolfish ruthlessness to navigate with any success, and which interacts with its unwitting subject peoples not once every four years but every day, in a variety of ways, seen and unseen. Like any big ship, America is run by people who understand how the vessel works. And the bigger the country gets, the fewer such people there are.

America's dirty little secret is that for this small group of plugged-in bubble lords, the political system works fine not just without elections, but without any political input from any people at all outside Manhattan. In bubble economics, actual human beings have only a few legitimate roles: they're either customers of the financial services industry (borrowers, investors, or depositors) or else they're wage earners whose taxes are used to provide both implicit and explicit investment insurance for the big casino-banks pushing the bubble scam.

People aren't really needed for anything else in the Griftopia, but since Americans require the illusion of self-government, we have elections.

To make sure those elections are effectively meaningless as far as Wall Street is concerned, two things end up being true. One is that voters on both sides of the aisle are gradually weaned off that habit of having real expectations for their politicians, consuming the voting process entirely as culture-war entertainment. The other is that millions of tenuously middle-class voters are conned into pushing Wall Street's own twisted greed ethos as though it were their own. The Tea Party, with its weirdly binary view of society as being split up cleanly into competing groups of producers and parasites—that's just a cultural echo of the insane greed-is-good belief system on Wall Street that's provided the foundation/excuse for a generation of brilliantly complex thievery. Those beliefs have trickled down to the ex-middle-class suckers struggling to stay on top of their mortgages and their credit card bills, and the real joke is that these voters listen to CNBC and Fox and they genuinely believe *they're* the producers in this binary narrative. They don't get that somewhere way up above, there's a group of people who've been living the Atlas dream for real—and building a self-dealing financial bureaucracy in their own insane image.

2

The Biggest Asshole
in the Universe

BAD POLITICAL SYSTEMS on their own don't always make societies fail. Sometimes what's required for a real social catastrophe is for one or two ingeniously obnoxious individuals to rise to a position of great power— get a one-in-a-billion asshole in the wrong job and a merely unfair system of government suddenly turns into seventies Guatemala, the Serbian despotate, the modern United States.

Former Federal Reserve chief Alan Greenspan is that one-in-a-billion asshole who made America the dissembling mess that it is today. If his achievements were reversed, if this gnomish bug-eyed party crasher had managed to convert his weird social hang-ups into positive accomplishments, then today we'd be calling his career one of the greatest political fairy tales ever witnessed, an unlikeliest of ugly ducklings who through sheer pluck, cunning, and determination made it to the top and changed the world forever.

But that isn't what happened. Greenspan's rise is instead a tale of a gerbilish mirror-gazer who flattered and bullshitted his way up the Matterhorn of American power and then, once he got to the top, feverishly jacked himself off to the attentions of Wall Street for twenty consecutive years—in the process laying the intellectual foundation for a generation of orgiastic greed and overconsumption and turning the Federal Reserve into a permanent bailout mechanism for the super-rich.

Greenspan was also the perfect front man for the hijacking of the democratic process that took place in the eighties, nineties, and the early part of the 2000s. During that time political power gradually shifted from the elected government to private and semiprivate institutions run by unelected officials whose sympathies were with their own class rather than any popular constituency. We suffered a series of economic shocks over the course of those years, and the official response from the institutions subtly pushed the country's remaining private wealth to one side while continually shifting the risk and the loss to the public.

This profoundly focused effort led to an intense concentration of private wealth on the one hand and the steady disenfranchisement of the average voter and the taxpayer on the other (who advanced inexorably, headfirst, into the resultant debt). But the true genius of this blunt power play was that it was cloaked in a process that everyone who mattered agreed to call the apolitical, "technocratic" stewardship of the economy.

Greenspan was the deadpan figurehead who as head of the "apolitical" Federal Reserve brilliantly played the part of that impartial technocrat. His impartiality was believable to the public precisely because of his long-demonstrated unscrupulousness and political spinelessness: he sucked up with equal ferocity to presidents of both parties and courted pundit-admirers from both sides of the editorial page, who all blessed his wrinkly pronouncements as purely nonpartisan economic wisdom.

Greenspan's rise to the top is one of the great scams of our time. His career is the perfect prism through which one can see the twofold basic deception of American politics: a system that preaches sink-or-swim laissez-faire capitalism to most but acts as a highly interventionist, bureaucratic welfare state for a select few. Greenspan pompously preached ruthless free-market orthodoxy every chance he got while simultaneously using all the powers of the state to protect his wealthy patrons from those same market forces. A perfectly two-faced man, serving a perfectly two-faced state. If you can see through him, the rest of it is easy.

Greenspan was born in 1926, just before the Depression, and boasts a background that reads a little like a generational prequel to the life of Woody Allen—a middle-class Jewish New Yorker from the outer rings of the city, a gaggle-eyed clarinet player who worshipped the big bands, used radio as an escape, obsessed over baseball heroes, and attended NYU (the latter with more success than Woody), eventually entering society in a state of semipanicked indecision over what career to pursue.

In his writings Greenspan unapologetically recalls being overwhelmed as a young man by the impression left by his first glimpses of the upper classes and the physical trappings of their wealth. In his junior year of college he had a summer internship at an investment bank called Brown Brothers Harriman:*

> Prescott Bush, father of George H. W. Bush and grandfather of George W. Bush, served there as a partner before and after his tenure in the U.S. Senate. The firm was literally on Wall Street near the stock exchange and the morning I went to see Mr. Banks was the first time I'd ever set foot in such a place. Walking into these offices, with their gilded ceilings and rolltop desks and thick carpets, was like entering a sanctum of venerable wealth—it was an awesome feeling for a kid from Washington Heights.

*Note the name-dropping at the start of this quote, a literary habit that through the years has infected Greenspan's writings and speeches like the world's most persistent case of herpes. His autobiography, *The Age of Turbulence,* features numerous passages in which his lists of dropped names ramble on with feverish, almost Gogolian intensity. Take for instance this one, in which he talks of the fiftieth birthday party his girlfriend Barbara Walters threw for him: "The guests were the people I'd come to think of as my New York friends: Henry and Nancy Kissinger, Oscar and Annette de la Renta, Felix and Liz Rohatyn, Brooke Astor (I knew her as a kid of seventy-five), Joe and Estée Lauder, Henry and Louise Grunwald, 'Punch' and Carol Sulzberger, and David Rockefeller." Needless to say, when the Federal Reserve Act was passed in 1913, Congress was probably not imagining that America would ultimately hire a central banker who dated anchorwomen and bragged about hanging out with Oscar de la Renta. Greenspan has always appeared constitutionally incapable of not letting people know who his friends are—it's always seemed to be a matter of tremendous importance to him—which is why it's absolutely reasonable to wonder if maybe that was a reason his Fed policies were so much more popular with the Hamptons set than those of a notoriously shabby recluse like Paul Volcker.

Greenspan left NYU to pursue a doctorate in economics at Columbia University, where one of his professors was economist Arthur Burns, a fixture in Republican administrations after World War II who in 1970 became chief of the Federal Reserve. Burns would be Greenspan's entrée into several professional arenas, most notably among the Beltway elite.

Remarkably, Greenspan's other great career rabbi was the objectivist novelist Ayn Rand, an antigovernment zealot who was nearly the exact ideological opposite of a career bureaucrat like Burns.

Greenspan met Rand in the early fifties after leaving Columbia, attending meetings at Rand's apartment with a circle of like-minded intellectual jerk-offs who called themselves by the ridiculous name the "Collective" and who provided Greenspan the desired forum for social ascent.

These meetings of the "Collective" would have an enormous impact on American culture by birthing a crackpot antitheology dedicated to legitimizing relentless self-interest—a grotesquerie called objectivism that hit the Upper East Side cocktail party circuit hard in the fifties and sixties.

It is important to spend some time on the seriously demented early history of objectivism, because this lunatic religion that should have choked to death in its sleep decades ago would go on, thanks in large part to Greenspan, to provide virtually the entire intellectual context for the financial disasters of the early twenty-first century.

Rand, the Soviet refugee who became the archpriestess of the movement, was first of all a perfect ancillary character in the black comedy that is Greenspan's life—a bloviating, arbitrary, self-important pseudo-intellectual who recalls the gibberish-spewing academic twits in Woody Allen spoofs like "No Kaddish for Weinstein" and "My Speech to the Graduates." In fact, some of Rand's quirks seemed to have been pulled more or less directly from Allen's movies; her dictatorial stance on facial hair ("She . . . regarded anyone with a beard or a mustache as inherently immoral," recalled one Rand friend) could have fit quite easily in the mouth of the Latin despot Vargas in *Bananas,* who demanded that his subjects change their underwear once an hour.

A typical meeting of Rand's Collective would involve its members challenging one another to prove they exist. "How do you explain the fact that you're here?" one Collective member recalls asking Greenspan. "Do you require anything besides the proof of your own senses?"

Greenspan played along with this horseshit and in that instance reportedly offered a typically hedging answer. "I think that I exist. But I don't know for sure," he reportedly said. "Actually, I can't say for sure that anything exists." (The Woody Allen version would have read, "I can't say for sure that I exist, but I do know that I have to call two weeks in advance to get a table at Sardi's.")

One of the defining characteristics of Rand's clique was its absolutist ideas about good and evil, expressed in a wildly off-putting, uncompromisingly bombastic rhetoric that almost certainly bled downward to the group ranks from its Russian émigré leader, who might have been one of the most humor-deprived people ever to walk the earth.

Rand's book *Atlas Shrugged,* for instance, remains a towering monument to humanity's capacity for unrestrained self-pity—it's a bizarre and incredibly long-winded piece of aristocratic paranoia in which a group of Randian supermen decide to break off from the rest of society and form a pure free-market utopia, and naturally the parasitic lower classes immediately drown in their own laziness and ineptitude.

The book fairly gushes with the resentment these poor "Atlases" (they are shouldering the burdens of the whole world!) feel toward those who try to use "moral guilt" to make them share their wealth. In the climactic scene the Randian hero John Galt sounds off in defense of self-interest and attacks the notion of self-sacrifice as a worthy human ideal in a speech that lasts *seventy-five pages.*

It goes without saying that only a person possessing a mathematically inexpressible level of humorless self-importance would subject anyone to a seventy-five-page speech about anything. Hell, even Jesus Christ barely cracked two pages with the Sermon on the Mount. Rand/Galt manages it, however, and this speech lays the foundation of objectivism, a term that was probably chosen because "greedism" isn't catchy enough.

Rand's rhetorical strategy was to create the impression of depth through overwhelming verbal quantity, battering the reader with a relentless barrage of meaningless literary curlicues. Take this bit from Galt's famous speech in *Atlas Shrugged*:

Rationality is the recognition of the fact that existence exists, that nothing can alter the truth and nothing can take precedence over that act of perceiving it, which is thinking—that the mind is one's only judge of values and one's only guide of action—that reason is an absolute that permits no compromise—that a concession to the irrational invalidates one's consciousness and turns it from the task of perceiving to the task of faking reality—that the alleged short-cut to knowledge, which is faith, is only a short-circuit destroying the mind—that the acceptance of a mystical invention is a wish for the annihilation of existence and, properly, annihilates one's consciousness.

A real page-turner. Anyway, Alan Greenspan would later regularly employ a strikingly similar strategy of voluminous obliqueness in his public appearances and testimony before Congress. And rhetorical strategy aside, he would forever more cling on some level to the basic substance of objectivism, expressed here in one of the few relatively clear passages in *Atlas Shrugged*:

A living entity that regarded its means of survival as evil, would not survive. A plant that struggled to mangle its roots, a bird that fought to break its wings would not remain for long in the existence they affronted. But the history of man has been a struggle to deny and to destroy his mind . . .

Since life requires a specific course of action, any other course will destroy it. A being who does not hold his own life as the motive and goal of his actions, is acting on the motive and standard of *death*. Such a being is a metaphysical monstrosity, struggling to oppose, negate and contradict the fact of his own existence, running blindly amuck on a trail of destruction, capable of nothing but pain.

This is pure social Darwinism: self-interest is moral, interference (particularly governmental interference) with self-interest is evil, a fancy version of the Gordon Gekko pabulum that "greed is good." When you dig deeper into Rand's philosophy, you keep coming up with more of the same.

Rand's belief system is typically broken down into four parts: metaphysics (objective reality), epistemology (reason), ethics (self-interest), and politics (capitalism). The first two parts are basically pure bullshit and fluff. According to objectivists, the belief in "objective reality" means that "facts are facts" and "wishing" won't make facts change. What it actually means is "When I'm right, I'm right" and "My facts are facts and your facts are not facts."

This belief in "objective reality" is what gives objectivists their characteristic dickish attitude: since they don't really believe that facts look different from different points of view, they don't feel the need to question themselves or look at things through the eyes of others. Since being in tune with how things look to other people is a big part of that magical unspoken connection many people share called a sense of humor, the "metaphysics" of objectivism go a long way toward explaining why there has never in history been a funny objectivist.

The real meat of Randian thought (and why all this comes back to Greenspan) comes in their belief in self-interest as an ethical ideal and pure capitalism as the model for society's political structure. Regarding the latter, Randians believe government has absolutely no role in economic affairs; in particular, government should never use "force" except against such people as criminals and foreign invaders. This means no taxes and no regulation.

To sum it all up, the Rand belief system looks like this:

1. Facts are facts: things can be absolutely right or absolutely wrong, as determined by reason.
2. According to my reasoning, I am absolutely right.
3. Charity is immoral.
4. Pay for your own fucking schools.

Rand, like all great con artists, was exceedingly clever in the way she treated the question of how her ideas would be employed. She used a strategic vagueness that allowed her to paper over certain uncomfortable contradictions. For instance, she denounced tax collection as a use of "force" but also quietly admitted the need for armies and law enforcement, which of course had to be paid for somehow. She de-

nounced the very idea of government interference in economic affairs
but also here and there conceded that fraud and breach of contract were
crimes of "force" that required government intervention.

She admitted all of this, but her trick was one of emphasis. Even as
she might quietly admit to the need for *some* economic regulation, for
the most part when she talked about "crime" and "force" she either
meant (a) armed robbers or pickpockets or (b) governments demanding taxes to pay for social services:

> Be it a highwayman who confronts a traveler with the ultimatum:
> "Your money or your life," or a politician who confronts a country
> with the ultimatum: "Your children's education or your life," the
> meaning of that ultimatum is: "Your mind or your life."

A conspicuous feature of Rand's politics is that they make absolutely perfect sense to someone whose needs are limited to keeping
burglars and foreign communists from trespassing on their Newport
manses, but none at all to people who might want different returns for
their tax dollar. Obviously it's true that a Randian self-made millionaire
can spend money on private guards to protect his mansion from B-and-E
artists. But exactly where do the rest of us look in the Yellow Pages to
hire private protection against insider trading? Against price-fixing in
the corn and gasoline markets? Is each individual family supposed to
hire Pinkertons to keep the local factory from dumping dioxin in the
county reservoir?

Rand's answer to all of these questions was to ignore them. There
were no two-headed thalidomide flipper-babies in Rand's novels, no
Madoff scandals, no oil bubbles. There *were*, however, a lot of lazy-ass
poor people demanding welfare checks and school taxes. It was belief in
this simplistic black-and-white world of pure commerce and bloodsucking parasites that allowed Rand's adherents to present themselves as
absolutists, against all taxes, all regulation, and all government interference in private affairs—despite the fact that all of these ideological ab-
solutes quietly collapsed whenever pragmatic necessity required it. In
other words, it was incoherent and entirely subjective. Its rhetoric flat-

tered its followers as Atlases with bottomless integrity, but the fine print allowed them to do whatever they wanted.

This slippery, self-serving idea ended up being enormously influential in mainstream American politics later on. There would be constant propaganda against taxes and spending and regulation as inherent evils, only these ideas would often end up being quietly ignored when there was a need for increased military spending, bans on foreign drug reimportation, FHA backing for mortgage lenders, Overseas Private Investment Corporation loans, or other forms of government largesse or interference for the right people. American politicians reflexively act as perfectly Randian free-market, antitax purists (no politician beyond the occasional Kucinich will admit to any other belief system) except when, quietly and behind the scenes, they don't.

The person of Alan Greenspan was where this two-sided worldview first became a polished political innovation. He was able to play the seemingly incompatible roles of believer and pragmatist fluidly; there were no core beliefs in there to gum up the works. It's not hard to imagine that even as Greenspan sat in Rand's apartment cheerfully debating the proofs of his own existence, he was inwardly cognizant of what complete goofballs his friends were, how quickly their absolutist dictums would wilt in actual practice. One of the surest proofs of this is Greenspan's schizophrenic posture toward his future employer, the Federal Reserve System.

Rand's objectivists were very strongly opposed to the very concept of the Federal Reserve, a quasi-public institution created in 1913 that allowed a federally appointed banking official—the Federal Reserve chairman—to control the amount of money in the economy.

When he was at Rand's apartment, Greenspan himself was a staunch opponent of the Federal Reserve. One of Rand's closest disciples, Nathaniel Branden, recalled Greenspan's feelings about the Fed. "A number of our talks centered on the Federal Reserve Board's role in influencing the economy by manipulating the money supply," Branden recalled. "Greenspan spoke with vigor and intensity about a totally free banking system."

Throughout the fifties and sixties Greenspan adhered strictly to

Rand's beliefs. His feelings about the Federal Reserve during this time are well documented. In 1966 he wrote an essay called "Gold and Economic Freedom" that blamed the Fed in part for the Great Depression:

> The excess credit which the Fed pumped into the economy spilled over into the stock market—triggering a fantastic speculative boom.

Foreshadowing alert! In any case, during this same period Greenspan drew closer to Rand, who as self-appointed pope of the protocapitalist religion had become increasingly unhinged, prone to Galtian rants and banishments. One of her rages centered around Branden, a handsome and significantly younger psychotherapist Rand met when she was forty-four and Branden was nineteen. The two had an affair despite the fact that both were married; in a cultist echo of David Koresh/Branch Davidian sexual ethics, both spouses reportedly consented to the arrangement to keep the movement leader happy.

But in 1968, eighteen years into their relationship, Rand discovered that Branden had used his pure reason to deduce that a young actress named Patrecia Scott was, objectively speaking, about ten thousand times hotter than the by-then-elderly and never-all-that-pretty-to-begin-with Rand, and was having an affair with her without Rand's knowledge.

Rand then used *her* pure reason and decided to formally banish both Branden and his wife, Barbara, from the movement for "violation of objectivist principles." This wouldn't be worth mentioning but for the hilarious fact that Greenspan signed the excommunication decree, which read:

> Because Nathaniel Branden and Barbara Branden, in a series of actions, have betrayed fundamental principles of Objectivism, we condemn and repudiate these two persons irrevocably.

The irony of a refugee from Soviet tyranny issuing such a classically Leninist excommunication appears to have been completely lost on Rand. But now here comes the really funny part. Almost exactly simultaneous to his decision to sign this preposterous decree, Greenspan did something that was anathema to any good Randian's beliefs: he went to work for a politician.

In 1968 he joined the campaign of Richard Nixon, going to work as an adviser on domestic policy questions. He then worked for Nixon's Bureau of the Budget during the transition, after Nixon's victory over Humphrey. This was a precursor to an appointment to serve on Gerald Ford's Council of Economic Advisers in 1974; he later ingratiated himself into the campaign of Ronald Reagan in 1980, served on a committee to reform Social Security, and ultimately went on to become Federal Reserve chief in 1987. There is a whole story about Greenspan's career as a private economist that took place in the intervening years, but for now the salient fact about Greenspan is that this is a person who grew up in an intellectual atmosphere where collaboration with the government in any way was considered a traitorous offense, but who nonetheless spent most of his adult life involved in government in one way or another. He told the *New York Times Magazine* in 1976 that he rationalized his decision to join the government thusly: "I could have a real effect."

Toward the end of her life, even Rand began to wonder about Greenspan's commitment to the faith, leading to one of the few genuinely salient observations she ever made in her whole silly life: "I think that Alan basically is a social climber," she said.

This ability to work both sides of the aisle at the same time would ultimately amaze even Barbara Walters, whom Greenspan somehow managed to make his girlfriend in the seventies. "How Alan Greenspan, a man who believed in the philosophy of little government interference and few rules of regulation, could end up becoming chairman of the greatest regulatory agency in the country is beyond me," Walters said in 2008.

How did it happen? Among other things, Alan Greenspan was one of the first Americans to really understand the nature of celebrity in the mass-media age. Thirty years before Paris Hilton, Greenspan managed to become famous for being famous—and levered that skill into one of the most powerful jobs on earth.

———

Alan Greenspan's political career was built on a legend—the legend of
the ultimate Wall Street genius, the Man with All the Answers. But the
legend wasn't built on his actual performance as an economist. It was
a reputation built on a reputation. In fact, if you go back and look at
his rise now, his career path has a lot less in common with economist
icons like Keynes or Friedman than it does with celebrity con artists
like L. Ron Hubbard, Tony Robbins, or Beatles guru Maharishi Ma-
hesh Yogi.

Like the Maharishi, Greenspan got his foot in the big door by daz-
zling deluded celebrities with voluble pseudo-mystical nonsense. One
of his big breaks came when a lawyer named Leonard Garment introduced him to Dick Nixon in 1968.

Garment would later describe Greenspan's bloviating on economic matters in that meeting as "Nepal Kathmandu language." Nixon,
nonetheless, was impressed, saying, "That's a very intelligent man." Later
he brought him into the campaign. And although Greenspan eventually
declined a formal role in Nixon's government, he would henceforth thrive
in a role as economic guru to men with power, a role that the press somehow never failed to be made aware of.

When he finally did come into government full-time as head of
Ford's Council of Economic Advisers, glowing accounts of Greenspan's
authority in the White House routinely appeared in the press.

"Greenspan has a unique relationship with the president," crowed
BusinessWeek, which added that, according to one aide, "on economic
policy, Alan is a heavyweight." Future right-wing Godzilla Dick Cheney,
then serving as Ford's chief of staff, added in the *New York Times Magazine* that President Ford attached "more weight to Greenspan's views
than those of any other among his economic advisers."

Sometimes Greenspan himself was the source of the compliments.
The *New Yorker* in 1974, addressing the inflation issue that was hot at
the time, offered this hilarious piece of praise: "Economists of all per-
suasions (with the exception of Alan Greenspan, an Ayn Rand disciple,
who heads the President's Council of Economic Advisers) admit to
being baffled by today's problems."

Not long after that, in 1975, Greenspan became the first economist
to grace the cover of *Newsweek;* by then he had also already been named

to *Time*'s illustrious Board of Economists, which met four times a year to harrumph about economic matters for the mag. Greenspan was even asked for an interview by *Penthouse* that same year, although he declined.

That Greenspan has always been intensely interested in press attention is something that virtually every source I spoke with accepts almost without question. His interest in the media can even be seen in his personal life; he dated in succession three different prominent television figures, moving from Barbara Walters in the late seventies to *MacNeil/Lehrer* producer Susan Mills in the eighties to the woman he ultimately married, NBC correspondent Andrea Mitchell.

One reporter for a major daily newspaper who covered the Fed in the nineties tells of getting frantic calls from Greenspan's office at 7:00 the morning after a negative piece appeared. "I was still half asleep, but the chairman was already unhappy," he said. Around the same time, Paul Weller, a University of Iowa professor who wrote a blisteringly critical paper on Greenspan, was hounded for a copy by Fed press aides before it was even published. "Alan himself wanted to see it," the author chuckles now.

Greenspan was exceptionally skilled at pushing his image of economic genius, particularly since his performance as an economic prognosticator was awful at best. "He was supposedly the smartest man in the world," laughs economist Brian Wesbury today. "He was the greatest, the Maestro. Only if you look at his record, he was wrong about almost everything he ever predicted."

Fed watchers and Greenspan critics all seem to share a passion for picking out which of Greenspan's erroneous predictions was most ridiculous. One of his most famous was his pronouncement in the *New York Times* in January 1973: "It's very rare that you can be as unqualifiedly bullish as you can now," he said. The market proceeded to lose 46 percent of its value over the next two years, plunging from above 1,000 the day of Greenspan's prediction to 571 by December 1974.

Greenspan was even bad at predicting events that had already happened. In April 1975, Greenspan told a New York audience that the recession wasn't over, that the "worst was yet to come." The economy swiftly improved, and the National Bureau of Economic Research later placed the end of the recession at March 1975, a month before Greenspan's speech.

Greenspan's career is full of such pronouncements. In July 1990, at the start of the recession that would ultimately destroy the presidency of George H. W. Bush, Greenspan opined: "In the very near term there's little evidence that I can see to suggest the economy is tilting over [into recession]." Months later, as the bad news continued, Greenspan soldiered on: "Those who argue that we are already in a recession I think are reasonably certain to be wrong."

By October, with the U.S. in the sixth of what would ultimately be ten consecutive months of job losses, Greenspan remained stubborn. "The economy," he said, "has not yet slipped into recession."

The economy has a lot in common with the weather, and even very good economists charged with the job of predicting market swings can become victims of unexpected turns, just like meteorologists. But Greenspan's errors were often historic, idiotic blunders, evidence of a fundamental misunderstanding of problems that led to huge disasters. In fact, if you dig under almost every one of the major financial crashes of our time, you can find some kind of Greenspan quote cheerfully telling people not to worry about where the new trends in the economy were leading.

Before the S&L crisis exploded Greenspan could be seen giving a breezy thumbs-up to now-notorious swindler Charles Keating, whose balance sheet Greenspan had examined—he said that Keating's Lincoln Savings and Loan "has developed a series of carefully planned, highly promising and widely diversified projects" and added that the firm "presents no foreseeable risk to the Federal Savings and Loan Corporation."

The mistake he made in 1994 was even worse. After a few (relatively) small-scale disasters involving derivatives of the sort that would eventually nearly destroy the universe in 2008, Greenspan told Congress that the risks involved with derivatives were "negligible," testimony that was a key reason the government left the derivatives market unregulated. His misreading of the tech bubble of the late nineties is legendary (more on that later); he also fell completely for the Y2K scare and at one point early in the George W. Bush presidency actually worried aloud that the national debt might be repaid too quickly.

But it wasn't Greenspan's economic skill that got him to the top banker job. Instead, it was his skill as a politician. During Ronald Reagan's first and second terms, while the irritatingly independent Paul Volcker sat on the Fed throne, Greenspan was quietly working the refs, attending as many White House functions as he could. Former Reagan aides told Greenspan's biographer Jerome Tuccille that "Alan made a point of regularly massaging the people who mattered." Another official, Martin Anderson, reported that "I don't think I was in the White House once where I didn't see him sitting in the lobby or working the offices. I was absolutely astounded by his omnipresence."

Greenspan had proved his worth to Reagan by using a commission he headed to perform one of the all-time budgetary magic tricks, an invisible tax hike that helped the supposedly antitax Reagan administration fund eight years of massive deficit spending.

In 1981 Reagan appointed Greenspan to head the National Commission on Social Security Reform, which had been created to deal with an alleged short-term funding crisis that would leave the Old-Age and Survivors Insurance Trust Fund bankrupt by 1983. It goes without saying that any political decision one makes with regard to Social Security is hazardous; cutting benefits is a shortcut to electoral death, and the alternative, raising taxes, isn't so palatable either.

Greenspan's solution was to recommend hikes in the Social Security tax, which of course is not considered a real "tax" (Reagan would hilariously later describe such hikes as "revenue enhancements") because the taxpayer theoretically gets that money back later on in benefits. The thinking here was that in the early eighties, with so many baby boomers now in their prime earning years, the Reagan administration would hike payments to build up a surplus that could in twenty or thirty years be used to pay out benefits when those same baby boomers reached retirement age. The administration accepted those proposals, and the Social Security tax rate went from 9.35 percent in 1981 to 15.3 percent by 1990.

Two things about this. One, Social Security taxes are very regressive, among other things because they only apply to wage income (if you're a hedge fund manager or a Wall Street investor and you make all your money in carried interest or capital gains, you don't pay) and they are also capped, at this writing at around $106,000, meaning that wages above a certain level are not taxed at all. That means that a married couple earning $100,000 total will pay roughly the same amount of Social Security taxes that Lloyd Blankfein or Bill Gates will (if not more, depending on how the latter two structure their compensation). So if you ignore the notion that Social Security taxes come back as benefits later on, and just think of them as a revenue source for the government, it's a way for the state to take money from working- and middle-class taxpayers at a highly disproportional rate.

Second, Greenspan's plan to build up a sort of Social Security war chest for use in paying out benefits to retirees twenty years down the road was based on a fallacy. When you pay money into Social Security, it doesn't go into a locked box that is separate from the rest of the budget and can't be used for other government spending. After the Greenspan reforms, the Social Security Administration bought T-bills with that money, essentially lending the cash back to the government for use in other appropriations. So if, let's say, your president wanted an extra few billion dollars or so of short-term spending money, he could just reach into the budget and take all that Social Security money, leaving whoever would be president two decades later holding not cash to pay out Social Security benefits, but government notes or bonds, i.e., IOUs.

And that's exactly what happened. The recommendations ushered in after Greenspan's commission effectively resulted in $1.69 trillion in new, regressive taxes over the next twenty years or so.

But instead of keeping their hands off that money and preserving it for Social Security payments, Reagan, Bush I, Clinton, and Bush II spent it—all of it—inspiring the so-called Social Security crisis of George W. Bush's presidency, in which it was announced suddenly that Social Security, far from having a surplus, was actually steaming toward bankruptcy. The bad news was released to the public by then–Treasury secretary Paul O'Neill, who let it slip that the Social Security fund had no assets at all, and instead just had pieces of paper in its account.

"I come to you as managing trustee of Social Security," O'Neill said. "Today we have no assets in the trust fund. We have the good faith and credit of the United States government that benefits will flow."

In other words, Greenspan and Reagan had conspired to hike Social Security payments, justifying it with the promise of building up a Social Security nest egg for subsequent decades, then used up that nest egg on current government spending.

Now, it was bad enough that Greenspan, who as a Randian was supposedly against all use of government "force," would propose such a big tax hike. But what made his role especially villainous was that when George W. Bush decided to start sounding alarm bells about the future of Social Security, it was none other than Alan Greenspan who came out and argued that maybe it was time to cut Social Security benefits. This is from a *Washington Post* story in February 2004:

> Greenspan offered several ways to curtail federal spending growth, including reducing Social Security and Medicare benefits. The Fed chairman again recommended raising the age at which retirees become eligible, to keep pace with the population's rising longevity. And he reminded lawmakers that they could link cost-of-living increases in benefits levels to a measure of inflation other than the consumer price index, a widely followed measure that some economists believe overstates the rise in overall prices. A measure that showed less inflation would cause benefit levels to rise more slowly.

To recap: Greenspan hikes Social Security taxes by a trillion and a half dollars or so, four presidents spend all that money on other shit (including, in George W. Bush's case, a massive tax cut for the wealthy), and then, when it comes time to start paying out those promised benefits, Greenspan announces that it can't be afforded, the money isn't there, benefits can't be paid out.

It was a shell game—money comes in the front door as payroll taxes and goes right out the back door as deficit spending, with only new payroll taxes over the years keeping the bubble from popping, continuing the illusion that the money had never left. Senator Daniel Patrick Moynihan, way back in 1983, had called this "thievery," but as the scam played out over the decades it earned a more specific title. "A classic Ponzi scheme" is how one reporter who covered Greenspan put it.

Coming up with a scheme like this is the sort of service that endears

one to presidents, and by the mid-eighties Greenspan got his chance at
the big job. Reagan had grown disenchanted with Volcker. The administration apparently wanted a Fed chief who would "collaborate more
intimately with the White House," as one Fed historian put it, and they
got him in Greenspan, whom Reagan put in the top job in 1987.
Greenspan "struggled inwardly to contain his glee," his biographer Tuccille wrote, and came into the job with great fanfare, including a *Time*
magazine cover story that anointed him "The New Mr. Dollar."

He breezed through the nomination process, despite a battering
by Wisconsin senator William Proxmire, who whaled on Greenspan's
record of failed forecasts during his tenure on Ford's Council of Economic Advisers. In one of the more humorous exchanges, Greenspan
attempted to deny that he had once predicted a T-bill rate of 4.4 percent for 1978 (it turned out to be 9.8 percent) or that the U.S. Consumer Price Index would rise 4.5 percent (it actually rose 9.5 percent).
"That is not my recollection of the way those forecasts went,"
Greenspan asserted.

Proxmire then went on to read out Greenspan's predictions one
by one.

"Well," Greenspan quipped, "if they're written down, those are the
numbers."

Proxmire kept at Greenspan, but it didn't take. On August 11,
1987, Alan Greenspan was sworn in as Federal Reserve chairman, effectively marking the beginning of the Bubble Generation.

The shorthand version of how the bubble economy works goes something like this:

Imagine the whole economy has turned into a casino. Investors are
betting on oil futures, subprime mortgages, and Internet stocks, hoping
for a quick score. In this scenario the major brokerages and investment
banks play the role of the house. Just like real casinos, they always win
in the end—regardless of which investments succeed or fail, they always
take their cut in the form of fees and interest. Also just like real casinos,
they only make more money as the number of gamblers increases: the

more you play, the more they make. And even if the speculative bubbles themselves have all the inherent value of a royal flush, the money the house takes out *is* real.

Maybe those oil futures you bought were never close to being worth $149 a barrel in reality, but the fees you paid to Goldman Sachs or Morgan Stanley to buy those futures get turned into real beach houses, real Maseratis, real Park Avenue town houses. Bettors chase imaginary riches, while the house turns those dreams into real mansions.

Now imagine that every time the bubble bursts and the gamblers all go belly-up, the house is allowed to borrow giant piles of money from the state for next to nothing. The casino then in turn lends out all that money at the door to its recently busted customers, who flock back to the tables to lose their shirts all over again. The cycle quickly repeats itself, only this time the gambler is in even worse shape than before; now he's not only lost his own money, he's lost his money *and* he owes the house for what he's borrowed.

That's a simplistic view of what happened to the American economy under Alan Greenspan. The financial services industry inflated one speculative bubble after another, and each time the bubble burst, Greenspan and the Fed swept in to save the day by printing vast sums of money and dumping it back on Wall Street, in effect encouraging people to "drink themselves sober," as Greenspan biographer William Fleckenstein put it.

That's why Alan Greenspan is the key to understanding this generation's financial disaster. He repeatedly used the financial might of the state to jet-fuel the insanely regressive pyramid scheme of the bubble economy, which like actual casinos proved to be a highly efficient method for converting the scattered savings of legions of individual schmuck-citizens into the concentrated holdings of a few private individuals.

"The one way you can have a particularly disastrous bubble is if it's fueled by the central bank," says Fleckenstein. "And that's what Greenspan did."

A person can easily go crazy trying to understand everything the

Fed does,* so in the interests of sanity it's probably best to skip the long version and focus on its magical money-creating powers, the key to the whole bubble scam. The bank has a great many functions—among other things, it enforces banking regulations and maintains and standardizes the currency—but its most obvious and important job has to do with regulating the money supply.

The basic idea behind the Fed's regulation of the money supply is to keep the economy as healthy as possible by limiting inflation on the one hand and preventing recession on the other. It achieves this by continually expanding and contracting the amount of money in the economy, theoretically tightening when there is too much buying and inflation and loosening when credit goes slack and the lack of lending and business stimulation threatens recession.

The Fed gets its pseudo-religious aura from its magical ability to create money out of nothing, or to contract the money supply as it sees fit. As a former Boston Fed chief named Richard Syron has pointed out, the bank has even fashioned its personnel structure to resemble that of the Catholic Church, with a pope (the chairman), cardinals (the regional governors), and a curia (the senior staff).

One way that money is created is through new issuance of private credit; when private banks issue new loans, they essentially create money out of thin air. The Fed supervises this process and theoretically monitors the amount of new loans issued by the banks. It can raise or lower the amount of new loans by raising or lowering margin requirements, i.e., the number of hard dollars each bank has to keep on hand every time it makes a loan. If the margin requirement is 10 percent, banks have to keep one dollar parked in reserve at the Fed for every ten they lend out. If the Fed feels like increasing the amount of money in circulation, it can lower the margin rate to, say, 9 percent, allowing banks to lend out about eleven dollars for every one kept in reserve at the Fed.

The bank can also inject money into the system directly, mainly through two avenues. One is by lending money directly to banks at a

---

*It's a heavy subject even in the literal sense. One of the definitive works on the Fed, William Greider's *Secrets of the Temple*, is such a legendarily dense and physically massive book that a group of editors I know jokingly dared one another to try to shoplift it.

thing called the *discount window,* which allows commercial banks to borrow from the Fed at relatively low rates to cover short-term financing problems.

The other avenue is for the Fed to buy Treasury bills or bonds from banks or brokers. It works like this: The government, i.e., the Treasury, decides to borrow money. One of a small group of private banks called *primary dealers* is contracted to raise that money for the Treasury by selling T-bills or bonds or notes on the open market. Those primary dealers (as of this writing there are eighteen of them, all major institutions, including Goldman Sachs, Morgan Stanley, and Deutsche Bank) on occasion sell those T-bills to the Fed, which simply credits that dealer's account when it buys the securities. Through this circular process the government prints money to lend to itself, adding to the overall money supply in the process.

In recent times, thanks to an utterly insane program spearheaded by Greenspan's successor, Ben Bernanke, called quantitative easing, the Fed has gotten into the habit of buying more than just T-bills and is printing billions of dollars every week to buy private assets like mortgages. In practice, however, the Fed's main tool for regulating the money supply during the Greenspan years wasn't its purchase of securities or control over margin requirements, but its manipulation of interest rates.

Here's how this works: When a bank falls short of the cash it needs to meet its reserve requirement, it can borrow cash either from the Fed or from the reserve accounts of other banks. The interest rate that bank has to pay to borrow that money is called the *federal funds rate,* and the Fed can manipulate it. When rates go up, borrowers are discouraged from taking out loans, and banks end up rolling back their lending. But when the Fed cuts the funds rate, banks are suddenly easily able to borrow the cash they need to meet their reserve requirements, which in turn dramatically impacts the amount of new loans they can issue, vastly increasing the money in the system.

The upshot of all of this is that the Fed has enormous power to create money both by injecting it directly into the system and by allowing private banks to create their own new loans. If you have a productive economy and an efficient financial services industry that rapidly marries money to solid, job-creating business opportunities, that stimulative power of a central bank can be a great thing. But if the national economy is a casino and the financial services industry is turning one market after another into a Ponzi scheme, then frantically pumping new money into such a destructive system is madness, no different from lending money to wild-eyed gambling addicts on the Vegas strip—and that's exactly what Alan Greenspan did, over and over again.

Alan Greenspan met with major challenges almost immediately after taking office in August 1987. The first was the stock market correction of October of that year, and the next was the recession of the early 1990s, brought about by the collapse of the S&L industry.

Both disasters were caused by phenomena Greenspan had a long track record of misunderstanding. The 1987 crash was among other things caused by portfolio insurance derivatives (Greenspan was still fighting against regulation of these instruments five or six derivative-based disasters later, in 1998, after Long-Term Capital Management imploded and nearly dragged down the entire world economy), while Greenspan's gaffes with regard to S&Ls like Charles Keating's Lincoln Savings have already been described. His response to both disasters was characteristic: he slashed the federal funds rate and flooded the economy with money.

Greenspan's response to the 1990s recession was particularly dramatic. When he started cutting rates in May 1989, the federal funds rate was 9 percent. By July 1991 he had cut rates 36 percent, to 5.75 percent. From there he cut rates another 44 percent, reaching a low of 3 percent in September 1992—and then he held rates at that historically low rate for fifteen more months. He showered Wall Street with money year after year. When he raised rates again in February 1994, it was the first time he had done so in five years.

Here we have to pause briefly to explain something about these rate cuts. When the Fed cuts the funds rate, it affects interest rates across the board. So when Greenspan cut rates for five consecutive years, it caused rates for bank savings, CDs, commercial bonds, and T-bills to drop as well.

Now all of a sudden you have a massive number of baby boomers approaching retirement age, and they see that all the billions they have tied up in CDs, money market funds, and other nest-egg investments are losing yields. Meanwhile Wall Street was taking that five consecutive years of easy money and investing it in stocks to lay the foundation for Greenspan's first bubble, the stock market mania of the nineties.

Baby boomers and institutional investors like pension funds and unions were presented with a simple choice: get into the rising yields of the stock market or stick with the declining yields of safer investments and get hammered. As economist Brian Wesbury puts it, it was as if Greenspan was holding up a green light, inviting people to rush into the equity markets.

"When you come to a green light in your car, how many of you have ever stopped your car, gotten out, gone around, and made sure that it's okay to go through?" says Wesbury.

Greenspan himself was fully aware that his rate cuts were pushing people into the stock markets. In testimony before the Senate on May 27, 1994, he said:

> Lured by consistently high returns in capital markets, people exhibited increasing willingness to take on market risk by extending the maturity of their investments . . . In 1993 alone, $281 billion moved into [stock and bond mutual funds], representing the lion's share of net investment in the U.S. bond and stock markets. A significant portion of the investments in longer-term mutual funds undoubtedly was diverted from deposits, money market funds, and other short-term lower-yielding, but less speculative investments.

So Greenspan was aware that his policies were luring ordinary people into the riskier investments of the stock market, which by 1994 was already becoming overvalued, exhibiting some characteristics of a bubble. But he was reluctant to slow the bubble by raising rates or increasing margin requirements, because . . . why? If you actually listen to his explanations at the time, Greenspan seems to say he didn't raise rates because he didn't want to be a bummer. In that same Senate testimony, he admits to seeing that investors were chasing a false dream:

Because we at the Federal Reserve were concerned about sharp re-
actions in the markets that **had grown accustomed to an unsustainable combination of high returns and low volatility** [emphasis
mine], we chose a cautious approach . . . We recognized . . . that
our shift could impart uncertainty to markets, and many of us were
concerned that a large immediate move in rates could create too big
a dose of uncertainty, which could destabilize the financial system.

Translation: everybody was used to making unrealistic returns, and
we didn't want to spoil the party by instituting a big rate hike. (Cue
Claude Rains in *Casablanca* after the Nazis shut down Rick's roulette
game: "But everybody's having such a good time!") Instead, Greenspan's
response to the growing bubble in the summer of 1994 was a very modest hike of one-half of one percentage point.

Now here comes the crazy part. At around the same time that
Greenspan was testifying before the Senate that a cautious approach
was fine, that no drastic action was needed, and there was no danger
out there of a bubble, he was saying virtually the exact opposite at a
meeting of the Federal Open Market Committee (FOMC), the hu-
morously secretive and Politburo-esque body charged with making rate
adjustments. Here is Greenspan on May 17, 1994:

I think there's still a lot of bubble around; we have not completely
eliminated it. Nonetheless, we have the capability, I would say at
this stage, to move more strongly than we usually do without crack-
ing the system.

This testimony is amazing in retrospect because about eight years
later, after the crash of the tech bubble, Greenspan would openly argue
that bubbles are impossible to see until they pop. It is, he would say
in 2002, "very difficult to definitively identify a bubble until after the
fact—that is, when its bursting confirmed its existence."

A few months after Greenspan warned the FOMC that there was
still some "bubble around," he suddenly announced that the bubble
had been popped. At an FOMC meeting in August 1994, he said that
the May rate hike of one-half a percentage point had solved the prob-

lem. "With the May move," he said, "I think we demonstrated that the bubble for all practical purposes had been defused."

About a half year later, in February 1995, Greenspan would raise rates for the last time for many years. "One can say that while the stock market is not low, it clearly is not anywhere close to being as elevated as it was a year or so ago," he said.

Within a few months after that, by July 1995, Greenspan was back to *cutting* rates, slashing the funds rate from 6 percent to 5.75 percent, flooding the economy with money at a time when the stock market was exploding. With easy credit everywhere and returns on savings and CDs at rock bottom, everyone and his brother rushed ass first into the tech-fueled stock market. "That's the beginning of the biggest stock market bubble in U.S. history," says Fleckenstein.

But Greenspan's biggest contribution to the bubble economy was psychological. As Fed chief he had enormous influence over the direction of the economy and could have dramatically altered history simply by stating out loud that the stock market was overvalued.

And in fact, Greenspan in somewhat hesitating fashion tried this—with his famous December 1996 warning that perhaps "irrational exuberance" had overinflated asset values. This was spoken in the full heat of the tech bubble and is a rare example of Greenspan speaking, out loud, the impolitic truth.

It's worth noting, however, that even as he warned that the stock market was overheated, he was promising to not do a thing about it. On the same day that he spoke about "irrational exuberance," Greenspan said that the Fed would only act if "a collapsing financial asset bubble does not threaten to impair the real economy." Since popping a bubble *always* impairs the real economy, Greenspan was promising never to do anything about anything.

Despite Greenspan's rather explicit promise to sit on his liver-spotted hands during the bubble, Wall Street reacted with unbridled horror at Greenspan's "irrational exuberance" quote, which made sense: the Internet stock party was just getting going and nobody wanted to see it end. A mini-panic ensued as the Street brutally responded to Greenspan's rhetoric, with the NYSE plunging 140 points in the first hour of trading the day after his comments. The *New York Times* even ran a front-page story with the headline "Stocks Worldwide Dive as Greenspan Questions Euphoria."

For a man who hated to be disliked on Wall Street, the reaction was a nightmare. "Greenspan was freaked out by the response," says one newspaper reporter who covered Greenspan on a daily basis at the time. "That [irrational exuberance business] was the one time he said something in a way that was clear enough and quotable enough to make the newspapers, and all hell broke loose."

And so, true to his psychological pattern, Greenspan spent much of the next four years recoiling from his own warning, turning himself all the way around to become head cheerleader to the madness.

In fact, far from expressing concern about "irrational" stock values, Greenspan subsequently twisted himself into knots finding new ways to make sense of the insane share prices of the wave of Worthless.com stocks that were flooding the market at the end of that decade. The same man who as early as 1994 was warning the FOMC about "a lot of bubble around" took to arguing that there *was* no bubble.

Greenspan's eventual explanation for the growing gap between stock prices and actual productivity was that, fortuitously, the laws of nature had changed—humanity had reached a happy stage of history where bullshit could be used as rocket fuel. In January 2000 Greenspan unveiled a theory, which he would repeat over and over again, that the economy had entered a new era, one in which all the rules were being rewritten:

> When we look back at the 1990s, from the perspective of say 2010, the nature of the forces currently in train will have presumably become clearer. We may conceivably conclude from that vantage point that, at the turn of the millennium, the American economy was experiencing a once-in-a-century acceleration of innovation, which propelled forward productivity . . . at a pace not seen in generations, if ever.

In a horrifyingly literal sense, Greenspan put his money where his mouth was, voting for the mania with the Fed's money. An example: On November 13, 1998, a company called theglobe.com went public, opening at $9 and quickly jumping to $63.50 at the close of the first day's trading. At one point during that day, the stock market briefly valued the shares in theglobe.com at over $5 billion—this despite the fact that the company's total earnings for the first three quarters of that year were less than $2.7 *million.*

Four days after that record-shattering IPO, which clearly demonstrated the rabid insanity of the tech-stock tulipomania, Alan Greenspan again doused the market with lighter fluid, chopping rates once more, to 4.75 percent. This was characteristic of his behavior throughout the boom. In fact, from February 1996 through October 1999, Greenspan expanded the money supply by about $1.6 trillion, or roughly 20 percent of GDP.

Even now, with the memory of the housing bubble so fresh, it's hard to put in perspective the craziness of the late-nineties stock market. Fleckenstein points out that tech stocks were routinely leaping by 100 percent of their value or more on the first day of their IPOs, and cites Cobalt Networks (482 percent), Foundry Networks (525 percent), and Akamai Technologies (458 percent) as examples. All three of those companies traded at one hundred times sales—meaning that if you bought the entire business and the sales generated incurred no expenses, it would have taken you one hundred years to get your money back.

According to Greenspan, however, these companies were not necessarily valued incorrectly. All that was needed to make this make sense was to rethink one's conception of "value." As he put it during the boom:

> [There is] an ever increasing conceptualization of our Gross Domestic Product—the substitution, in effect, of ideas for physical value.

What Greenspan was saying, in other words, was that there was absolutely nothing wrong with bidding up to $100 million in share value some hot-air Internet stock, because the lack of that company's "physical value" (i.e., the actual money those three employees weren't earning) could be overcome by the inherent value of their "ideas."

To say that this was a radical reinterpretation of the entire science of economics is an understatement—economists had never dared measure "value" except in terms of actual concrete production. It was equivalent to a chemist saying that concrete becomes gold when you paint it yellow. It was lunacy.

Greenspan's endorsement of the "new era" paradigm encouraged all the economic craziness of the tech bubble. This was a pattern he fell into repeatedly. When a snooty hedge fund full of self-proclaimed geniuses called Long-Term Capital Management exploded in 1998, thanks to its managers' wildly irresponsible decision to leverage themselves one hundred or two hundred times over or more to gamble on risky derivative bets, Greenspan responded by orchestrating a bailout, citing "systemic risk" if the fund was allowed to fail. The notion that the Fed would intervene to save a high-risk gambling scheme like LTCM was revolutionary. "Here, you're basically bailing out a hedge fund," says Dr. John Makin, a former Treasury and Congressional Budget Office official. "This was a bad message to send. It basically said to people, take more risk. Nobody is going to stop you."

When the Russian ruble collapsed around the same time, causing massive losses in emerging markets where investors had foolishly committed giant sums to fledgling economies that were years from real productivity, Greenspan was spooked enough that he announced a surprise rate cut, again bailing out dumb investors by letting them borrow their way out of their mistakes. "That's what capitalism is supposed to be about—creative destruction," says Fleckenstein. "People who take too much risk are supposed to fail sometimes." But instead of letting nature take its course, Greenspan came to the rescue every time some juiced-up band of Wall Street greedheads drove their portfolios into a tree.

Greenspan was even dumb enough to take the Y2K scare seriously, flooding the markets with money in anticipation of a systemwide computer malfunction that, of course, never materialized. We can calculate how much money Greenspan dumped into the economy in advance of Y2K; between September 20 and November 10, 1999, the Fed printed about $147 billion extra and pumped it into the economy. "The crucial issue . . . is to recognize that we have a Y2K problem," he said at the century's final FOMC meeting. "It is a problem about which we don't want to become complacent."

Again, all of these rate cuts and injections—in response to LTCM, the emerging markets crash, and Y2K—were undertaken in the middle of a raging stock market bubble, making his crisis strategy somewhat like trying to put out a forest fire with napalm.

By the turn of the century, the effect of Greenspan's constant money printing was definite and contagious, as it was now widely understood that every fuckup would be bailed out by rivers of cheap cash. This was where the term "Greenspan put" first began to be used widely.

Aside: a "put" is a financial contract between two parties that gives the buyer the option to sell a stock at a certain share price. Let's say IBM is trading at 100 today, and you buy 100 puts from Madonna at 95. Now imagine the share price falls to 90 over the course of the next two weeks. You can now go out and buy 100 shares at 90 for $9,000, and then exercise your puts, obligating Madonna to buy them back at 95, for $9,500. You've then earned $500 betting against IBM.

The "Greenspan put" referred to Wall Street's view of cheap money from the Fed playing the same hedging role as a put option; it's a kind of insurance policy against a declining market you keep in your back pocket. Instead of saying, "Well, if IBM drops below ninety-five, I can always sell my put options," Wall Street was saying, "Well, if the market drops too low, Greenspan will step in and lend us shitloads of money." A Cleveland Fed official named Jerry Jordan even expressed the idea with somewhat seditious clarity in 1998:

> I have seen—probably everybody has now seen—newsletters, advisory letters, talking heads at CNBC, and so on saying there is no risk that the stock market is going to go down because even if it started down, the Fed would ease policy to prop it back up.

Eventually, the Iowa professor Paul Weller, along with University of Warwick professors Marcus Miller and Lei Zhang, would formally identify this concept in a paper called "Moral Hazard and the U.S. Stock Market: Analyzing the 'Greenspan Put.'" By then, however, the term "Greenspan put" had been around for years, and the very fact that it was now being formally studied is evidence of the profound effect it had on the markets.

"Investors came to believe in something the Fed couldn't really deliver," says Weller now. "There was this belief that the Fed would always provide a floor to the market."

"His effect on the psychology is the most important thing you have to look at," says the manager of one well-known hedge fund. "There was this belief that Greenspan would always be the lender of last resort, that we would always have the government bail us out."

"It was all psychological. If people just *thought* Greenspan was in charge, things would be okay," says Wesbury. "Even John McCain said that if Greenspan were ever to die, he would just prop him up in the corner and put sunglasses on him, like in *Weekend at Bernie's*.* The belief that he would be there is the thing."

"It's a two-pronged problem," says Fleckenstein. "Number one, he's putting in this rocket fuel to propel the speculation. And number two, he's giving you the confidence that he's going to come in and save the day . . . that the Fed will come in and clean up the mess."

The idea that Greenspan not even covertly but overtly encouraged irresponsible speculation to a monstrous degree is no longer terribly controversial in the financial world. But what isn't discussed all that often is how Greenspan's constant interventions on behalf of Wall Street speculators dovetailed with his behavior as a politician and as a regulator during the same period.

Even as Greenspan was using the vast power of the state to bail out the very assholes who were selling back-of-the-napkin Internet start-ups to pension funds or betting billions in borrowed cash on gibberish foreign exchange derivative trades, he was also working round the clock, with true Randian zeal, to destroy the government's regulatory infrastructure.

As chief overseer of all banking activity the Fed was ostensibly the top cop on the financial block, but during his years as Fed chief Greenspan continually chipped away—actually it was more like hacking away, with an ax—at his own regulatory authority, diluting the Fed's power to enforce margin requirements, restrict derivative trades, or prevent unlawful

---

*"I would not only reappoint Mr. Greenspan; if Mr. Greenspan should happen to die, God forbid . . . I would prop him up and put a pair of dark glasses on him."—then–presidential candidate John McCain, 2000.

mergers. What he was after was a sort of cynical perversion of the already perverse Randian ideal. He wanted a government that was utterly powerless to interfere in the workings of private business, leaving just one tool in its toolbox—the ability to funnel giant sums of money to the banks. He turned the Fed into a Santa Claus who was legally barred from distributing lumps of coal to naughty kids.

Greenspan's reigning achievement in this area was his shrewd undermining of the Glass-Steagall Act, a Depression-era law that barred insurance companies, investment banks, and commercial banks from merging. In 1998, the law was put to the test when then–Citibank chairman Sandy Weill orchestrated the merger of his bank with Travelers Insurance and the investment banking giant Salomon Smith Barney.

The merger was frankly and openly illegal, precisely the sort of thing that Glass-Steagall had been designed to prevent—the dangerous concentration of capital in the hands of a single megacompany, creating potential conflicts of interest in which insurers and investment banks might be pressed to promote stocks or policies that benefit banks, not customers. Moreover, Glass-Steagall had helped prevent exactly the sort of situation we found ourselves subject to in 2008, when a handful of companies that were "too big to fail" went belly up thanks to their own arrogance and stupidity, and the government was left with no choice but to bail them out.

But Weill was determined to do this deal, and he had the backing of Bill Clinton, Clinton's Treasury secretary Bob Rubin (who would go on to earn $100-plus million at postmerger Citigroup), and, crucially, Alan Greenspan. Weill met with Greenspan early in the process and received what Weill called a "positive response" to the proposal; when the merger was finally completed, Greenspan boldly approved the illegal deal, using an obscure provision in the Bank Holding Company Act that allowed the merger to go through temporarily. Under the arrangement, the newly created Citigroup would have two years to divest itself of its illegal insurance company holdings, plus three additional years if Greenspan approved a series of one-year grace periods. That gave all the parties involved time to pass a new law in Congress called the Gramm-Leach-Bliley Act, which would legalize the deal post factum.

It was a move straight out of *Blazing Saddles:* Greenspan basically had this newly formed megafirm put a gun to its own head and pull the "One move and the nigger gets it!" routine before Congress.

Greenspan himself put it in even starker terms, not so subtly threatening that if Congress failed to play ball, the state would be forced to pay for a wave of insurance and banking failures. "Without congressional action to update our laws," he said in February 1999, "the market will force ad hoc administrative responses that lead to inefficiencies and inconsistencies, expansion of the federal safety net, and potentially increased risk exposure to the federal deposit insurance funds."

Congress had fought off pressure to repeal Glass-Steagall numerous times in the eighties and early nineties, but this time, in the face of Greenspan's threats and this massive deal that had already been end-run into existence, it blinked. Gramm-Leach-Bliley thus became law, a move that would lead directly to the disasters of 2008.

And once he was finished with Glass-Steagall, Greenspan took aim at the derivatives market, where a rogue government official named Brooksley Born had committed the cardinal sin of suggesting that derivatives, like foreign exchange swaps and credit default swaps, posed a potential danger to the economy and might be necessary to regulate. Born, at the time the head of the Commodity Futures Trading Commission, which has purview over derivatives, had in the spring of 1998 issued something called a *concept release,* sort of the government bureaucracy version of a white paper, calling for suggestions on potential regulation of the over-the-counter derivatives market. The twenty-odd-page paper detailed many of the potential risks of derivative trading and today looks a lot like a Nostradamus testament, so accurately does it predict derivative-fueled disasters like the collapse of AIG.

When a draft of Born's concept release began circulating on the Hill in March and April of that year, Bill Clinton's inner circle on economic matters—including former Goldman chief and then–Treasury secretary Bob Rubin, his deputy Gary Gensler, Greenspan at the Fed, and then–SEC chief Arthur Levitt—all freaked out. This was despite the fact that Born hadn't even concretely proposed any sort of regulation yet—she was just trying to initiate a discussion about the *possibility* of regulation. Nonetheless, a furor ensued, and at a critical April 21, 1998, meeting of the President's Working Group on Financial Markets—a group that includes primarily the heads of the Treasury (at the time, Rubin), the SEC (Levitt), the CFTC (Born), and the Fed (Greenspan)—the other members openly pressured Born to retrench.

"It was a great big conference table in this ornate room that the secretary of the Treasury had," says Michael Greenberger, who at the time worked under Born as the head of the CFTC's Division of Trading and Markets. "Not only were the four principals there, but everybody in the government who has any regulatory responsibility for financial affairs was there—the comptroller of the currency, the chairman of the FDIC, the Office of Thrift Supervision, the White House adviser, the OMB, the room was packed with people.

"And if you were a staff member, you sat behind your principal," he goes on. "My seat was directly behind Brooksley and Greenspan. I could have reached out and touched either one of them. And Greenspan turned to her, and his face was red, and he wasn't hollering, but he was quite insistent that she was making a terrible mistake and that she should stop."

Born had complete legal authority to issue her concept release without interference from the Working Group, the president, or anyone else—in fact, the seemingly overt effort to interfere with her jurisdiction was "a violation, maybe even rising to the level of a criminal violation," according to Greenberger. Despite these legally questionable efforts of Rubin and Greenspan, Born did eventually release her paper on May 7 of that year, but to no avail; Greenspan et al. eventually succeeded not only in unseating Born from the CFTC the next year, but in passing a monstrosity called the Commodity Futures Modernization Act of 2000, which affirmatively deregulated the derivatives market.

The new law, which Greenspan pushed aggressively, not only prevented the federal government from regulating instruments like collateralized debt obligations and credit default swaps, it even prevented the states from regulating them using gaming laws—which otherwise might easily have applied, since so many of these new financial wagers were indistinguishable from racetrack bets.

The amazing thing about the CFMA was that it was passed immediately after the Long-Term Capital Management disaster, a potent and obvious example of the destructive potential inherent in an unregulated derivatives market. LTCM was a secretive hedge fund that was making huge bets without collateral and keeping massive amounts of debt off its balance sheet, à la Enron—the financial equivalent of performing open heart surgery with unwashed hands, using a Super 8 motel bedspread as an operating surface.

None of this fazed Greenspan, who apparently never understood what derivatives are or how they work. He saw derivatives like credit default swaps—insurance-like contracts that allow a lender to buy "protection" from a third party in the event his debtor defaults—as brilliant innovations that not only weren't risky, but reduced risk.

"Greenspan saw credit derivatives as a device that enhanced a risk-free economic environment," says Greenberger. "And the theory was as follows: he's looking at credit derivatives, and he's saying everyone is going to have insurance against breakdowns . . . But what he didn't understand was that the insurance wasn't going to be capitalized."

In other words, credit default swaps and the like allowed companies to sell something like insurance protection without actually having the money to pay that insurance—a situation that allowed lenders to feel that they were covered and free to take more risks, when in fact they were not. These instruments were most often risk enhancers, not risk eliminators.

"It wasn't like buying insurance, car insurance, life insurance, something else, where it's regulated and the companies have to be capitalized," Greenberger goes on. "These guys were selling insurance without being capitalized." AIG, which imploded in 2008 after selling nearly a half billion dollars' worth of insurance despite having practically no money to pay off those bets, would end up being the poster child for that sort of risk.

But this problem should have been obvious way before AIG, particularly to someone in Greenspan's position. In fact, even by 1998, by the time LTCM was over, the country had already experienced numerous derivatives-based calamities: the 1987 crash, the Orange County bankruptcy of 1994, the Bankers Trust scandal of 1995, and LTCM. Nonetheless, Greenspan refused to see the danger. In March 1999, just months after he himself had orchestrated a bailout for LTCM, he said that "derivatives are an increasingly important vehicle for unbundling risk." He then said he was troubled that the "periodic emergence of financial panics" had inspired some to consider giving regulators more power to monitor derivative risk, instead of leaving the banks to monitor risk on their own.

An example of the kind of private "monitoring" that Greenspan championed was Long-Term Capital Management's risk models. According to the fund's initial calculations, it would lose 50 percent of its portfolio only once every 10^{30} days, i.e., one would have to sit and wait for several billion times the life of the universe for such a disaster to happen. The fund would actually lose pretty much its entire portfolio just a few years into its existence.

Nonetheless, Greenspan just months after this collapse said that regulators' risk models were "much less accurate than banks' risk measurement models." This was the line he sold to Congress before it passed the CFMA; he also insisted that the derivatives market needed exemptions from regulation in order to remain competitive internationally. But he made clear his real reasons for pushing derivatives deregulation in a speech to the Futures Industry Association in March 1999:

> It should come as no surprise that the profitability of derivative products . . . is a factor in the significant gain of the overall finance industry's share of American corporate output during the past decade. In short, the value added of derivatives themselves derives from their ability to enhance the process of wealth creation.

Translating that into English: I recognize that derivatives are making everyone shitloads of money, so I'll leave them alone.

It was in the immediate wake of all these historically disastrous moves—printing 1.7 trillion new dollars in the middle of a massive stock bubble, dismantling the Glass-Steagall Act, deregulating the derivatives market, blowing off his regulatory authority in the middle of an era of rampant fraud—that Greenspan was upheld by the mainstream financial and political press as a hero of almost Caesarian stature. In February 1999, *Time* magazine even put him on the cover, flanked by

Clinton officials Bob Rubin and Larry Summers, next to the preposterous headline "The Committee to Save the World: The inside
story of how the Three Marketeers have prevented a global economic
meltdown—so far."

That these guys were actually *anti*-Marketeers who had not prevented but *caused* an economic meltdown was an irony that even in retrospect was apparently lost on *Time,* which would make the exact same
idiotic mistake in 2009, when it made Greenspan's similarly bubble-
manic successor, Ben Bernanke, its Person of the Year. In any case, the
1999 *Time* cover captured Greenspan at his peak; he had used the Fed's
power to turn himself into the great indispensable superhero of the investor class, worshipped on the one hand for the uncompromising free-
market orthodoxy of his crotchety public statements, and giddily
prized on the other hand for his under-the-table subsidies of the nation's bankers.

But even as Greenspan sheltered Wall Street from changes in the
weather, when it came to using the Fed's powers to rein in abuses he
proclaimed helplessness before the forces of the free market. The same
person who intervened to counteract the market's reaction to the implosion of Long-Term Capital Management and the Russian ruble
even had the balls to tell Congress that he, Alan Greenspan, did not
have the right to question the wisdom of the market, when for instance the market chose to say that a two-slackers-in-a-cubicle operation like theglobe.com was worth $5 billion.

"To spot a bubble in advance," he told Congress in 1999, "requires
a judgment that hundreds of thousands of informed investors have it all
wrong." He added, with a completely straight face, "Betting against
markets is usually precarious at best."

Some said he was just naïve, or merely incompetent, but in the end,
Greenspan was most likely just lying. He castrated the government as a
regulatory authority, then transformed himself into the Pablo Escobar
of high finance, unleashing a steady river of cheap weight into the crack
house that Wall Street was rapidly becoming.

———

Greenspan's response to the horrific collapse of the tech bubble in 2000–2001 was characteristic and predictable. More than $5 trillion worth of wealth had been destroyed in worthless tech stocks, but instead of letting investors feel the pain they deserved, Greenspan did what he had always done: he flooded the market with money all over again and inflated a new bubble. Only this was the biggest "Greenspan put" of all: in the wake of the tech bubble he cut rates eleven consecutive times, all the way down to 1 percent, an all-time low, and began talking out loud about housing and mortgages as the new hot table in the casino.

"When the real estate bubble came along as a consequence of the money printing that was used to sort of drink ourselves sober after the equity bubble, I knew it was going to be an even bigger disaster," says Fleckenstein.

Looking back now at the early years in the 2000s, Greenspan's comments almost seem like the ravings of a madman. The nation's top financial official began openly encouraging citizens to use the equity in their homes as an ATM. "Low rates have also encouraged households to take on larger mortgages when refinancing their homes," he said. "Drawing on home equity in this manner is a significant source of funding for consumption and home modernization."

But he went really crazy in 2004, when he told America that adjustable-rate mortgages were a good product and safer, fixed-rate mortgages were unattractive. He said the following in a speech to the Credit Union National Association Governmental Affairs Conference in February 2004:

> Indeed, recent research within the Federal Reserve suggests that many homeowners might have saved tens of thousands of dollars had they held adjustable-rate mortgages rather than fixed-rate mortgages during the past decade, though this would not have been the case, of course, had interest rates trended sharply upward . . .
>
> American consumers might benefit if lenders provided greater mortgage product alternatives to the traditional fixed-rate mortgage. To the degree that households are driven by fears of payment

shocks but are willing to manage their own interest rate risks, the traditional fixed-rate mortgage may be an expensive method of financing a home.

The most revolting thing about Greenspan's decision to wave a flag for adjustable-rate mortgages was the timing.

Greenspan was nearing the end of his reign as Fed chief. He would be renominated one more time by George W. Bush, but his last term would end in January 2006.

So the timing of that speech to the Credit Union National Association Conference in February 2004 is remarkable. He had been cutting rates or holding them flat for years. The economy at the time was full of easy money and people everywhere were borrowing fortunes and buying beyond their means. Greenspan himself knew he was on his way out soon, but he also knew one other thing: he was about to start raising interest rates.

In fact, in June 2004, just a few months after he encouraged Americans to shun fixed-rate mortgages for adjustable-rate mortgages, Greenspan raised rates for what would be the first of seventeen consecutive times. He would raise rates at every FOMC meeting between June 2004 and the time he left office two years later, more than quadrupling interest rates, moving them from 1 percent to 4.5 percent. In other words, he first herded people into these risky mortgage deals and then, seemingly as a gift to the banks on his way out of town, spent two straight years jacking up rates to fatten the payments homeowners had to make to their lenders.

"He made that argument [about adjustable-rate mortgages] right before he started raising interest rates. Are you kidding me?" said one hedge fund manager. "All he was doing was screwing the American consumer to help the banks . . . If you had had people on thirty-year fixed mortgages, you wouldn't have had half these houses blowing up, because mortgages would have remained steady. Instead . . . it was the most disingenuous comment I've ever heard from a government official."

Greenspan's frantic deregulation of the financial markets in the late nineties had led directly to the housing bubble; in particular, the deregulation of the derivatives market had allowed Wall Street to create a vast infrastructure for chopping up mortgage debt, disguising bad loans as AAA-rated investments, and selling the whole mess off on a secondary market as securities. Once Wall Street perfected this mechanism, it was suddenly able to create hundreds of billions of dollars in crap mortgages and sell them off to unsuspecting pension funds, insurance companies, unions, and other suckers as grade-A investments, as I'll detail in the next chapter.

The amount of new lending was mind-boggling: between 2003 and 2005, outstanding mortgage debt in America grew by $3.7 trillion, which was roughly equal to the entire value of all American real estate in the year 1990 ($3.8 trillion). In other words, Americans in just two years had borrowed the equivalent of two hundred years' worth of savings.

Any sane person would have looked at these numbers and concluded that something was terribly wrong (and some, like Greenspan's predecessor Paul Volcker, did exactly that, sounding dire warnings about all that debt), but Greenspan refused to admit there was a problem. Instead, incredibly, he dusted off the same old "new era" excuse, claiming that advances in technology and financial innovation had allowed Wall Street to rewrite the laws of nature again:

> Technological advances have resulted in increased efficiency and scale within the financial services industry . . . With these advances in technology, lenders have taken advantage of credit-scoring models and other techniques for efficiently extending credit to a broader spectrum of consumers.

The kinds of technological advances Greenspan was talking about were actually fraud schemes. In one sense he was right: prior to the 2000s, the technology did not exist to make a jobless immigrant with no documentation and no savings into an AAA-rated mortgage risk. But now, thanks to "technological advances," it was suddenly possible to lend trillions of dollars to millions of previously unsuitable borrowers! This was Greenspan's explanation for the seemingly inexplicable surge in new home buying.

The results of all these policies would be catastrophic, of course, as the collapse of the real estate market in 2007–8 would wipe out roughly 40 percent of the world's wealth, while Greenspan's frantic printing of trillions of new dollars after the collapse of the tech boom would critically devalue the dollar. In fact, from 2001 to 2006, the dollar would lose 24 percent of its value versus the foreign currencies in the dollar index and 28 percent of its value versus the Canadian dollar. Even tinpot third world currencies like the ruble and the peso gained against the dollar during this time. And yet Greenspan insisted at the end of this period that the devaluation of the dollar was not really a problem—so long as you didn't travel abroad!

> So long as the dollar weakness does not create inflation . . . then I think it's a market phenomenon, which aside from those who travel the world, has no real fundamental consequences.

No real fundamental consequences? For Greenspan to say such a thing proved he was either utterly insane or completely dishonest, since even the world's most stoned college student understands that a weak dollar radically affects real wealth across the board: we buy foreign oil in dollars, and since energy costs affect the price of just about everything, being able to buy less and less oil with a dollar as time goes on makes the whole country that much poorer. It's hard to overstate how utterly mad it is for a Fed chairman in the age of the global economy to claim that a weak currency only affects *tourists*. It's a little bit like saying a forest fire only really sucks if you're a woodpecker.

In any case, by the time Greenspan left the Fed in 2006, Americans had lost trillions upon trillions of dollars in two gigantic bubble scams, and we had gone from being a nation with incredible stored wealth in personal savings to being a country that collectively is now way over its head in hock, with no way out in sight. As of this writing, America's international debt is somewhere in the region of $115 trillion, with our debt now well over 50 percent of GDP. This is debt on a level never before seen in a modern industrialized country.

It sounds facile to pin this all on one guy, but Greenspan was the crucial enabler of the bad ideas and greed of others. He blew up one bubble and then, when the first one burst, he printed money to inflate the next one. That was the difference between the tech and the housing disasters. In the tech bubble, America lost its own savings. In the housing bubble, we borrowed the shirts we ended up losing, leaving us in a hole twice as deep.

It's important to note that throughout this entire time, while Greenspan was printing trillions of dollars and manipulating the economy to an elaborate degree, he was almost completely unaccountable to voters. Except for the right of an elected president to nominate the Fed chief, voters have no real say over what the Fed does. Citizens do not even get to see transcripts of FOMC meetings in real time; we're only now finding out what Greenspan was saying during the nineties. And despite repeated attempts to pry open the Fed's books, Congress as of this writing has been unsuccessful in doing so and still has no idea how much money the Fed has lent out at the discount window and to whom.

Congress's authority over the Fed is so slight that when Los Angeles congressman Brad Sherman passed an amendment capping the amount of emergency assistance to banks the Fed could loan out at a still-monstrous $4 trillion, it was considered a big victory.

"We were lucky to get that," Sherman says.

Really the only time the public could even get an audience with Greenspan was through his compulsory appearances before Congress, which Greenspan plainly loathed and for which he set strict time limits. Texas congressman Ron Paul explains that Greenspan was so tight with his time that members of Congress would have to wait in line for months just to get this or that question before His Highness in committee hearings.

"He might come at ten a.m. and say his limit was one or two [congressmen]," Paul says now. "So if you were at the bottom of the list, you wouldn't get a chance to ask the question."

As a result, Paul says, members who didn't get questions in would have to wait months until their next shot. "If you didn't get to ask your question, you'd be high on the list the next time," he says. "That was the best you could hope for."

All of which makes Greenspan's exit from power that much harder to swallow. He was unrepentant almost to the bitter end. Even as late as

November 2007, with the international financial community already beginning to erupt in panic thanks to the latest bubble explosion, Greenspan shrugged. "I have no particular regrets," he told audiences in Norway. "The housing bubble is not a reflection of what we did."

It wasn't until October 2008, after the collapses of Bear Stearns and Lehman Brothers and AIG, after massive federal bailouts were implemented to stave off total panic, that Greenspan budged—sort of. In testimony before Henry Waxman's Committee on Oversight and Government Reform, he admitted, sort of, that his Randian faith in the eternal efficacy of self-regulating markets had been off, a little.

"I've found a flaw," he told Waxman. "I don't know how significant or permanent it is. But I've been very distressed by that fact."

Waxman at that instant found himself in an unusual position, representing a whole generation of infuriated Greenspan critics and opponents who had never gotten the Maestro to apologize for a damn thing. It would have been understandable had he been overwhelmed by the pressure of the moment. Instead Waxman calmly pressed Greenspan.

"Were you wrong?"

Greenspan's answer to this question was priceless—a landmark moment in the annals of political narcissism, the Bobby Thomson walk-off homer of unrepentant dickdom. Was he wrong?

"Partially," Greenspan answered.

That moment is what passes for a major victory for American democracy these days—an elected official getting at least one semistraight answer out of an unaccountable financial bureaucrat.

But that's about as good as it gets. In reality, even if Greenspan got taken down a fraction of an inch toward the end of his life, his belief system—or what passes for his belief system—remains ascendant, if not dominant, in the international finance culture. He raised a generation of Wall Street bankers who under his tutelage molded themselves in the image of Randian supermen, pursuing the mantra of personal profit with pure religious zeal.

In fact, what made the bubbles possible was that the people who ran banks like Goldman Sachs and Morgan Stanley and Citigroup during the Greenspan era were possessed by this cultist fervor, making them genuinely blind to the destructive social consequences of their actions and infuriatingly immune to self-doubt. The Randian mindset was so widespread in the finance world that even after the horrific 2008 crash, executives from Goldman Sachs could be seen insisting in public that Jesus himself would have approved of their devotion to personal profit ("The injunction of Jesus to love others as ourselves is an endorsement of self-interest," Goldman international adviser Brian Griffiths told parishioners of London's St. Paul's Cathedral). That sort of moral blindness turbocharged the greed on the private banking side, but it was Greenspan's cynical construction of a vast and unaccountable welfare state that made the theft scheme virtually unstoppable.

The important thing to remember about the Alan Greenspan era is that despite all the numbers and the inside-baseball jargon about rates and loans and forecasts, his is not a story about economics. The Greenspan era instead is a crime story. Like drug dealing and gambling and Ponzi schemes, bubbles of the sort he oversaw are rigged games with preordained losers and inherently corrupting psychological consequences. You play, you get beat, in more ways than one.

Greenspan staked the scam, printing trillions upon trillions of dollars to goad Americans into playing a series of games they were doomed from the start to lose to the dealer. In the end the printed wealth all disappeared and only the debts remained. He probably did this just because he wanted to see his face on magazine covers and be popular at certain Upper East Side cocktail parties. His private hang-ups in this way shaped the entire scam of modern American politics: a pure free market for the suckers, golden parachutes for the Atlases.

3

Hot Potato
The Great American Mortgage Scam

THE GRIFT IN America always starts out with a little hum on the airwaves, some kind of dryly impersonal appeal broadcast over the skies from a high tower, an offer to sell something—help, advice, a new way of life, a friend at a time of need, the girl of your dreams. This is the way the ordinary American participates in this democracy: he buys. Most of us don't vote more than once every four years, but we buy stuff every day. And every one of those choices registers somewhere, high up above, in the brain of the American Leviathan.

Back in early 2005 a burly six-foot seven-inch black sheriff's deputy named Eljon Williams was listening to the radio on the way home from his nightmare job wrestling with Boston-area criminals at the city's notorious South Bay House of Correction. The station was WILD, Boston's black talk-radio station, which at the time featured broadcasts by Al Sharpton and the *Two Live Stews* sports radio show. While driving Williams heard an interview with a man named Solomon Edwards,* a self-described mortgage expert, who came on the air to educate the lis-

*Name changed for legal reasons.

tening public about a variety of scams that had been used of late to target minority homebuyers.

Williams listened closely. He had some questions about the mortgage he held on his own three-decker home in Dorchester, a tough section of Boston. Williams rented out the first and third floors of his house and lived in the middle with his wife and his son, but he was thinking of moving out and buying a new home. He wondered if he should maybe get some advice before he made the move. He listened to the end of the broadcast, jotted down Edwards's number, and later gave him a call.

He made an appointment with Edwards and went to meet him. "Nice young black man, classy, well-dressed," Williams recalls now. "He was the kind of guy I would have hung out with, could have been friends with."

In fact, they did become friends. Edwards, Williams recalled, took a look at the mortgage on the three-decker and did indeed find some irregularities. He told Williams about RESPA, the Real Estate Settlement Procedures Act, designed to prevent scam artists from burying hidden commissions in the closing costs for urban and low-income homebuyers in particular. And Edwards found some hidden costs in Eljon's mortgage and helped him get some of that money back. "He saved me money," Williams recalls now. "I really trusted him."

Edwards ended up getting so close to Williams that he came over to his house from time to time, even stopping by for his son Eljon Jr.'s birthday party. ("Even brought a present," Williams recalls.) In their time together Edwards sold Williams on the idea that he was an advocate for the underprivileged. "He would talk to me about how a rich man doesn't notice when a biscuit is stolen from his cupboard, but a poor man does," he says now. "He had the whole rap."

Fast-forward a year. Williams and his wife decide to make their move. They find a small two-bedroom home in Randolph, a quiet middle-class town a little farther outside Boston. Williams had a little money saved up, plus the proceeds from the sale of his three-decker, but he still needed a pair of loans to buy the house, an 80/20 split, with the 80 percent loan issued by a company called New Century, and the 20 issued by a company called Ocwen.

Edwards helped him get both loans, and everything seemed kosher. "I was an experienced homeowner," Williams recalls. "I knew the difference between a fixed-rate mortgage and an adjustable-rate mortgage. And I specifically asked him, I made sure, that these were fixed-rate mortgages."

Or so he thought. The Williamses moved in to their new home and immediately fell into difficulty. In late 2006, Eljon's wife, Clara Bernardino, was diagnosed with ovarian cancer. She was pregnant at the time. Urgent surgery was needed to save her life and her baby's life, and the couple was for a time left with only Eljon's income to live on. Money became very, very tight—and then the big hammer dropped.

In mid-2007 the family got a notice from ASC (America's Servicing Company), to whom New Century had sold their 80 percent loan. New Century by then was in the process of going out of business, its lenders pulling their support and its executives under federal investigation for improper accounting practices, among other things—but that's another story. For now, the important thing was that Eljon and Clara woke up one morning in June 2007 to find the following note from ASC in their mailbox:

> This notice is to inform you of changes to your adjustable rate mortgage loan interest rate and payment . . .
>
> The principal and interest due on your loan will be adjusted from $2,123.11 to $2,436.32 . . .
>
> Effective with your August 01, 2007 payment your interest rate will be adjusted from 7.225% to 8.725% . . .

Eljon, not yet completely flipping out, figured a mistake had been made. He called up Edwards, who was "weird" on the phone at first, mumbling and not making sense. When Eljon insisted that it was not possible that their mortgage was adjustable, since Edwards himself had told them it was fixed, Edwards demurred, saying he, Eljon, was wrong, that it was adjustable and he'd been told that.

Soon after that, Edwards stopped answering his phone. And soon after that, Edwards disappeared entirely. He was no longer at his office, he was no longer anywhere on earth. And the Williamses were left facing cancer, a newborn baby, and foreclosure. They subsequently found out that Edwards had taken more than $12,000 in commissions through their house deal—among other things by rigging the appraisal. Edwards, it turned out, was the appraiser. This long-conning grifter had taken a perfectly decent, law-abiding, hardworking person and turned him and his mortgage into a time bomb—a financial hot potato that he'd managed to pass off before the heat even hit his fingers.

Realizing that he'd been scammed, Eljon now went into bunker mode. He called everyone under the sun for help, from the state attorney general to credit counselors to hotlines like 995-HOPE. At one point he called ASC and, in an attempt to convince them to modify their loan, simply begged, telling them about his wife's bout with cancer, the dishonest loan, their situation in general. "I offered to bring them documentation from the doctors, proof that we were in this spot because of a medical emergency, that what they were doing would put us into a life-and-death situation," he says. "And they were like, 'Whatever.' They just didn't care, you know."

The family missed several payments and were, technically, in default. Williams dug in and prepared for an Alamo-like confrontation. "I would have barricaded myself in the house," he says. "I was not leaving. Not for anything."

In the end . . . but let's leave the end for later. Because that's where the story gets really ugly.

Every country has scam artists like Solomon Edwards, but only in a dying country, only at the low end of the most distressed third world societies, are people like that part of the power structure. That's what makes the housing bubble that burst all over Eljon Williams so extraordinary. If you follow the scam far enough, it will literally go all the way to the top. Solomon Edwards, it turns out, is not an aberration, not even a criminal really, but a kind of agent of the highest powers in the land, on whose behalf the state was eventually forced to intercede, in the fall of 2008, on a gigantic scale—in something like a quiet coup d'état.

At the lower levels anyway, the subprime market works almost exactly like a Mafia protection racket.

Anyone who's seen *Goodfellas* knows how it works. A mobster homes in on a legit restaurant owner and maxes out on his credit, buying truckloads of liquor and food and other supplies against his name and then selling the same stuff at half price out the back door, turning two hundred dollars in credit into one hundred dollars in cash. The game holds for two or three months, until the credit well runs dry and the trucks stop coming—at which point you burn the place to the ground and collect on the insurance.

Would running the restaurant like a legit business make more money in the long run? Sure. But that's only if you give a fuck. If you *don't* give a fuck, the whole equation becomes a lot simpler. Then every restaurant is just a big pile of cash, sitting there waiting to be seized and blown on booze, cars, and coke. And the marks in this game are not the restaurant's customers but the clueless, bottomless-pocketed societal institutions: the credit companies, the insurance companies, the commercial suppliers extending tabs to the mobster's restaurant.

In the housing game the scam was just the same, only here the victims were a little different. It was an ingenious, almost impossibly complex sort of confidence game. At the bottom end of the predator chain were the brokers and mortgage lenders, raking in the homeowners, who to the brokers were just unwitting lists of credit scores attached to a little bit of dumb fat and muscle. To the brokers and lenders, every buyer was like a restaurant to a mobster—just a big pile of cash waiting to be seized and liquidated.

The homeowner scam was all about fees and depended upon complex relationships that involved the whole financial services industry. At the very lowest level, at the mortgage-broker level, the game was about getting the target homeowner to buy as much house as he could at the highest possible interest rates. The higher the rates, the bigger the fees for the broker. They greased the homeowners by offering nearly unlimited sums of cash.

Prior to 2002, when so-called subprime loans were rare ("subprime" just refers to anyone with a low credit score, in particular anyone with a score below 660; before 2002 fewer than $100 billion worth of mortgages a year were to subprime borrowers), you almost never had people without jobs or a lengthy income history buying big houses. But that all changed in the early part of this decade. By 2005, the year Eljon bought his house, fully $600 billion worth of subprime mortgage money was being lent out every year. The practice of giving away big houses to people with no money became so common that the industry even coined a name for it, NINJA loans, meaning "no income, job, or assets."

A class-action lawsuit against Washington Mutual offered a classic example. A Mexican immigrant named Soledad Aviles with no English skills, who was making nine dollars an hour as a glass cutter, was sold a $615,000 house, the monthly payments for which represented 96 percent of his take-home income. How did that loan go through? Easy: the lender simply falsified the documentation, giving Aviles credit for $13,000 a month in income.

The falsification mania went in all directions, as Eljon and Clara found out. On one hand, their broker Edwards doctored the loan application to give Clara credit for $7,000 in monthly income, far beyond her actual income; on the other hand, Edwards falsified the couple's credit scores downward, putting them in line for a subprime loan when they actually qualified for a real, stable, fixed bank loan. Eljon and his wife actually got a worse loan than they deserved: they were prime borrowers pushed down into the subprime hell because subprime made the bigger commission.

It was all about the commissions, and the commissions were biggest when the mortgage was adjustable, with the so-called option ARM being particularly profitable. Buyers with option-ARM mortgages would purchase their houses with low or market loan rates, then wake up a few months later to find an adjustment upward—and then perhaps a few years after that find another adjustment. The jump might be a few hundred dollars a month, as in the case of the Williams family, or it might be a few thousand, or the payment might even quadruple. The premium for the brokers was in locking in a large volume of buyers as quickly as possible.

Both the lender and the broker were in the business of generating commissions. The houses being bought and sold and the human borrowers moving in and out of them were completely incidental, a tool for harvesting the financial crop. But how is it possible to actually make money by turning on a fire hose and blasting cash by the millions of dollars into a street full of people with low credit scores?

This is where the investment banks came in. The banks and the mortgage lenders had a tight symbiotic relationship. The mortgage guys had a job in this relationship, which was to create a vast volume of loans. In the past those great masses of loans would have been a problem, because nobody would have wanted to sit on millions' worth of loans lent out to immigrant glass cutters making nine dollars an hour.

Enter the banks, which devised a way out for everybody. A lot of this by now is ancient history to anyone who follows the financial story, but it's important to quickly recap in light of what would happen later on, in the summer of 2008. The banks perfected a technique called securitization, which had been invented back in the 1970s. Instead of banks making home loans and sitting on them until maturity, securitization allowed banks to put mortgages into giant pools, where they would then be diced up into bits and sold off to secondary investors as securities.

The securitization innovation allowed lenders to trade their long-term income streams for short-term cash. Say you make a hundred thirty-year loans to a hundred different homeowners, for $50 million worth of houses. Prior to securitization, you couldn't turn those hundred mortgages into instant money; your only access to the funds was to collect one hundred different meager payments every month for thirty years. But now the banks could take all one hundred of those loans, toss them into a pool, and sell the future revenue streams to another party for a big lump sum—instead of making $3 million over thirty years, maybe you make $1.8 million up front, today. And just like that, a traditionally long-term business is turned into a hunt for short-term cash.

But even with securitization, lenders had a limiting factor, which was that even in securitized pools, no one wanted to buy mortgages unless, you know, they were actually good loans, made to people unlikely to default.

To fix that problem banks came up with the next innovation—derivatives. The big breakthrough here was the CDO, or collateralized debt obligation (or instruments like it, like the collateralized mortgage obligation). With these collateralized instruments, banks took these big batches of mortgages, threw them into securitized pools, and then created a multitiered payment structure.

Imagine a box with one hundred home loans in it. Every month, those one hundred homeowners make payments into that box. Let's say the total amount of money that's supposed to come in every month is $320,000. What banks did is split the box up into three levels and sell shares in those levels, or "tranches," to outside investors.

All those investors were doing was buying access to the payments the homeowners would make every month. The top level is always called senior, or AAA rated, and investors who bought the AAA-level piece of the box were always first in line to get paid. The bank might say, for instance, that the first $200,000 that flowed into the box every month would go to the AAA investors.

If *more* than $200,000 came in every month, in other words if most of the homeowners did not default and made their payments, then you could send the next payments to the BBB or "mezzanine"-level investors—say, all the money between $200,000 and $260,000 that comes into the box. These investors made a higher rate of return than the AAA investors, but they also had more risk of not getting paid at all.

The last investors were the so-called "equity" investors, whose tranche was commonly known as toxic waste. These investors only got their money if everyone paid their bills on time. They were more likely to get nothing, but if they did get paid, they'd make a very high rate of return.

These derivative instruments allowed lenders to get around the loan-quality problem by hiding the crappiness of their loans behind the peculiar alchemy of the collateralized structure. Now the relative appeal of a mortgage-based investment was not based on the individual borrower's ability to pay over the long term; instead, it was based on computations like "What is the likelihood that more than ninety-three out of one hundred homeowners with credit scores of at least 660 will default on their loans next month?"

These computations were highly subjective and, like lie-detector tests, could be made to say almost anything the ratings agencies wanted them to say. And the ratings agencies, which were almost wholly financially dependent upon the same big investment banks that were asking them to rate their packages of mortgages, found it convenient to dole out high ratings to almost any package of mortgages that crossed their desks.

Most shameful of all was the liberal allotment of investment-grade ratings given to combinations of subprime mortgages. In a notorious example, Goldman Sachs put together a package of 8,274 mortgages in 2006 called GSAMP Trust 2006-S3. The average loan-to-value in the mortgages in this package was an astonishing 99.21 percent. That meant that these homeowners were putting less than 1 percent in cash for a down payment—there was virtually no equity in these houses at all. Worse, a full 58 percent of the loans were "no-doc" or "low-doc" loans, meaning there was little or no documentation, no proof that the owners were occupying the homes, were employed, or had access to any money at all.

This package of mortgages, in other words, was almost pure crap, and yet a full 68 percent of the package was given an AAA rating, which technically means "credit risk almost zero." This was the result of the interdependent relationship between banks and the ratings agencies; not only were the ratings agencies almost totally dependent financially on the very banks that were cranking out these instruments that needed rating, they also colluded with the banks by giving them a road map to game the system.

"The banks were explicitly told by ratings agencies what their models required of the banks to obtain a triple-A rating," says Timothy Power, a London-based trader who worked with derivatives. "That's fine if you're telling a corporation that they need to start making a profit or you'll downgrade them. But when we're in the world of models and dodgy statistics and a huge incentive to beat the system, you just invite disaster."

The ratings agencies were shameless in their explanations for the seemingly inexplicable decision to call time-bomb mortgages risk free for years on end. Moody's, one of the two agencies that control the vast majority of the market, went public with one of the all-time "the dog ate my homework" moments in financial history on May 21, 2008, when it announced, with a straight face, that a "computer error" had led to a misclassification of untold billions (not millions, billions) of junk instruments. "We are conducting a thorough review of the matter," the agency said.

It turns out the company was aware of the "error" as early as February 2007 and yet continued overrating the crap instruments (specifically, they were a beast called *constant proportion debt obligations*) with the AAA label through January 2008, during which time senior management pocketed millions in fees.

Why didn't it fix the grade on the misrated instruments? "It would be inconsistent with Moody's analytical standards and company policies to change methodologies in an effort to mask errors," the company said. Which translates as: "We were going to keep this hidden forever, except that we got outed by the *Financial Times*."

In this world, everybody kept up the con practically until they were in cuffs. It made financial sense to do so: the money was so big that it was cost-efficient (from a personal standpoint) for executives to chase massive short-term gains, no matter how ill-gotten, even knowing that the game would eventually be up. Because you got to keep the money either way, why not?

There is an old Slavic saying: one thief sits on top of another thief and uses a third thief for a whip. The mortgage world was a lot like that. At every level of this business there was some sort of pseudo-criminal scam, a transaction that either bordered on fraud or actually was fraud. To sort through all of it is an almost insanely dull exercise to anyone who does not come from this world, but the very dullness and complexity of that journey is part of what made this cannibalistic scam so confoundingly dependable.

The process starts out with a small-time operator like Solomon Edwards, who snares you, the schmuck homeowner, and slaps your name on a loan that gets sent up the line. In league with Edwards is the mortgage lender, the originator of the loan, who like Edwards is just in it for the fees. He lends you the money and immediately looks for a way to sell that little stake in you off to a big national or international investment bank—whose job it is to take that loan of yours and toss it into a big securitized pool, where it can then be chopped up and sold as securities to the next player in the sequence.

This was a crucial stage in the process. It was here that the great financial powers of this country paused and placed their bets on the various classes of new homeowner they'd created with this orgy of new lending. Amazingly, these bigger players, who ostensibly belonged to the ruling classes and were fighting over millions, were even more dishonest and underhanded and petty than the low-rent, just-above-street-level grifters who bought cheap birthday presents for the kids of the Eljon Williamses of the world in pursuit of a few thousand bucks here and there.

A trader we'll call Andy B., who worked at one of those big investment banks and managed one of these mortgage deals, describes the process. In the waning months of the boom, in the early part of 2007, Andy was put in charge of a monster deal, selling off a billion-dollar pool of securitized mortgages. Now retired from not only that bank but from banking altogether, he can talk about this deal, which at the time was one of the great successes in his career.

A big, garrulous family man with a wicked sense of humor, Andy B. had, for most of his career, been involved in fairly run-of-the-mill work, trading in CMOs, or collateralized mortgage obligations—"that's like noncredit stuff, just trading around on interest-rate risk," he says, "the blocking-the-tackle work of Wall Street." But in the years leading up to the financial crisis he took a new job at a big bank and suddenly found himself in charge of a giant deal involving option-ARM mortgages, something he had almost no experience with.

"Option ARMs used to be a wealthy person's product," he explains now. "It was for people who had chunky cash flows. For instance, on Wall Street you get paid a bonus at the end of the year," he said, describing one of the option ARM's traditional customer profiles, "so I'll pay a little now, but at the end of the year I'll pay down the principal, true everything up—a wealthy person's product. Then it became the ultimate affordability product."

The option ARM evolved into an arrangement where the homebuyer could put virtually nothing down and then have a monthly payment that wasn't just interest only, but, in some cases, *less than* interest only. Say the market interest rate was 5 percent; you could buy a house with no money down and just make a 1 percent payment every month, for years on end. In the meantime, those four points per month you're not paying just get added to the total amount of debt. "The difference between that 5 percent and the 1 percent just gets tacked on later on in the form of a negative amortization," Andy explains.

Here's how that scenario looks: You buy a $500,000 house, with no money down, which means you take out a mortgage for the full $500,000. Then instead of paying the 5 percent monthly interest payment, which would be $2,500 a month, you pay just $500 a month, and that $2,000 a month you're not paying just gets added to your mortgage debt. Within a couple of years, you don't owe $500,000 anymore; now you owe $548,000 plus deferred interest. "If you're making the minimum payment, you could let your mortgage go up to 110 percent, 125 percent of the loan value," says Andy. "Sometimes it went as high as 135 percent or 140 percent. It was crazy."

In other words, in the early years of this kind of mortgage, you the homeowner are not actually paying off anything—you're really borrowing more. It was this perverse reality that, weirdly enough, made Andy's collection of mortgages more attractive to other buyers.

Again, in the kind of tiered deal that was used to pool these mortgages, Andy had to find buyers for three different levels of the pool— the "senior" or AAA stuff at the top, the B or "mezzanine" stuff in the middle, and the unrated "equity" or "toxic waste" portion at the bottom. (In reality each of these levels might in turn have been broken down into three or more sublevels, but the basic structure was threefold: senior, mezzanine, equity.)

Selling the AAA stuff was never a problem, because there was no shortage of institutional investors and banks that needed large percentages of AAA-rated investments in their portfolios in order to satisfy regulatory requirements. And since the AAA-rated slices of these mortgage deals paid a much higher rate of return than traditional AAA investments like Treasury bills, it was not at all hard to find homes for that section of the deal.

Selling the mezzanine level or "tranche" of the deal was another story, one outrageous enough in itself—but let's just say for now that it wasn't a problem, that a trader like Andy B. would always be able to find a home for that stuff.

That left the bottom tier. The key to any of these huge mortgage deals was finding a buyer for this "equity" tranche, the so-called toxic waste. If the investment banks could sell that, they could make huge up-front money on these deals. In the case of the $1 billion pool of mortgages Andy was selling, the toxic waste represented the homeowners in the pool who were the worst risks—precisely the people buying those insane negative amortization mortgage deals, making 1 percent payments against a steadily growing debt nut, borrowing against money they had already borrowed.

But Andy was fortunate: there were indeed clients out there who had some appetite for toxic waste. In fact, they were friends of his, at a hedge fund. "There were two companies that were buying tons of this stuff, Deutsche Bank and this hedge fund," he says now. "These were smart guys. In fact, [the hedge fund guys] taught me about tiering this kind of risk—they were actually teaching my traders as we were buying these packages."

The reason this hedge fund wanted to buy the crap at the bottom was that they'd figured that even a somewhat lousy credit risk could make a 1 percent monthly payment for a little while. Their strategy was simple: buy the waste, cash in on the large returns for a while (remember, the riskier the tranche, the higher rate of return it pays), and hope the homeowners in your part of the deal can keep making their pathetic 1 percent payments just long enough that the hedge fund can eventually unload their loans on someone else before they start defaulting. "It was a timing game," Andy explains. "They figured that these guys at the bottom would be able to make their payments even later than some of the guys higher up in the deal."

Before we even get to why these "smart guys" got it wrong, it's worth pointing out how consistent the thinking is all along this chain. Everybody involved is thinking short-term: Andy's hedge fund clients, Andy himself and his bank, certainly the originator-lender, and in many cases even the homeowner—none of them actually believed that this or that subprime loan was going to make it to maturity, or even past 2008 or 2009. Everybody involved was, one way or another, making a bet not on whether or not the loan would default, but when (and specifically when in the near future) it would default. In the transaction between Andy and his hedge fund clients, Andy was betting short and his clients were betting long, "long" in this case being a few months or maybe a year. And even that proved to be too long in that market.

Meanwhile a lot of the homeowners taking out these loans were buying purely as a way of speculating on housing prices: their scheme was to keep up those 1 percent payments for a period of time, then flip the house for a profit before the ARM kicked in and the payments adjusted and grew real teeth. At the height of the boom this process in some places was pushed to the level of absurdity. A *New Yorker* article cited a broker in Fort Myers, Florida, who described the short resale history of a house that was built in 2005 and first sold on December 29, 2005, for $399,600. It sold the next day for $589,900. A month later it was in foreclosure and the real estate broker bought it all over again for $325,000. This clearly was a fraudulent transaction of some kind—the buyers on those back-to-back transactions were probably dummy buyers, with the application and appraisal process rigged somehow (probably with the aid of a Solomon Edwards type) to bilk the lenders, which in any case probably didn't mind at all and simply sold off the loans immediately, pocketing the fees—but this is the kind of thing that went on. The whole industry was infested with scam artists.

Neither Andy nor his clients were even aware of the degree of that infestation, which was their crucial mistake. In this new world they should've realized they could no longer trust anything, not even the most seemingly solid pillars of the traditional lending infrastructure.

For example, part of the reason Andy's hedge fund clients had such faith in these homeowners in the toxic-waste tranche is that their credit scores weren't so bad. As most people know, the scores used in the mortgage industry are called FICO scores and are based on a formula invented back in the late fifties by an engineer named Bill Fair and a mathematician named Earl Isaac. The Fair Isaac Corporation, as their company was eventually called, created an algorithm that was intended to predict a home loan applicant's likelihood of default. The scores range from 300 to 850, with the median score being 723 at this writing. Scores between 620 and 660 are considered subprime, and above 720 is prime; anything in between is considered "Alt-A," a category that used to be a catchall term for solid borrowers with nontraditional jobs, but which morphed into something more ominous during the boom.

Wall Street believed in FICO scores and over the years had put a lot of faith in them. And if you just looked at the FICO scores, the homeowners in Andy's deal didn't look so bad.

"Let's say the average FICO in the whole deal, in the billion dollars of mortgages, was 710," Andy says. "The hedge fund guys were getting the worst of the worst in the deal, and they were getting, on average, 675, 685 FICO. That's not terrible."

Or so they thought. Andy's bank assembled the whole billion-dollar deal in February 2007; Andy ended up selling the bottom end of the pool to these hedge fund clients for $30 million in May. That turned out to be just in the nick of time, because almost immediately afterward, the loans started blowing up. This was doubly bad for Andy's clients, because they'd borrowed half of the money to buy this crap . . . from Andy's bank.

"Yeah, we financed fifteen million dollars of it to them at a pretty attractive rate," he recalls. Which for Andy's clients wasn't even enough, apparently, compared to other similar deals they'd done. "We're lending fifty percent, and they're getting better rates from other guys. Like they're bitching about us only giving fifty percent."

But now all that borrowing would come back to kill them. "So now they've got all this leverage, and the loans start coming on line," Andy says. "And we're noticing there are guys going delinquent. And we're thinking, why are they going delinquent? They only have to make a one-percent payment!"

It turns out that the FICO scores themselves were a scam. A lot of the borrowers were gaming the system. Companies like TradeLine Solutions, Inc., were offering, for a $1,399 fee, an unusual service: they would attach your name to a credit account belonging to some stranger with a perfect credit history, just as the account was about to close. Once this account with its perfect payment history was closed, it could add up to 45 points to your score. TradeLine CEO Ted Stearns bragged on the company's website: "There is one secret the credit scoring granddaddy and the credit bureaus do not want you to know: Good credit scores can be bought!"

In an alternative method, an applicant would take out five new credit cards with $5,000 limits and only run a $100 balance. "So FICO goes, oh, this guy's got $25,000 of available credit, and he's only drawing down $500," Andy explains. "He's very liquid."

What was happening, it turned out, was that many of these people with their souped-up credit scores had bought their houses purely as speculative gambles—and once they saw home prices start to go down, they abandoned ship rather than pay even the meager 1 percent payment. Andy's hedge fund clients were toast, and within a few months they were selling huge chunks of their portfolio to raise cash to cover their losses in the deal. "I'm looking at [the list of the holdings up for sale], and I'm thinking, they're done," recalls Andy.

Even crazier was how Andy sold off the middle tranche of the pool. The AAA portion was never really a problem to sell, as the institutional investors like pension funds back then had a nearly unlimited appetite for the less-risky part of these deals. And the bottom of the deal, the toxic stuff, he'd sold off to his hedge fund guys. "I'm kind of stuck with the middle pieces," says Andy.

Which theoretically was a problem, because who wanted the middle portion of a billion-dollar package of option-ARM mortgages? After all, the market for this portion—the mezzanine—was kind of limited. "The AAA guy can't buy them, because they're only triple-B, and the hedge funds, there's not enough juice in them to buy that stuff," says Andy.

So what did they do with the BBB part? That's easy: they re-rated it as AAA paper!

How? "They would take these BBBs, and then take the BBBs from the last five deals or so," says Andy, "and put it into a CDO squared."

What's a CDO squared? All it is is a CDO full of . . . other CDOs!

It's really an awesome piece of financial chicanery. Say you have the BBB tranche from that first deal Andy did. You lump it in with the BBB tranches from five, six, seven other deals. Then you just repeat the same tiering process that you started with, and you say, "Well, the first hundred thousand dollars of the revenue from all these BBB tiers that goes into the box every month, that goes to the AAA investors in this new CDO."

"And now the ratings agencies would say, okay, let's do a first, second, and third loss," referring to the same three-part structure of the overall pool, "and now let's call seventy percent of these AAA," says Andy.

This sounds complicated, but all you have to do is remember the ultimate result here. This technique allowed Andy's bank to take all the unsalable BBB-rated extras from these giant mortgage deals, jiggle them around a little using some mathematical formulae, and—presto! All of a sudden 70 percent of your unsalable BBB-rated pseudo-crap ("which in reality is more like B-minus-rated stuff, since the FICO scores aren't accurate," reminds Andy) is now very salable AAA-rated prime paper, suitable for selling to would-be risk-avoidant pension funds and insurance companies. It's the same homeowners and the same loans, but the wrapping on the box is different.

"You couldn't make this stuff up if you tried, in your most diabolical imagination," says Andy now.

But it wasn't the toxic waste or the mezzanine deals that blew up the financial universe. It was the AAA-rated tiers of the mortgage-backed deals that crushed America's financial hull, thanks to an even more sophisticated and diabolical scam perpetrated by some of the wealthiest, most powerful people in the world.

At around the same time Andy was doing his billion-dollar deal, another trader at a relatively small European bank—let's call him Miklos—stumbled on to what he thought, at first, was the find of a lifetime.

"So I'm buying bonds," he says. "They're triple-A, supersenior tranche bonds. And they're paying, like, LIBOR plus fifty."

Jargon break:

LIBOR, or the London Interbank Offered Rate, is a common reference tool used by bankers to determine the price of borrowing. LIBOR refers to the interest rate banks in London charge one another to borrow unsecured debt. The "plus" in the expression "LIBOR plus," meanwhile, refers to the amount over and above LIBOR that bankers charge one another for transactions, with the number after "plus" refer- ring to hundredths of a percentage point. These hundredths of a point are called *basis points*.

So when Miklos says, "LIBOR plus fifty," he means the rate Lon- don banks charge to borrow money from one another, plus 0.50 per- cent more. If the LIBOR rate is 0.50 percent that day, then LIBOR plus fifty means, basically, 1 percent interest.

So Miklos was buying the AAA portions of deals like Andy's at LIBOR plus fifty, and all you really need to know about that price is that it is slightly higher than what he would have been paying back then for a Treasury bill. The whole bubble game in the years leading up to the financial meltdown was driven by this small difference in the yield between Treasuries, which are more or less absolutely safe, and the AAA-rated slices of these collateralized securities.

Why? Because what few regulations there are remaining are based upon calculations involving AAA-rated paper. Both banks and insur- ance companies are required by regulators to keep a certain amount of real capital on hand, to protect their depositors. Of course, these insti- tutions do not simply hold their reserves in cash; instead, they hold interest-bearing investments, so that they can make money at the same time they are fulfilling their reserve obligations.

Knowing this, the banking industry regulators—in particular a set of bylaws called the Basel Accords, which all major banking nations ad- here to—created rules to make sure that those holdings these institu- tions kept were solid. These rules charged institutions for keeping their holdings in investments that were not at least AAA rated. In order to avoid these *capital charges,* institutions needed to have lots of "safe" AAA-rated paper. And if you could find AAA-rated paper that earns LIBOR plus fifty, instead of buying the absolutely safe U.S. Treasury notes that might earn LIBOR plus twenty, well, then, you jumped on that chance—because that was 0.30 more percentage points you were making. In banks and insurance companies with holdings in the bil- lions, that subtle discrepancy meant massive increases in revenue.

It was this math that drove all the reckless mortgage lending. Thanks to the invention of these tiered, mortgage-backed, CDO-like derivative deals, banks could now replace all the defiantly unsexy T-bills

and municipal bonds they were holding to fulfill their capital requirements with much higher earning mortgage-backed securities. And
what happens when most of the world's major financial institutions
suddenly start replacing big chunks of their "safe" reserve holdings
with mortgage-backed securities?

To simplify this even more: The rules say that banks have to have a
certain amount of cash on hand. And if not cash, something as valuable
as cash. But the system allowed banks to use home loans as their reserve
capital, instead of cash, Banks were therefore meeting their savings
requirements by . . . lending. Instead of the banking system being buttressed by real reserve capital, it was buttressed by the promised mortgage payments of a generation of questionable homebuyers.

Everyone and his brother starts getting offered mortgages. At its
heart, the housing/credit bubble was the rational outcome of a nutty
loophole in the regulatory game. The reason Vegas cocktail waitresses
and meth addicts in Ventura were suddenly getting offered million-
dollar homes had everything to do with Citigroup and Bank of America and AIG jettisoning their once-safe AAA reserves, their T-bills and
municipal bonds, and exchanging them for these mortgage-backed
"AAA"-rated securities—which, as we've already seen, were sometimes
really BBB-rated securities turned into AAA-rated paper through the
magic of the CDO squared. And which in turn perhaps should originally have been B-minus-rated securities, because the underlying FICO
scores of the homeowners in deals like Andy's might have been fakes.

Getting back to the story: So Miklos is buying AAA bonds. These
bonds are paying his bank LIBOR plus fifty, which isn't bad. But it becomes spectacular when he finds a now-infamous third party, AIG, to
make the deal absolutely bulletproof.

"So I'm getting LIBOR plus fifty for these bonds," he says. "Then
I turn around and I call up AIG and I'm like, 'Hey, where would you
credit default swap this bond?' And they're like, 'Oh, we'll do that for
LIBOR plus ten.' ".

Miklos pauses and laughs, recalling the pregnant pause on his end
of the phone line as he heard this offer from AIG. He couldn't believe
what he'd just heard: it was either a mistake, or they had just handed
him a mountain of money, free of charge.

"I hear this," he says, "and I'm like, 'Uh . . . okay. Sure, guys.'"

Here we need another digression. The *credit default swap* was a kind of insurance policy originally designed to get around those same regulatory capital charges. Ironically, Miklos had once been part of a famed team at JPMorgan that helped design the modern credit default swap, although the bank envisioned a much different use for them back then.

A credit default swap is just a bet on an outcome. It works like this: Two bankers get together and decide to bet on whether or not a homeowner is going to default on his $300,000 home loan. Banker A, betting against the homeowner, offers to pay Banker B $1,000 a month for five years, on one condition: if the homeowner defaults, Banker B has to pay Banker A the full value of the home loan, in this case $300,000.

So Banker B has basically taken 5–1 odds that the homeowner will not default. If he does not default, Banker B gets $60,000 over five years from Banker A. If he does default, Banker B owes Banker A $300,000.

This is gambling, pure and simple, but it wasn't invented with this purpose. Originally it was invented so that banks could get around lending restrictions. It used to be that, in line with the Basel Accords, banks had to have at least one dollar in reserve for every eight they lent; the CDS was a way around that.

Say Bank A is holding $10 million in A-minus-rated IBM bonds. It goes to Bank B and makes a deal: we'll pay you $50,000 a year for five years and in exchange, you agree to pay us $10 million if IBM defaults sometime in the next five years—which of course it won't, since IBM never defaults.

If Bank B agrees, Bank A can then go to the Basel regulators and say, "Hey, we're insured if something goes wrong with our IBM holdings. So don't count that as money we have at risk. Let us lend a higher percentage of our capital, now that we're insured." It's a win-win. Bank B makes, basically, a free $250,000. Bank A, meanwhile, gets to lend out another few million more dollars, since its $10 million in IBM bonds is no longer counted as at-risk capital.

That was the way it was supposed to work. But two developments helped turn the CDS from a semisensible way for banks to insure themselves against risk into an explosive tool for turbo leverage across the planet.

One is that no regulations were created to make sure that at least one of the two parties in the CDS had some kind of stake in the underlying bond. The so-called *naked default swap* allowed Bank A to take out insurance with Bank B not only on its own IBM holdings, but on, say, the soon-to-be-worthless America Online stock Bank X has in its portfolio. This is sort of like allowing people to buy life insurance on total strangers with late-stage lung cancer—total insanity.

The other factor was that there were no regulations that dictated that Bank B had to have any money at all before it offered to sell this CDS insurance. In other words, Bank A could take out insurance on its IBM holdings with Bank B and get an exemption from lending restrictions from regulators, even if Bank B never actually posted any money or proved that it could cover that bet. Wall Street is frequently compared by detractors to a casino, but in the case of the CDS, it was far worse than a casino—a casino, at least, does not allow people to place bets they can't cover.

These two loopholes would play a major role in the madness Miklos was now part of. Remember, Miklos was buying the AAA-rated slices of tiered bonds like the ones Andy was selling, and those bonds were paying LIBOR plus fifty. And then he was turning around and buying default swap insurance on those same bonds for LIBOR plus ten.

To translate that into human terms, Miklos was paying one-tenth of a percentage point to fully insure a bond that was paying five-tenths of a percentage point. Now, the only reason a bond earns interest at all is because the person buying it faces the risk that it might default, but the bonds Miklos was buying were now 100 percent risk free. The four-tenths of a percentage point he was now earning on the difference between the bond and the default swap was pure, risk-free profit. This was the goose that laid the golden egg, the deal of the decade. Once he bought the AIG default swap protection on his bonds, Miklos couldn't lose. The only thing to compare it to would be a racetrack whose odds-makers got stoned and did their math wrong—imagine if you could put a dollar on all twenty horses in the Kentucky Derby and be guaranteed to make at least $25 no matter who wins the race. That's what it's like to buy bonds at LIBOR plus fifty that you can credit-default-swap at LIBOR plus ten.

"So I've basically got forty basis points *in my pocket,*" Miklos recalls, giggling even now. "It's free money. I mean, I'm getting those forty basis points running, for the life of the bond."

Making matters even more absurd, the bonds Miklos was buying were already insured; they had, built in to the bonds themselves, something called *monoline insurance*. Monoline insurance refers to the insurance provided by companies like Ambac and MBIA. These companies, for a fee, will guarantee that the buyer of the bond will receive all his interest and principal on time. Miklos's bonds contained MBIA/Ambac insurance; in the event of a default, they were supposed to cover the bond.

So Miklos's bond deal was, in a sense, almost triple insured. It was AAA rated to begin with. Then it had the monoline insurance built in to the bond itself. Then it had credit default swap insurance from AIG. And yet there was that forty-basis-point spread, just sitting there. It was bizarre, almost like Wall Street had reached into Miklos's office and started handing him money, almost without his even asking. Perhaps not coincidentally, it was very much like the situation for ordinary homeowners, who around the same time found themselves suddenly and inexplicably offered lots of seemingly free money. It sounded too good to be true—was it?

Miklos's bank thought so. "It was so unreal, my bosses wouldn't let me book this stuff as profit," he recalls now. "They just didn't believe it could be true. I explained it to them over and over, but they wouldn't mark it as profit."

That didn't mean, however, that they didn't want him to do more of those trades. But no sooner had Miklos tried to buy more of the bonds than he found that another, much bigger party had discovered his little secret. "Suddenly someone is buying like five hundred million dollars of this stuff and getting the same swap deal from AIG," he says. "I'm getting blown out of the water."

Miklos starts hearing that the other party is one of the top five investment banks on Wall Street. And the rumor is that the money behind the deals is "partner money"—that the higher-ups in the Wall Street colossus had caught on to this amazing deal and were buying it

all up for themselves, with their personal money, via the firm's proprietary trading desk. "They started tagging AIG with all of this stuff," he
recalls. "And we got squeezed out."

So here's the question: why would AIG do this? Andy, though not
involved with that deal, has a theory.

"The question is, were they stupid—or were they just never intending to pay?" he asks.

Before we get to the final part of the story—the part that involves a
meeting of the very highest officials in government and heads of the
most powerful financial companies in the world colluding on one final,
unprecedented, grand-scale heist—we have to back up just a little and
talk about another continent of Wall Street scams. Because what happened with AIG, what brought the financial crisis to a head, was really
an extraordinary merger of the two different schools of cutting-edge
Wall Street scammery, taking place under the one roof of AIG.

One school was the part we've already seen, the credit default scam
that Miklos tapped into. This was the monster created by a pinhead
American financier named Joe Cassano, who was running a tiny unit
within AIG called AIG Financial Products, or AIGFP (FP for short).
Cassano, a beetle-browed, balding type in glasses, worked for years
under Mike Milken at the notorious Drexel Burnham Lambert investment bank, the poster child for the 1980s era of insider manipulations.
He moved to AIG in 1987 and helped set up AIGFP.

The unit originally dealt in the little-known world of interest rate
swaps (which would later become notorious for their role in the collapse of countries like Greece and localities like Jefferson County, Alabama). But in the early part of this decade it moved into the credit
default swap world, selling protection to the Mikloses and Goldman
Sachses of the world, mainly for supersenior AAA-rated tranches of the
tiered, structured deals of the type Andy put together.

How you view Cassano's business plan largely depends on whether
you think he was hugely amoral or just really stupid. Again, thanks
largely to the fact that credit default swaps existed in a totally unregulated area of the financial universe—this was the result of that 2000 law,

the Commodity Futures Modernization Act, sponsored by then-senator Phil Gramm and supported by then–Treasury chief Larry Summers and his predecessor Bob Rubin—Cassano could sell as much credit protection as he wanted without having to post any real money at all. So he sold hundreds of billions of dollars' worth of protection to all the big players on Wall Street, despite the fact that he didn't have any money to cover those bets.

Cassano's business was rooted in the way these structured deals were set up. When investment banks assembled their pools of mortgages, they would almost always sell the high-yield toxic waste portions at the bottom of the deals as quickly as possible—few banks wanted to hold on to that stuff (although some did, to disastrous effect). But they would often keep the AAA-rated portions of the pools because they were useful in satisfying capital requirements. Instead of keeping low-yield Treasuries or municipal bonds to satisfy regulators that they had enough reserves on hand, banks could keep the AAA tranches of these mortgage deals and get a much higher rate of return.

Another thing that happened is that sometime around the end of 2005 and 2006, the banks started finding it harder to dump their excess AAA tranches on the institutional clients. So the banks ended up holding on to this stuff temporarily, in a practice known as warehousing. Theoretically, investment banks didn't mind warehousing, because they earned money on these investments as they held them. But since they represented a somewhat larger risk of default than normal AAA investments (although, of course, this was not publicly conceded), the banks often went out and bought credit protection from the likes of Cassano to hedge their risk.

Banks like Goldman Sachs and Deutsche Bank were holding literally billions of dollars' worth of these AAA-rated mortgage deals, and they all went to Cassano for insurance, offering to pay him premiums in exchange for a promise of compensation in the event of a default. The money poured in. In 1999, AIGFP only had $737 million in revenue. By 2005, that number jumped to $3.26 billion. Compensation at the tiny unit (which had fewer than five hundred employees total) was more than $1 million per person.

Cassano was thinking one of two things. Either he thought that these instruments would never default, or else he just didn't care and never really planned to pay out in the event that they did. It's probably the latter, for things worked out just fine for Cassano; he made $280 million in personal compensation over eight years and is still living in high style in a three-floor town house in Knightsbridge in London, while beyond his drawing room windows, out in the world, the flames keep kicking higher. Moreover, reports have also surfaced indicating that the Justice Department will not prosecute him.

That's what Andy means when he asks if, in offering guys like Miklos their crazy insurance deals, AIG was being stupid, or whether they were just collecting premiums without ever intending to pay. It would fit perfectly with the narrative of the grifter era if it turned out to be the latter.

That was one scam AIG had running, and it was a big one. But even as Cassano was laying nearly $500 billion in bets with the biggest behemoths on Wall Street, there was another big hole opening on the other side of the AIG hull. This was in AIG's Asset Management department, headed by yet another egomaniacal buffoon, this one by the name of Win Neuger.

Semi-notorious in insurance circles for his used-car-salesman/motivational-speaker rhetorical style, Neuger is a sixty-year-old executive who came up in AIG in the mid-1990s and, much like Cassano, spearheaded a major new profit-seeking initiative within the traditionally staid and boring insurance business. Via the magic of an internal memo system he whimsically called "Neuger Notes," the executive set out a target for his two-thousand-plus employees: they were to make "one thousand million" dollars in annual profit, a nice round number Neuger liked to refer to as "ten cubed."

In quest of that magical "ten cubed" number, Neuger wasn't going to brook any dissent. In his Neuger Notes back in December 2005, Neuger wrote, "There are still some people who do not believe in our mission . . . If you do not want to be on this bus it is time to get off . . . Your colleagues are tired of carrying you along."

How was he going to make that money? Again, just like Cassano, he was going to take a business that should have and could have been easy, almost risk-free money and turn it into a raging drunken casino.

Neuger's unit was involved in securities lending. In order to understand how this business makes money, one first needs to understand some basic Wall Street practices, in particular short selling—the practice of betting against a stock.

Here's how shorting works. Say you're a hedge fund and you think the stock of a certain company—let's call it International Pimple—is going to decline in value. How do you make money off that knowledge?

First, you call up a securities lender, someone like, say, Win Neuger, and ask if he has any stock in International Pimple. He says he does, as much as you want. You then borrow a thousand shares of International Pimple from Neuger, which let's say is trading at 10 that day. So that's $10,000 worth of stock.

Now, in order to "borrow" those shares from Neuger, you have to give him collateral for those shares in the form of cash. For his trouble, you have to pay him a slight markup, usually 1–2 percent of the real value. So perhaps instead of sending $10,000 to Neuger, you send him $10,200.

Now you take those thousand shares of International Pimple, you go out onto the market, and you sell them. Now you've got $10,000 in cash again. Then, you wait for the stock to decline in value. So let's say a month later, International Pimple is now trading not at 10 but at 7½. You then go out and buy a thousand shares in the company for $7,500. *Then* you go back to Win Neuger and return his borrowed shares to him; he returns your $10,000 and takes the stock back. You've now made $2,500 on the decline in value of International Pimple, less the $200 fee that Neuger keeps. That's how short selling works, although there are endless nuances. It's a pretty simple business model from the short seller's end. You identify securities you think will fall in value, you borrow big chunks of those securities and sell them, then you buy the same stock back after the value has plummeted.

But how does a securities lender like Neuger make money? Theoretically, with tremendous ease. The first step to being a successful securities lender is having lots and lots of securities. AIG had mountains of the stuff, through its subsidiary insurance companies, annuities, and retirement plans. An insurance company, after all, is just a firm that takes money from a policyholder and invests it in long-term securities.

It then takes those mountains of securities and holds on to them as they appreciate over periods of years and years. The insurer makes money when the securities it buys with the policyholder's money appreciate to the point that the company has something left over when it comes time to pay out policyholders' claims.

It's a good, solid business, but AIG wanted to make more money with those securities. So they formed a company that took those securities and lent them, en masse, to short sellers. From the point of view of the securities lender, the process is supposed to be simple and completely risk free. If you're the lender, borrowers come to you for shares; you make money first of all because they pay you that 1–2 percent markup (called the *general collateral,* or *GC, rate*). You lend out a thousand shares, but the borrowers give you 102 percent of what those shares cost as collateral—that extra 2 percent is the GC rate, which you get really for nothing, just for having lots of securities to lend.

So now you've got all this cash, and you don't know when you're going to have to take back those securities you lent out, but the understanding is that it could be anytime and will usually be in the near future. So say Borrower A takes a thousand shares of International Pimple from you and gives you that $10,000 as collateral—you have to be prepared to take those thousand shares back and give him his money back at any time. Because of this, you normally don't want to invest in anything risky at all, anything that requires a long commitment. After all, why bother? You can take that money, buy U.S. Treasury notes with it, twiddle your thumbs, and make nice money basically for free—without any risk at all.

"The collateral shouldn't be subject to market volatility," says David Matias of Vodia Capital, who notes that more conservative sec lenders basically only put their collateral into short-term, ironclad safe investments like U.S. Treasuries, because there's no reason not to. "Say you can make a fifty bps spread [i.e., one-half of 1 percent]. That's enormous in this business. If you've got $100 billion in collateral and you can make a fifty bps on an annualized basis . . . that's like a half-a-billion-dollar business right there."

That's the way it's supposed to work. If Win Neuger and AIG had just taken the mountain of securities their subsidiary life insurance companies held, lent it out on the market, taken that collateral and invested it in the usual boring stuff—Treasuries, for instance—they would have made a small fortune without any risk at all. But that isn't what Win Neuger did, because Win Neuger is a moron.

What Neuger did, instead, is take that collateral and invest it in *residential-mortgage-backed securities*! In other words, he took cash and plunged it into the very risky, not-really-AAA AAA-rated securities that bankers like Andy were cranking out by the metric ton, thanks to the insane explosion of mortgage lending.

This was par for the course during an era when you could never really be entirely sure where your money was or how safe it was. The high yields that these structured deals were offering to investors proved a monster temptation to people up and down the financial services industry. Larry Tabb of the TABB Group, a financial advisory company, gives an example.

"So take me," he says. "I own a bank account. The money for my payroll, it either stays in my account or earns no interest . . . So what my banker says is, why don't we, every night, we'll roll that into an interest-bearing account. And then the next morning you'll get it back, and we'll give you interest overnight on it. And I'm like, 'Okay, that sounds wonderful.'

"So along comes the credit crisis," he says, "and, being in the industry, I say, okay, well, what are these guys putting my money into? So I called up my bank and I say, what are you guys putting my overnight money into? And the answer is like, agency and agency-backed securities.* And I'm like, oh, how much interest are they getting me? Oh, about one percent a year. So these are toxic securities that you're putting me into, and you're giving me one percent interest."

"Great. And how much were they making?" I ask.

"Exactly," Tabb says, explaining that in the end he was left with two options—go without any additional interest, or put all his money at risk while getting ripped off by other bankers.

Neuger's scheme was a variation on the same business model. They were taking cash collateral in the billions from all the major investment

*"Agency-backed" securities refers to securities backed by government-sponsored entities, e.g., Fannie Mae or Freddie Mac.

banks on earth—Deutsche, Goldman, Société Générale—and plunging it into the riskiest instruments imaginable. What's especially crazy about what he did is that the nature of his business dictated that he should have stayed away from all but the very shortest-term investments, because the people he was lending his securities to might at any time have decided they wanted their collateral back.

But Neuger did just the opposite. He borrowed short, taking collateral that technically he had to be prepared to give back overnight, and invested long, in instruments that take ten, fifteen, thirty years to mature. This was a business model that only worked if new business was continually coming in—and we all know what that's called.

"It's kind of a Ponzi scheme, actually," says Matias of Vodia Capital. "If your business is growing, that point at which you have to pay it back is postponed into the future. As long as your business is growing, you have more collateral, not less. But as soon as your business contracts, your collateral starts to decrease and you actually have to make good on that collateral payback. They were betting the money as if they had years to ride through the market. But they didn't."

So within AIG in the period leading up to the total collapse of the housing bubble, you had two major operations running that depended entirely on the continued insane inflation of that bubble. On one hand, Joe Cassano was selling billions of dollars in credit default swap protection to banks like Goldman and Deutsche Bank without having any money to cover those obligations. On the other hand, Win Neuger was lending out billions of dollars of securities to more or less the same customers, then taking the collateral he was getting in return and investing it in illiquid, residential-mortgage-backed, toxic securities.

This was the backdrop for the still largely secret events that took place during the weekend of September 14, 2008, when the government stepped in to rescue AIG and changed the face of the American economy forever.

The CDS insurance Joe Cassano was selling started to show cracks as early as 2005. The reason Cassano could sell this insurance without putting up any money in the first place was that AIG, a massive financial behemoth as old as the earth itself, had a rock-solid credit rating and seemingly inexhaustible resources. When Cassano did deals with the likes of Goldman and Deutsche Bank (to say nothing of Miklos and his smaller Euro bank), all he needed in the way of collateral was AIG's name.

But in March 2005, AIG's name took a hit. The firm's then-CEO, Maurice "Hank" Greenberg, was forced to step down when then–New York attorney general Eliot Spitzer charged Greenberg with a series of accounting irregularities. Those allegations, and Greenberg's departure, led the major ratings agencies to downgrade AIG's credit rating for the first time ever, dropping it from AAA to AA.

When that happened, it triggered clauses in the CDS deals Cassano was writing to all his counterparties, forcing the parent company to post collateral to prove its ability to repay—$1.16 billion, to be exact, in the wake of that first downgrade.

In 2007, as the housing market began to collapse, some of Cassano's clients started to become nervous. They argued that the underlying assets in the deals had seriously declined in value and demanded that Cassano post still more collateral. Importantly, it was Goldman Sachs that freaked out first, demanding in August 2007 that AIG/Cassano fork over $1.5 billion in collateral.

AIG disputed that claim, the two sides argued, and ultimately AIG handed over $450 million. This was right around the time that Cassano was busy lying his ass off about the dangers of his portfolio. In the same month that he agreed to hand over $450 million to cover the depreciation in value of the assets underlying his CDS deals, Cassano told investors in a conference call that everything was hunky-dory. "It is hard for us, without being flippant, to even see a scenario within any kind of [rhyme] or reason that would see us losing one dollar in any of those transactions," he said.

A month later, Cassano fired an accountant named Joseph W. St. Denis, who discovered irregularities in the way AIG valuated a target company's hedge fund accounts; Cassano openly told St. Denis that he wanted to keep him away from his CDS portfolio. "I have deliberately excluded you from the valuation of the Super Seniors [CDSs] because I was concerned that you would pollute the process," he says.

Then, in October 2007, Goldman Sachs came back demanding more money, this time asking for $3 billion. The two sides again argued and again settled on a compromise, as Cassano and AIG this time agreed to pony up $1.5 billion. This was a key development, because when AIG's outside auditor (PricewaterhouseCoopers) heard about Goldman's demands, it downgraded Cassano's swaps portfolio, writing down some $352 million in value that quarter.

Despite this very concrete loss of value, Cassano and his superiors at AIG continued lying their asses off. In yet another conference call in early December 2007, Cassano repeated his earlier position: "It is very difficult to see how there can be any losses in these portfolios."

But it was too late to stave off disaster. By the time Cassano made that December statement, two other major counterparties, Merrill Lynch and Société Générale SA, had come knocking, demanding collateral to cover their deals. By late December, four more banks piled on: UBS, Barclays, Crédit Agricole's Calyon investment-banking unit, and Royal Bank of Scotland Group. Deutsche Bank and a pair of Canadian Banks, CIBC and the Bank of Montreal, would join in later.

AIGFP by that point was, for all intents and purposes, dead. In February 2008, PwC, the auditor, found a "material weakness" in AIG's books, and that quarter AIG announced an extraordinary $5.3 billion loss for the fourth quarter of 2007. Cassano was finally axed that same month, although, amazingly, he was still being paid a $1 million monthly retainer. Then, in May, AIG posted yet another record quarterly loss, of $7.8 billion. The company's then-CEO, Martin Sullivan, was forced to step down in June. The nightmare was officially beginning.

And the collateral calls kept coming. By July 31, 2008, AIG had handed over $16.5 billion in collateral to Cassano's clients. But some of them, in particular Goldman Sachs, were not satisfied. Goldman still had about $20 billion in exposure to AIG and it wanted its money. The management of AIG, however, disputed the amount it owed Goldman as per Cassano's agreements. This was normal, but the lengths to which Goldman went to fight its cause were extraordinary.

"Collateral calls are somewhat subjective because they are based on the caller's [i.e., Goldman's] valuation of the CDS," says one government official who would later be involved in the AIG bailout negotiations. "There may be a degree of negotiation, and since the called [AIG] has the money and the caller [Goldman] wants it, the called has a certain amount of power in the negotiations . . . This is what happened between AIG and Goldman."

As is well known by now, these collateral disputes were a big part of the reason the government was ultimately forced to step in and take action to prop up AIG on the weekend of September 13–14, 2008. One of the key precipitating incidents, in fact, was the decision by the various credit agencies to downgrade AIG a second time. When AIG learned that Moody's and Standard and Poor's intended to downgrade them again on September 15, AIG knew it was in serious trouble, as the downgrade would trigger still more collateral clauses in Cassano's crazy-ass deals. Already in a desperate fight to stave off Goldman and other clients that were screaming for the collateral ostensibly owed thanks to the *last* downgrade, AIG was now going to be on the hook to those same people for tens of billions more. It was this impending ratings holocaust that got the Treasury and the Fed scrambling, beginning Friday, September 12, to figure a way out for everyone concerned.

That part of the story is well known by now. What is less well known is the role that the other AIG crisis—the one caused by Win Neuger—played in the same mess.

Just a few months before, in late June and early July 2008, at roughly the same time Sullivan was stepping down and AIG was announcing a massive $7.8 billion first-quarterly loss, Neuger was announcing problems in his own unit. It seems that by July 2007 Neuger had lent out about $78 billion worth of securities and invested nearly two-thirds of the collateral he received in mortgage-backed crap. By March 31, 2008, the value of his portfolio had dropped to $64.3 billion. In late June, AIG made it public: Neuger, rather than make his "ten cubed" in profits, had actually lost $13 billion in the course of a year.

What is interesting about this is how the world came to find out about it. Neuger, remember, made his money by pulling securities out of the holdings of AIG's subsidiary life companies, lending them out to Wall Street, then taking the cash put up as collateral and investing it. Unlike Cassano's CDS deals, the securities he was lending were actually quite solid, so the parties he was lending them to—in large part the same people who were Cassano's counterparties, i.e., Goldman, Deutsche, Société Générale, etc.—were in theory not at risk of taking great losses. After all, they were still holding the securities, the ordinary stocks and bonds in the portfolios of the subsidiary life companies, and those things were still worth something.

But a funny thing began happening in late 2007 and early 2008. Suddenly Neuger's customers started returning their securities to him en masse. Banks like Goldman Sachs started returning huge chunks of securities and demanding their collateral back. In what quickly struck some regulators as a somewhat too convenient coincidence, many of these banks that started returning Neuger's sec-lending cash were also counterparties to Cassano's Financial Products division.

"Many of the counterparties who were involved with the securities-lending business, they were knowledgeable as to what was going on with [Cassano's] Financial Products division," says Eric Dinallo, at the time the head of the New York State Insurance Department. "You had people who were counterparties to the credit default swap side who were also able to pull cash out of [Neuger's] sec-lending business."

Early in that summer of 2008, Dinallo would chair a multistate task force charged with helping AIG "wind down" its crippled securities-lending business in such a way that AIG's subsidiary insurance companies (and by extension the holders of policies issued by those companies) would not be harmed by any potential bankruptcy. The threat that a run on Neuger's sec-lending business would result in these insurance companies getting bankrupted or seized by state insurance commissioners was like a guillotine that hung over the entire American economy in the summer of 2008—and, in ways that to this day remain unknown to most Americans, that guillotine would become a crucial factor in the decision to bail out AIG and AIG's counterparties amid the implosion of September 2008.

Neuger had been borrowing from AIG subsidiary companies like American General, SunAmerica, and United States Life, companies that insured tens of thousands, if not hundreds of thousands, of ordinary policyholders and retirees. If enough of Neuger's securities-lending clients demanded their money back at once, suddenly there was a real threat that the parent company AIG would have to reach down and liquidate the assets of these mom-and-pop insurance companies, leaving those tens of thousands of people out in the wilderness. All in order to cover Neuger's colossally stupid and unnecessary bets on the mortgage market.

Faced with this terrifying possibility, the regulators in numerous states—led by New York but also including Texas, which contained many thousands of ordinary people with American General policies—suddenly took notice. It was little noted at the time, but when AIG announced that $13 billion loss, Texas insurance officials said publicly that they were not aware of the liabilities involved with Neuger's portfolio. "We were aware of this portfolio, but we didn't have transparency on what was in it because it was off-balance-sheet" in the company's statutory accounting reports, said Doug Slape, chief analyst at the Texas Department of Insurance.

It was around this time, in June and July, that Dinallo and insurance officials from the states scrambled to step in and make sure that AIG had enough funds to cover the messes in the securities-lending business. The states had a mandate to make sure that no one would be allowed to take value out of these mom-and-pop insurance companies; before they would ever let that happen, they would step in and take the companies over.

They had the power to do that, but in July the officials were trying everything they could to avoid taking that drastic step. The situation was so serious that the federal government also stepped in to help convince the states not to seize any of the AIG subsidiaries if they could avoid it. "Treasury was calling the governors of the states and getting the governors to get their insurance commissioners to stay on board," says Dinallo. "I was in the middle of these eleven-state conference calls—eleven states being the number of states that had AIG subsidiary companies—and we were making sure that everybody was saying the same thing: that if we start seizing life or property insurers because they file for bankruptcy, it will be bad for everybody."

In the end, the task force worked with AIG and got them to sign a "make-whole" agreement in which they pledged to put some money into the subsidiary pool and throw in another $5 billion or so to cover any potential future losses. The states thought this would be more than enough.

"As of June thirtieth, everything was still more or less fine," says one state official involved in those negotiations. "It wasn't the end of the world yet."

But AIG and its subsidiary life companies were only "fine" up to a point. The garbage Neuger had invested in—and about a third of his portfolio was mortgage-based toxic crap—had plummeted in value, perhaps irreversibly. He couldn't sell the stuff and he couldn't really replace it in his portfolio with something safer. All he could do was hold on to his big folder full of worthless paper and hope it recovered its value. Meanwhile, he had to cross his fingers and hope his customers/counterparties wouldn't start returning their securities and demanding their money back.

This, incidentally, was not an unreasonable expectation. Under normal circumstances a sec-lending business like Neuger's wouldn't have to deal with a lot of customers returning their securities (also called closing out their accounts) all at once. Normally the lender would lend out his securities on short-term contracts—say, sixty to ninety days—and at the end of that time the client would either renew the deal or else the securities would be lent to someone else. In either case the securities would remain lent out. This is called rolling the deal. Since the securities Neuger had lent out were still valuable, and the parties holding them didn't have that much real risk of a loss, it was reasonable to expect that his clients would keep rolling them into the future.

And as long as the deals kept rolling, Neuger's losses would remain hidden, or at least intermittent and therefore manageable. At the very least, this is what the state insurance officials, examining things jointly in June, expected.

"We didn't see any reason why the counterparties should worry," says the state official. "The stuff was still valuable. There wasn't much risk."

But then something surprising happened. The counterparties did start closing out their accounts with Neuger. One in particular was extremely aggressive in returning securities to AIG: Goldman Sachs. Goldman had been leading the charge throughout the year in closing out its accounts with Neuger; now, in the summer of 2008, it stepped up the pace, hurling billions of dollars' worth of Neuger's securities back in his car-salesman face and demanding its money back.

Dinallo here interjects with what he calls a "powerful" piece of information—that during this period when Goldman and all the other counterparties suddenly started pulling cash out of AIG's securities-lending business, no other sec-lending firm on Wall Street was having anything like the same problems. If Neuger's counterparties were pulling their cash out en masse, it didn't seem to be because they were worried about the value of the securities they were holding. Something else was going on.

"We analyzed every single other sec-lending business that was under our jurisdiction," Dinallo says. "And not any one of them had problems. To this day they don't have problems . . . You had Met Life, and AXA, and all these others—there were twenty-three others—and they had no issues. It was just AIG."

So of all the billions of dollars' worth of securities that had been lent out, it seemed the big Wall Street banks in the summer of 2008 suddenly found reason to worry only about those lent out by just one company—the same company that just so happened to owe these same banks billions via its unrelated credit-default-swap business.

"So what's the coincidence of that?" asks Dinallo. "It was clearly a result of what was going on in the financial products division."

Once the sec-lending counterparties started pulling out, the run on AIG was on. Already besieged with requests for cash to cover nutjob Joe Cassano's bets, AIG now needed to come up with billions more to cover the losses of the firm's other idiot stepchild, Win Neuger.

Lacking the funds to cover Neuger's losses, AIG once again rang up the state insurance regulators along with the Federal Reserve, this time with a more urgent request. The parent company wanted permission from the regulators to reach down into its subsidiary companies and liquidate some of their holdings—imperiling the retirement accounts and insurance policies of thousands—in order to pay off the likes of Goldman and Deutsche Bank.

The states balked, however. In fact, the situation grew dire enough that by the first week of September, Texas—which was home to some of AIG's biggest subsidiary insurance companies and would have been affected disproportionately if AIG tried to raid those companies' holdings—had drawn up a draft letter outlining its plans to seize control of four AIG subsidiary companies, including American General.

"We got active in stepping in to protect those companies from being swallowed up in what was happening with the overall AIG picture," says Doug Slape of the Texas Department of Insurance.

"Texas was definitely very aggressive," says Dinallo.

The seizure of AIG subsidiaries would have been an extraordinary, unprecedented event. It was an extreme step, the nuclear option: had this occurred, the state would have simply stepped in, frozen the companies' business, and then distributed the assets to the policyholders as equitably as possible. If the assets weren't sufficient to cover those policies (and they almost certainly would have covered just a fraction of the company's obligations), then the state also had public guaranty associations that would have kicked in to help rescue the policies. But without a doubt, had Texas stepped in to seize American General and other companies, policyholders and retirees who might already have paid premiums for a lifetime would have been left basically with pennies on the dollar.

"Thousands would have been affected," says Slape.

It gets worse. Had Texas gone ahead and seized those subsidiaries, all the other states that had AIG subsidiaries headquartered within their borders would almost certainly have followed suit. A full-blown run on AIG's subsidiary holdings would likely have gone into effect, creating a real-world financial catastrophe. "It would have been ugly," says Dinallo. Thousands if not tens or hundreds of thousands of people would have seen their retirement and insurance nest eggs depleted to a fraction of their value, overnight.

The Texas letter was prepared and ready to go on the weekend of September 13–14. That was when an extraordinary collection of state officials and megapowerful Wall Street bankers had gathered in several locations in New York to try to figure out how best to handle the financial storm that had gathered around a number of huge companies—not only AIG, but Lehman Brothers, Merrill Lynch, and others.

The key gathering with regard to AIG took place at the offices of the New York Federal Reserve Bank. The government/state players in-

cluded a group from the Fed, led by then–New York Fed official Timothy Geithner, as well as officials from the Treasury (then run by former
Goldman Sachs chief Henry Paulson) and regulators from Dinallo's office at the New York Insurance Department. The private players of
course included AIG executives and teams of bankers from, primarily,
three private companies: JPMorgan, Morgan Stanley, and Goldman
Sachs. For most of the weekend, the AIG meetings took place in the
Fed building, with Fed officials in one corner, Dinallo's people in a conference room in the center, and bankers from the three banks in each of
the remaining corners.

Now, JPMorgan had a good reason to be there: it had been hired as
a banking consultant by AIG some weeks before to try to salvage its financial health. Morgan Stanley, meanwhile, had been (since the Bear
Stearns rescue) hired to consult with the U.S. Treasury. Why Goldman
was there is one of the key questions of the whole bailout era. Goldman
did not represent anyone at this gathering but Goldman.

Ostensibly, Goldman was there because of its status as one of AIG's
largest creditors. But then Deutsche Bank and Société Générale were
also similarly large creditors, and they weren't there. "I don't know why
they were there and other large counterparties weren't there," says Dinallo. There was something special about Goldman's status, and what
that thing was was about to come out, in a big way.

On that Saturday, one state regulatory official present for these
meetings—we'll call him Kolchak—saw the prepared Texas letter for
the first time and immediately realized its implications. In conference
calls with other state officials Kolchak understood that the Texas letter was like a giant bomb waiting to be set off. If Texas moved on the
companies, the other states would follow and a Main Street disaster
would be under way. And that bomb was going to blow under one
specific circumstance. Texas was waiting to see if AIG was determined to reach into those subsidiary companies, and AIG was only
going to do that if Neuger's counterparties insisted on a massive collateral call. But among those counterparties, most were willing to be
cool and hold on to the securities. Only one was making noise like it
was not going to be patient and was willing to pull the plug: Goldman Sachs.

That fact was made clear the next morning, on Sunday, when all the main parties met in the grand old conference room on the first floor of the Fed building. "It's like this weird, medieval lobby," says Kolchak. "No one ever goes in there, ever. That made it even weirder." The sight of this seldom-used hall, packed with fifty or sixty of the most powerful financiers in the world, was surreal—as was the angry announcement made by Goldman CEO Lloyd Blankfein at the outset of the meeting. Kolchak reports that Blankfein was the dominant presence at the meeting; he stood up and threw down the gauntlet, demanding that AIG cough up the disputed collateral in the CDS/Cassano mess.

"Blankfein was basically like, 'They [AIG] can start by giving us our money,' " Kolchak says. "He was really pissed. He just kept coming back to that, that he wanted his fucking money."

After that meeting Kolchak suddenly grasped, he thought, the dynamic of the whole weekend. Goldman was really holding a gun not only to the head of AIG but to the thousands of policyholders who, somewhere outside the room and all across America, had no idea what was going on. Basically what was happening was that Blankfein and the other Goldman partners wanted the money AIGFP and Cassano owed them so badly that they were willing to blow up the other end of AIG, if needed, to make that happen. Even though they weren't really in danger of losing any money by holding on to Neuger's securities, they were returning them anyway, just to force AIG into a crisis.

With Texas ready at any moment to move in and seize the AIG subsidiaries, all Goldman had to do to create a national emergency was make that one last giant collateral call on Neuger's business. If it did that, all the other banks would follow, the run on Neuger's business would continue, and AIG would be forced to try to raid its subsidiaries. That in turn would force the states to step in and seize the subsidiary insurance companies.

Blankfein's announcement that Sunday morning was a declaration that Goldman had no intention of relenting. It was going to pull the pin not only on AIG but on the financial universe if *someone* didn't come up with the money it felt it was owed by AIG.

"That's what the whole weekend was about," says Kolchak. "We're all basically there to try to figure out if Goldman is going to stand down. There's literally a whole army of bankers there trying to figure out a way to get Goldman to call off the dogs."

After that Sunday morning announcement, the scene became even more surreal. Literally hundreds of bankers from the three banks had already descended upon AIG's headquarters at nearby 70 Pine Street (which has since been sold off for pennies on the dollar to Korean investors—but that's another story, for later) and begun poring over AIG's books in search of value. But there wasn't much left.

"Honestly, pretty much everything that hadn't been nailed down had already been liquidated and invested in RMBS [residential-mortgage-backed securities] and stuff like that," says one source close to AIG who was there that weekend. The only stuff left was a lot of weird, eclectic crap. "We're talking ski resorts in Vail, little private equity partnerships, nothing that you could sell off fast," he says.

The bankers who were poring over this stuff were working feverishly to see if there was enough there that could be turned into ready money to fight off the collateral calls. "They're working to see if there's enough value, enough liquidity, to pay up," says Kolchak. "And at the end of this, Goldman comes back and basically says no. There's not enough there to satisfy them. They're going to turn the jets up."

AIG, meanwhile, was begging state officials to intercede on its behalf with Goldman with regard to the collateral demands on the Neuger business. "They're like, 'Can you get Goldman to lay off?' " says one state regulator who was there that weekend.

All of this pressure from the collateral calls on the Win Neuger/sec-lending side were matched by the extremely aggressive collateral calls Goldman in particular had been making all year on the Cassano/CDS side of the business. In fact, two years later, the question of whether or not Goldman had used those collateral calls to accelerate AIG's demise would be a subject of open testimony at hearings of the Financial Crisis Inquiry Commission in Washington. I was at those hearings on June 30, 2010, sitting just a few seats away from the homuculoid Cassano, who was making his first public appearance since the crash. And one of the first things that Cassano was asked, by the commission's chairman, Phil Angelides, was whether or not Goldman had been over-aggressive in its collateral calls. The author apologizes on behalf of Angelides for the reckless mixing of metaphors here, but his question is all about whether AIG fell into crisis or was pushed by banks like Goldman:

> ANGELIDES: The chronology . . . appears to indicate that there's some pretty hard fighting with Goldman Sachs in particular through March of 2008, and then after. I used the analogy when I started here: was there a cheetah hunting down a weak member of the herd? . . . I am trying to get to this very issue of was a first domino pushed over? Or did someone light a fuse here?

Another FCIC commissioner put it to Cassano this way: "Was Goldman out to get you?"

Angelides during the testimony referred to Goldman's aggressiveness in making collateral calls to AIG. At one point he quotes an AIGFP official who says that a July 30 margin call from Goldman "hit out of the blue, and a fucking number that's well bigger than we ever planned for." He called Goldman's numbers "ridiculous."

Cassano that day refused to point a finger at Goldman, and Goldman itself, through documents released to the FCIC later in the summer of 2010 and via comments by Chief Operating Officer Gary Cohn ("We are not pushing markets down through marks"), denied that it had intentionally hastened AIG's demise by being overaggressive with its collateral demands.

Nonetheless, it's pretty clear that the unwavering collateral demands by Goldman and by the other counterparties (but particularly Goldman) left the Fed and the Treasury with a bleak choice. Once the bankers came back and pronounced AIG not liquid enough to cover the collateral demands for *either* AIGFP or Neuger's business, there was only one real option. Either the state would pour massive amounts of public money into the hole in the side of the ship, or the Goldman-led run on AIG's sec-lending business would spill out into the real world. In essence, the partners of Goldman Sachs held the thousands of AIG policyholders hostage, all in order to recover a few billion bucks they'd bet on Joe Cassano's plainly crooked sweetheart CDS deals.

Within a few days, the crisis had been averted, but at the cost of a paradigm-changing event in American history. Paulson and the Fed came through with an $80 billion bailout, which would later be expanded to more than $200 billion in public assistance. Once that money was earmarked to fill the hole, Texas stood down and withdrew its threat to seize AIG's subsidiary life companies, since AIG would now have plenty of money from the Federal Reserve to pay off Neuger's stupidities.

As is well known now, the counterparties to Joe Cassano's CDS deals received $22.4 billion via the AIG bailout, with Goldman and Société Générale getting the biggest chunk of that money.

Less well known is that the counterparties to Neuger's securities-lending operations would receive a staggering $43.7 billion in public money via the AIG bailout, with Goldman getting the second-biggest slice, at $4.8 billion (Deutsche Bank, with $7 billion, was number one).

How they accomplished that feat was somewhat complicated. First, the Fed put up the money to cover the collateral calls against Neuger from Goldman and other banks. Then the Fed set up a special bailout facility called Maiden Lane II (named after the tiny street in downtown Manhattan next to the New York Federal Reserve Bank), which it then used to systematically buy up all the horseshit RMBS assets Neuger and his moronic "ten cubed"–chasing employees had bought up with all their billions in collateral over the years.

The mechanism involved in these operations—whose real mission was to filter out the unredeemable crap from the merely temporarily distressed crap and stick the taxpayer with the former and Geithner's buddies with the latter—would be enormously complex, a kind of labyrinthine financial sewage system designed to stick us all with the raw waste and pump clean water back to Wall Street.

The AIG bailout marked the end of a chain of mortgage-based scams that began, in a way, years before, when Solomon Edwards set up a long con to rip off an unsuspecting sheriff's deputy named Eljon Williams. It was a game of hot potato in which money was invented out of thin air in the form of a transparently bogus credit scheme, converted through the magic of modern financial innovation into highly combustible, soon-to-explode securities, and then quickly passed up the chain with lightning speed—from the lender to the securitizer to the major investment banks to AIG, with each party passing it off as quickly as possible, knowing it was too hot to hold. In the end that potato would come to rest, sizzling away, in the hands of the Federal Reserve Bank.

Eljon Williams is still in his house. He scored an extraordinary reprieve when two things happened. One, the state of Massachusetts in the person of Attorney General Martha Coakley launched an investigation of some of the mortgage-lending companies in her state, including Litton Loans—a wholly owned subsidiary of Goldman Sachs that ended up owning the smaller of Eljon's two mortgage loans. Coakley accused Goldman Sachs of facilitating the kind of fraud practiced by Solomon Edwards by providing a market for these bad loans through the securitization process, by failing to weed out bad or unfair loans, and by failing to make information about the bad loans available to potential investors on the other end. By the time Coakley settled negotiations with Goldman Sachs, the latter had already been the beneficiary of at least $13 billion in public assistance through the AIG bailout, with $10 billion more coming via the Troubled Asset Relief Program and upwards of $29 billion more in cheap money coming via FDIC backing for new debt under another Geithner bailout program, the Temporary Liquidity Guarantee Program.

Despite all that cash, Goldman drove a very hard bargain with Coakley. It ultimately only had to pay the state a $50 million fine, pennies compared to what the bank made every month trading in mortgage-backed deals. Moreover, it did not have to make a formal admission of wrongdoing. A month or so after Coakley and Goldman went public with the terms of their settlement, Goldman announced that it had earned a record $3.44 billion in second-quarter profits in 2009.

But there was one benefit to this mess, and that was this: Goldman, through Litton, forgave entirely the smaller of Eljon Williams's two mortgage loans. Meanwhile his other lender, ASC, agreed under public pressure to a modification, allowing Eljon and his family to return to a relatively low fixed rate. A religious man, Williams talks of the events that led to his keeping his home as though they involved divine intervention. "I prayed on it, and prayed on it," he says. "And it happened."

What is most amazing about the mortgage-scam era is how consistent the thinking was all the way up the chain. At the very bottom, lowlifes like Solomon Edwards, the kind of shameless con man who preyed on families and kids and whom even other criminals would look down on, simply viewed each family as assets to be liquidated and converted into one-time, up-front fees. They were incentivized to behave that way by a kink in the American credit system that made it easier, and more profitable, to put a torch to a family's credit rating and collect a big up-front fee than it was to do the job the right way.

And, amazingly, it was the same thing at the very top. When the CEO of Goldman Sachs stood up in the conference room of the New York Federal Reserve Bank and demanded his money, he did so knowing that it was more profitable to put AIG to the torch than it was to try to work things out. In the end, Blankfein and Goldman literally did a mob job on AIG, burning it to the ground for the "insurance" of a government bailout they knew they would get, if that army of five hundred bankers could not find the money to arrange a private solution. In their utter pessimism and complete disregard for the long term, they were absolutely no different from Solomon Edwards or the New Century lenders who trolled the ghettos and the middle-class suburbs for home-buying suckers to throw into the meat grinder, where they could be ground into fees and turned into Ford Explorers and flat-screen TVs or weekends in Reno or whatever else helps a back-bench mortgage scammer get his rocks off. The only difference with Goldman was one of scale.

Two other things are striking about the mortgage-scam era. One was that nobody in this vast rogues' gallery of characters was really engaged in building anything. If Wall Street makes its profits by moving money around from place to place and taking a cut here and there, in a sense this whole mess was a kind of giant welfare program the financial services industry simply willed into being for itself. It invented a moun-

tain of money in the form of a few trillion dollars' worth of bogus mortgages and rolled it forward for a few years, until reality intervened—
and suddenly it was announced that We the Taxpayer had to *buy* it
from them, at what they called face value, for the good of the country.

In the meantime, and this is the second thing that's so amazing, almost everyone who touched that mountain turned out to be a crook of
some kind. The mortgage brokers systematically falsified information
on loan applications in order to secure bigger loans and hawked explosive option-ARM mortgages to people who either didn't understand
them or, worse, did understand them and simply never intended to pay.
The loan originators cranked out massive volumes of loans with plainly
doctored applications, not giving a shit about whether or not the borrowers could pay, in a desperate search for short-term rebates and fees.
The securitizers used harebrained math to turn crap mortgages into
AAA-rated investments; the ratings agencies signed off on that harebrained math and handed out those AAA ratings in order to keep the
fees coming in and the bonuses for their executives high. But even the
ratings agencies were blindsided by scammers who advertised and sold,
openly, help in rigging FICO scores to make broke and busted borrowers look like good credit risks. The corrupt ratings agencies were undone by ratings corrupters!

Meanwhile, investment banks tried to stick pensioners and insurance companies with their toxic investments, or else they held on to
their toxic investments and tried to rip off idiots like Joe Cassano by
sticking him with the liability of default. But they were undone by the
fact that Joe Cassano probably never even intended to pay off, just like
the thousands of homeowners who bought too-big houses with option-
ARM mortgages and never intended to pay. And at the tail end of all
this frantic lying, cheating, and scamming on all sides, during which
time no good jobs were created and nothing except a few now-empty
houses (good for nothing except depressing future home prices) got
built, the final result is that we all ended up picking up the tab, subsidizing all this crime and dishonesty and pessimism as a matter of national policy.

We paid for this instead of a generation of health insurance, or an
alternative energy grid, or a brand-new system of roads and highways.

With the $13-plus trillion we are estimated to ultimately spend on the bailouts, we could not only have bought and paid off every single sub-prime mortgage in the country (that would only have cost $1.4 trillion), we could have paid off every remaining mortgage of any kind in this country—and still have had enough money left over to buy a new house for every American who does not already have one.

But we didn't do that, and we didn't spend the money on anything else useful, either. Why? For a very good reason. Because we're no good anymore at building bridges and highways or coming up with brilliant innovations in energy or medicine. We're shit now at finishing massive public works projects or launching brilliant fairy-tale public policy ventures like the moon landing.

What are we good at? Robbing what's left. When it comes to that, we Americans have no peer. And when it came time to design the bailouts, a monster collective project spanning two presidential administrations that was every bit as vast and far-reaching (only not into the future, but the past) as Kennedy's trip to the moon, we showed it.

4

Blowout
The Commodities Bubble

In the summer of 2008, Priscilla Carillo, a twenty-four-year-old living near San Bernardino, had some rough luck. She had been working as a temp at a warehouse and also going to school at Chaffey Community College, about forty minutes away from where she was living at the time. She was humping it back and forth in a beat-up Nissan Altima, making a go of it. She says her mom, thinking she was being helpful, had booted her out of the house when she turned eighteen, told her to make her own way. You know, the American way.

"I always thought Latinos lived with their parents until they were forty," she says now. "I guess I was different."

Then, at the beginning of 2008, Priscilla started to notice a problem. Gas prices were going up—*way* up. They were steaming past four dollars a gallon. Since the trip to her community college was a long one, it soon became unaffordable. She dumped school and went to work full-time. But then her temp agency went under and she lost her job. Now Priscilla was broke and unable to pay rent. In June and July 2008, she was living in her car.

"I'd park at a library or in a park or something," she says now. "I didn't know I couldn't sleep in residential neighborhoods at night. I got picked up by the cops a bunch of times. They thought I was a prostitute. I told them, man, I'm just sleeping."

Halfway across the country, at almost exactly the same time, a businessman named Robert Lukens was starting to feel a squeeze. He ran a contracting firm called Lukens Construction in Reading, Pennsylvania. Lukens had seven employees and his business had been in his family for three generations, founded by his grandfather close to forty years back.

He hadn't wanted to get into the family business, but circumstances made that decision for him. Way back in 1981 he'd moved to Richmond, Virginia, and in the space of a week had gotten married and then was laid off by Ryan Homes, one of the biggest contracting companies in America.

Now, with a new wife and no job, he reluctantly went back to work for his father, who had taken over Lukens Construction from his own father and with whom he had a difficult relationship. But father and son smoothed it out, stuck it out, and made it work. Some fourteen years later, in 1995, Robert Lukens took over the business himself, and in describing the firm he sounded like a man deeply proud of his family's business. "We do high-end contracting, really nice work," he says. Not cookie-cutter houses, he says, but custom additions and "lots of word-of-mouth referrals." Heading into 2008, Lukens says, he was doing fine.

"But then all of a sudden I started having high energy costs," he says. "Used to be I'd pay five hundred, six hundred dollars a week for gas. Now, in July of 2008, I'm suddenly paying twelve hundred dollars a week for gas. And not only that—all my vendors are suddenly hitting me with fuel costs. Used to be if I got a delivery of lumber, the delivery would be figured into the price. Now they'd hit me with a surcharge— a hundred and twenty-five bucks for the delivery or whatever. Lumber. Concrete. Stuff like that."

About the same time that Lukens was seeing those price hikes, a biology student with dreams of becoming a doctor named Sam Sereda was heading home for the summer. Sereda was doing his undergrad at Gordon College on the North Shore of Massachusetts, but his home was in Sunnyvale, in the Bay Area out in California. Sereda was doing everything right in his young life. His grades were good, he was making money in his spare time by tutoring kids from Hamilton Wenham High in AP Bio. For the summer he had an internship set up with a Bay Area company called Genentech in San Francisco, and was planning on taking an advanced calc class at West Valley College in Saratoga, to pick up a few extra credits for his upcoming senior year.

"But then gas prices, they went from like three bucks to over four bucks a gallon," he says now. "My family was going through some financial problems at the time, too. I ended up having to cancel the internship. The forty-minute drive was too long, it cost me too much money."

The calc class went out the window, too. "Couldn't afford that drive either," he says now. "I ended up having to do twenty credits in one semester when I got back to Massachusetts. I know how this sounds, but with gas prices the way they were . . . my only real option for that summer was to sit in the house and do nothing. My brother was ill at the time—my family and I made the decision, the best thing for me was just to stay home."

And while all of this was going on, a woman named Diane Zollinger was gainfully employed, no serious economic worries on the horizon. Her problem was that she lived in Montana. In Montana, everything is far from everything else. She had a good job in Bozeman, but Bozeman was thirty-five miles from her home in Livingston. She was driving seventy miles a day to work when the price of gas shot up to $4.85 a gallon. Her car got twenty-five miles a gallon. She was paying nearly seventy bucks a week for gas at the height of the oil spike that summer. "When the world crashed and I got laid off in November," she says now, "we had more money in our pockets at the end of the day with me on unemployment."

It didn't matter where you lived or what you did for a living—in the summer of 2008, the cost of energy almost certainly hit you hard. There was no serious attempt by either the national media or the national political establishment to explain the cause of the problem. Most people assumed it had to do with some combination of shortages and/or increased demand from the Chinese industrial machine, and most TV reports were more than willing to encourage that perception, despite the fact that there were no long lines at the gas stations, no seventies-style rage-fests while waiting for gas, no obvious evidence of scarcity. We were told about a crisis of supply that existed somewhere other than where we could see it—someplace in the abstract.

"I remember watching CNN, and they were trying to tell us about shortages," says Sereda. "They were showing lines in Canada, or somewhere else, someplace."

I mostly spent that summer covering the McCain-Obama presidential campaign for *Rolling Stone,* during which time I heard varying explanations for why this gas price spike was happening, why people like Priscilla were suddenly living out of cars.

McCain, amazingly, spent all summer telling us reporters that the reason for the spike in gas prices was that socialists like Barack Obama were refusing to permit immediate drilling for oil off the coast of Florida.

Like all reporters that summer, I found my attention dominated not by interjections into the commodities market but by a seemingly endless series of made-up controversies involving either warring tribes within the Democratic Party (the Clintonicons versus the Obamaniacs) or blue/red hot-button issues like the Reverend Wright business.

But I do remember that gas was an issue, sort of, and it sort of got talked about by both candidates. I remember being in Kenner, Louisiana, on the night McCain de facto won the nomination and he gave a speech against a hideous puke-green background saying that "no problem is more urgent today than America's dependence on foreign oil." I remember the somber ads McCain started airing that summer talking about how "some in Washington are still saying no to drilling in America."

I remember after that night, the press pool rolled out of its caged-in area after the speech and all us hacks were snickering in the bus about McCain's latest whopper.

"What a bunch of bullshit," one of them, a TV guy I'd known and disliked for years, said. "As if gas prices were going up because of an off-shore drilling ban."

"Yeah, nobody's gonna buy that," added another.

This went on for a few minutes. Campaign reporters love to rip the candidates they cover, it's their favorite sport—until the candidate actually walks back into their section of the plane, at which point they go weak in the knees like high school girls and start kissing his skirts like he's the pope. Anyway, at one point of this latest rip session about McCain's drilling gambit, I piped in. "Hey," I said. "Does anyone here actually *know* why gas prices are going up? I sure as hell don't."

There was a brief discussion at this, and theories were offered, but in the end it became clear that none of us in the pool had a fucking clue what was causing the gas spike. I later whispered to another print reporter: "Doesn't that make all of us frauds? I mean, if we're covering this stuff anyway."

His answer: "You're just figuring that out now?"

Later on, I was in Minnesota for the Republican convention in September of that summer and listening—squeezed up against a wall of other suckers with jobs as lousy as mine and with backgrounds in economics as shaky as mine—as McCain explained the problem in explicit terms:

> Senator Obama thinks we can achieve energy independence without more drilling and without more nuclear power. But Americans know better than that. We must use all resources and develop all technologies necessary to rescue our economy from the damage caused by rising oil prices.

How about Barack Obama? He offered a lot of explanations, too. In many ways the McCain-Obama split on the gas prices issue was a perfect illustration of how left-right politics works in this country.

McCain blamed the problem, both directly and indirectly, on a combination of government, environmentalists, and foreigners.

Obama knew his audience and aimed elsewhere. He blamed the problem on greedy oil companies and also blamed ordinary Americans for their wastefulness, for driving SUVs and other gas-guzzlers. I remember him in the pivotal Pennsylvania primary, when Hillary had him running scared for a while, and he was honing a strategy of chalking up the high gas prices to greedy oil companies that, one supposed, were simply bumping up prices to pay for bigger bonuses.

"They have been in fat city for a long time," Obama said in Wilkes-Barre during that campaign, referring to Exxon and other gas companies. "They are not necessarily putting that money into refinery capacity, which could potentially relieve some of the bottlenecks in our gasoline supply. And so that is something we have to go after. I think we can go after the windfall profits of some of these companies."

Both candidates presented the solution as just sitting there waiting to be unleashed, if only one or the other would get the political go-ahead. McCain said the lower gas prices were sitting somewhere under the Gulf of Mexico. Obama said they were sitting in the bank accounts of companies like Exxon in the form of windfall profits to be taxed.

The formula was the same formula we see in every election: Republicans demonize government, sixties-style activism, and foreigners. Democrats demonize corporations, greed, and the right-wing rabble.

Both candidates were selling the public a storyline that had nothing to do with the truth. Gas prices were going up for reasons completely unconnected to the causes these candidates were talking about. What really happened was that Wall Street had opened a new table in its casino. The new gaming table was called *commodity index investing.* And when it became the hottest new game in town, America suddenly got a very painful lesson in the glorious possibilities of taxation without representation. Wall Street turned gas prices into a gaming table, and when they hit a hot streak we ended up making exorbitant involuntary payments for a commodity that one simply cannot live without. Wall Street gambled, you paid the big number, and what they ended up doing with some of that money you lost is the most amazing thing of all. They got America—you, me, Priscilla Carillo, Robert Lukens—to pawn itself to pay for the gas they forced us to buy in the first place. Pawn its bridges, highways, and airports. Literally sell our sovereign territory. It was a scam of almost breathtaking beauty, if you're inclined to appreciate that sort of thing.

The scam was a two-part squeeze. Part one was the commodities bubble, a completely avoidable speculative mania that drove oil prices through the roof. It is perhaps the first bubble in history that badly wounded a mighty industrial empire without anyone even realizing it happened. Most Americans do not even know that it took place. That was part of the beauty of the grift—the oil supply crisis that never was.

This was never supposed to happen. All the way back in 1936, after gamblers disguised as Wall Street brokers destroyed the American economy, the government of Franklin D. Roosevelt passed a law called the Commodity Exchange Act that was specifically designed to prevent speculators from screwing around with the prices of day-to-day life necessities like wheat and corn and soybeans and oil and gas. The markets for these necessary, day-to-day consumer items—called commodities— had suffered serious manipulations in the twenties and thirties, mostly downward.

The most famous of these cases involved a major Wall Street power broker named Arthur Cutten, who was known as the "Wheat King." The government accused Cutten of concealing his positions in the wheat market to manipulate prices. His case eventually went to the Supreme Court as *Wallace v. Cutten* and provided the backdrop for passage of the new 1936 commodity markets law, which gave the government strict watchdog powers to oversee the functioning of this unique kind of trading.

The commodities markets are unlike any other markets in the world, because they have two distinctly different kinds of participants. The first kind of participants are the people who either produce the commodities in question or purchase them—actual wheat farmers, say, or cereal companies that routinely buy large quantities of grain. These participants are called *physical hedgers.* The market primarily functions as a place where the wheat farmers meet up with the cereal companies and do business, but it also allows these physical hedgers to buy themselves a little protection against market uncertainty through the use of futures contracts.

Let's say you're that cereal company and your business plan for the next year depends on your being able to buy corn at a maximum of $3.00 a bushel. And maybe corn right now is selling at $2.90 a bushel, but you want to insulate yourself against the risk that prices might skyrocket in the next year. So you buy a bunch of futures contracts for corn that give you the right—say, six months from now, or a year from now—to buy corn at $3.00 a bushel.

Now, if corn prices go up, if there's a terrible drought and corn becomes scarce and ridiculously expensive, you could give a damn, because you can buy at $3.00 no matter what. That's the proper use of the commodities futures market.

It works in reverse, too—maybe you grow corn, and maybe you're worried about a glut the following year that might, say, drive the price of corn down to $2.50 or below. So you sell futures for a year from now at $2.90 or $3.00, locking in your sale price for the next year. If that drought happens and the price of corn skyrockets, you might lose out, but at least you can plan for the future based on a reasonable price.

These buyers and sellers of real stuff are the physical hedgers. The FDR administration recognized, however, that in order for the market to properly function, there needed to exist another kind of player—the speculator. The entire purpose of the speculator, as originally envisioned by the people who designed this market, was to guarantee that the physical hedgers, the real players, could always have a place to buy and/or sell their products.

Again, imagine you're that corn grower but you bring your crop to market at a moment when the cereal company isn't buying. That's where the speculator comes in. He buys up your corn and hangs on to it. Maybe a little later, that cereal company comes to the market looking for corn—but there are no corn growers selling anything at that moment. Without the speculator there, both grower and cereal company would be fucked in the instance of a temporary disruption.

With the speculator, however, everything runs smoothly. The corn grower goes to the market with his corn, maybe there are no cereal companies buying, but the speculator takes his crop at $2.80 a bushel. Ten weeks later, the cereal guy needs corn, but no growers are there—so he buys from the speculator, at $3.00 a bushel. The speculator makes money, the grower unloads his crop, the cereal company gets its commodities at a decent price, everyone's happy.

This system functioned more or less perfectly for about fifty years. It was tightly regulated by the government, which recognized that the influence of speculators had to be watched carefully. If speculators were allowed to buy up the *whole* corn crop, or even a big percentage of it, for instance, they could easily manipulate the price. So the government set up position limits, which guaranteed that at any given moment, the trading on the commodities markets would be dominated by the physical hedgers, with the speculators playing a purely functional role in the margins to keep things running smoothly.

With that design, the commodities markets became a highly useful method of determining what is called the spot price of commodities. Commodities by their nature are produced all over the world in highly varying circumstances, which makes pricing them very trying and complicated. But the modern commodities markets simplified all that.

Corn, wheat, soybean, and oil producers could simply look at the futures prices at centralized commodities markets like the NYMEX (the New York Mercantile Exchange) to get a sense of what to charge for their products. If supply and demand were the ruling factors in determining those futures prices, the system worked fairly and sensibly. If something other than supply and demand was at work, though, then the whole system got fucked—which is exactly what happened in the summer of 2008.

The bubble that hit us that summer was a long time in coming. It began in the early eighties when a bunch of Wall Street financial companies started buying up stakes in trading firms that held seats on the various commodities exchanges. One of the first examples came in 1981, when Goldman Sachs bought up a commodities trading company called J. Aron.

Not long after that, in the early nineties, these companies quietly began to ask the government to lighten the hell up about this whole position limits business. Specifically, in 1991, J. Aron—the Goldman subsidiary—wrote to the Commodity Futures Trading Commission (the government agency overseeing this market) and asked for one measly exception to the rules.

The whole definition of physical hedgers was needlessly restrictive, J. Aron argued. Sure, a corn farmer who bought futures contracts to hedge the risk of a glut in corn prices had a legitimate reason to be hedging his bets. After all, being a farmer was risky! Anything could happen to a farmer, what with nature being involved and all!

Everyone who grew any kind of crop was taking a risk, and it was only right and natural that the government should allow these good people to buy futures contracts to offset that risk.

But what about people on Wall Street? Were not they, too, like farmers, in the sense that they were taking a risk, exposing themselves to the whims of economic nature? After all, a speculator who bought up corn also had risk—investment risk. So, Goldman's subsidiary argued, why not allow the poor speculator to escape those cruel position limits and be allowed to make transactions in unlimited amounts? Why even call him a speculator at all? Couldn't J. Aron call itself a physical hedger too? After all, it was taking *real* risk—just like a farmer!

On October 18, 1991, the CFTC—in the person of Laurie Ferber, an appointee of the first President Bush—agreed with J. Aron's letter. Ferber wrote that she understood that Aron was asking that its speculative activity be recognized as "bona fide hedging"—and, after a lot of jargon and legalese, she accepted that argument. This was the beginning of the end for position limits and for the proper balance between physical hedgers and speculators in the energy markets.

In the years that followed, the CFTC would quietly issue sixteen similar letters to other companies. Now speculators were free to take over the commodities market. By 2008, fully 80 percent of the activity on the commodity exchanges was speculative, according to one congressional staffer who studied the numbers—"and that's being conservative," he said.

What was even more amazing is that these exemptions were handed out more or less in secret. "I was the head of the Division of Trading and Markets, and Brooksley Born was the chair [of the CFTC in the late nineties]," says Michael Greenberger, now a professor at the University of Maryland, "and neither of us knew this letter existed."

And these letters might never have seen the light of day, either, but for an accident. It's a story that reveals just how total the speculators' hold over government is.

One congressional staffer, a former aide to the Energy and Commerce Committee, just happened to be there when certain CFTC officials mentioned the letters offhand in a hearing. "I had been invited by the Agriculture Committee to a hearing the CFTC was holding on energy," the aide recounts. "And suddenly in the middle of it they start saying, 'Yeah, we've been issuing these letters for years now.' And I raised my hand and said, 'Really? You issued a letter? Can I see it?' And they were like, 'Uh-oh.'

"So we had a lot of phone conversations with them, and we went back and forth," he continues. "And finally they said, 'We have to clear it with Goldman Sachs.' And I'm like, 'What do you mean, you have to clear it with Goldman Sachs?'"

The aide showed me an e-mail exchange with a then-CFTC official who was telling him he needed to clear the release of the letters with Goldman. The aide wrote first:

We are concerned there is a reluctance to release this 1991 letter involving hedge exemptions for swaps dealers that we requested.

Please let me know the name and date of this letter.

Please advise on the cftc posture on this letter. We cannot fathom the need for secrecy.

The CFTC official wrote back:

Can you give people a couple of days to agree with you?

"People," in this case, referred to the recipients of the letters, specifically Goldman Sachs. To which the congressional staffer wrote back:

what is the sensitivity of a 17 year old letter which shaped agency policy? I am baffled.

Adding to the problem were a series of other little-known exceptions, including the so-called swaps loophole (which allowed speculators to get around position limits if they traded through a swaps dealer), the Enron loophole (which eliminated disclosure and trading limits for trades conducted on electronic exchanges—like Goldman's ICE), and the London loophole (loosening regulation of trades on foreign exchanges—like the one Goldman owned part of in London). The loopholes were political/regulatory absurdities, not at all unlike the fictional old British laws lampooned in the classic British TV satire *Brass Eye*, in which the sale of dangerous narcotics was strictly prohibited, unless it was done "through a mandrill."

"The concepts here were ridiculous," says another congressional aide. "You've got something that's illegal if you do it one way, but perfectly okay if you do it through a swap. How does that make sense?"

All of these loopholes created—out of thin air, almost in a literal sense—a massive government subsidy for those few companies like Goldman's J. Aron that got those semisecret letters from the CFTC. Because at the same time these companies were getting those letters, they were creating a new kind of investment vehicle, a new table at the casino as it were, and the way that vehicle was structured forced everyone who wanted to play to give them a cut.

The new investment vehicle was called *index speculation*. There were two main indices that investors could bet on. One was called the GSCI, or the Goldman Sachs Commodity Index. The other was the Dow Jones–AIG Commodity Index. The S&P GSCI traditionally held about two-thirds of the index speculation market, while the Dow-AIG Index had the other third, roughly.

It's a pretty simple concept on the surface. The S&P GSCI tracks the prices of twenty-four commodities—some agricultural (cocoa, coffee, cotton, sugar, etc.), some involving livestock (hogs, cattle), some involving energy (crude oil, gasoline), and some involving metals, precious and otherwise (copper, zinc, gold, silver).

The percentages of each are different—the S&P GSCI, for instance, is heavily weighted toward the price of West Texas Intermediate Crude (the price of oil sold in the United States), which makes up 36.8 percent of the S&P GSCI. Wheat, on the other hand, only makes up 3.1 percent of the S&P GSCI. So if you invest money in the S&P GSCI and oil prices rise and wheat prices fall, and the net movement of all the other commodities on the list is flat, you're going to make money.

What you're doing when you invest in the S&P GSCI is buying monthly futures contracts for each of these commodities. If you decide to simply put a thousand dollars into the S&P GSCI and leave it there, the same way you might with a mutual fund, this is a little more complicated—what you're really doing is buying twenty-four different monthly futures contracts, and then at the end of each month you're selling the expiring contracts and buying a new set of twenty-four contracts. After all, if you didn't sell those futures contracts, someone would actually be delivering barrels of oil to your doorstep. Since you don't really need oil, and you're just investing to make money, you have to continually sell your futures contracts and buy new ones in what amounts to a ridiculously overcomplex way of betting on the prices of oil and gas and cocoa and coffee.

This process of selling this month's futures and buying the next month's futures is called *rolling*. Unlike shares of stock, which you can simply buy and hold, investing in commodities involves gazillions of these little transactions made over time. So you can't really do it by yourself: you usually have to outsource all of this activity, typically to an investment bank, which makes fees handling this process every month. This is usually achieved through yet another kind of diabolical derivative transaction called a *rate swap*. Roughly speaking, this infuriatingly complex scheme works like this:

1. You the customer take a concrete amount of money—let's say a thousand dollars—and "invest" it in your commodity index. That thousand dollars does not go directly to the index, however. Instead, you're buying, say, a thousand dollars' worth of U.S. Treasury notes. The money you make from those T-bills goes, every month, to your investment bank, along with a management fee.

2. Your friendly investment bank, which might very well be Goldman Sachs, then takes that money and buys an

equivalent amount of futures on the S&P GSCI, following
the price changes.
3. When you cash out, the bank pays you back whatever you
   invested, plus whatever increases there have been in
   commodity prices over that period of time.

If you really want to get into the weeds of how all this works,
there's plenty of complexity there to delve into, if you're bored as hell.
The monthly roll of the S&P GSCI has achieved an almost mythical
status—it is called the Goldman roll, and there are lots of folks who believe that knowing when and how it works gives investors an unfair advantage (particularly Goldman)—but in the interest of not having the
reader's head explode, we'll skip that topic for now.

Minus all of that, the concept of index commodity speculation is
pretty simple. When you invest in commodities indices, you are not actually buying cocoa, gas, or oil. You're simply betting that prices in
these products will rise over time. It might be a short period of time or
a long period of time. But that's all you're doing, gambling on price.

To look at this another way—just to make it easy—let's create
something we call the McDonaldland Menu Index (MMI). The MMI
is based upon the price of eleven McDonald's products, including the
Big Mac, the Quarter Pounder, the shake, fries, and hash browns. Let's
say the total price of those eleven products on November 1, 2010, is
$37.90. Now let's say you bet $1,000 on the McDonaldland Menu
Index on that date, November 1. A month later, the total price of those
eleven products is now $39.72.

Well, gosh, that's a 4.8 percent price increase. Since you put $1,000
into the MMI on November 1, on December 1 you've now got $1,048.
A smart investment!

Just to be clear—you didn't actually buy $1,000 worth of Big Macs
and fries and shakes. All you did is bet $1,000 on the prices of Big
Macs and fries and shakes.

But here's the thing: if you were just some schmuck on the street
and you wanted to gamble on this nonsense, you couldn't do it, because
your behavior would be speculative and restricted under that old 1936
Commodity Exchange Act, which supposedly maintained that delicate

balance between speculator and physical hedger (i.e., the real producers/consumers). Same goes for a giant pension fund or a trust that didn't have one of those magic letters. Even if you wanted into this craziness, you couldn't get in, because it was barred to the Common Speculator.

The only way for you to get to the gaming table was, in essence, to rent the speculator-hedger exemption that the government had quietly given to companies like Goldman Sachs via those sixteen letters.

If you wanted to speculate on commodity prices, you had to do so through a government-licensed speculator like Goldman Sachs. It was the ultimate scam: not only did Goldman and the other banks undermine the 1936 law and upset the delicate balance that had prevented bubbles for decades, unleashing a flood of speculative money into a market that was not designed to handle it, these banks managed to secure themselves exclusive middleman status for the oncoming flood.

Now, once upon a time, this kind of "investing" was barred to institutional investors like trusts and pension funds, which by law and custom are supposed to be extremely conservative in outlook. If you're the manager of a pension fund for Ford autoworkers, it kind of makes sense that when you invest the retirement money of a bunch of guys who spent their whole lives slaving away at hellish back-breaking factory work, that money should actually be buying something. It should go into blue-chip stocks, or Treasury bills, or some other safe-as-hell thing you can actually hold. You shouldn't be able to put that money on red on the roulette wheel.

In fact, for most of the history of the modern American economy, there had been laws specifically barring trusts and pension funds and other such entities from investing in risky/speculative ventures. For trusts, the standard began to be set with an influential Massachusetts Supreme Court case way back in 1830 called *Harvard College v. Amory,* which later became the basis for something called the prudent man rule.

What the Harvard case and the ensuing prudent man rule established was that if you're managing a trust, if you're managing someone else's money, you had to follow a general industry standard of prudence.

You couldn't decide, say, that your particular client had a higher appetite for risk than the norm and go off and invest your whole trust portfolio in a Mexican gold mine. There were numerous types of investments that one simply could not go near under the prudent man rule, commodity oil futures being a good example of one.

The system seemed to work well enough for a long period of time, but by the early nineties there was a new class of economists who had come to believe that the prudent man rule was needlessly restrictive. When I spoke with John Langbein, a Yale professor who helped draft the law that would eventually turn the prudent man rule on its head, he was dismissive, almost to the point of sneering, of the prudent man standard.

"It tended to use a sort of . . . widows and orphans standard," he said in an irritated voice.

I paused. "What do you mean by widows and orphans?" I asked.

"Well, what that means is that there was an extreme aversion to loss," he said. "Everyone had to do a lot of bonds and real estate, you understand."

While I was sitting there trying to figure out what was so bad about that, Langbein proceeded to tell me about how he helped draft something called the Uniform Prudent Investor Act of 1994, some form of which would eventually be adopted by every state in the union. The Prudent Investor Act was something of a financial version of the Clear Skies Act or the Healthy Forests Restoration Act, a sweeping deregulatory action with a cheerily Orwellian name that actually meant close to the opposite of what it sounded like.

The rule now said that there was no one-size-fits-all industry standard of prudence and that trusts were not only not barred from investing in certain asset classes, they were actually duty bound to diversify as much as possible.

"It made diversification a presumptive responsibility" of the trust manager, Langbein said proudly, adding, "It abolished all categoric prohibitions on investment types."

This revolution in institutional investment laws on the state level coincided with similar actions on the federal level—including yet another series of very quiet changes to the rules in 2003 by the CFTC, which for the first time allowed pension funds (which are regulated not by the states but by the federal government) to invest in, among other things, commodity futures. At that same time, the CFTC also loosened the rules about who could buy and sell commodity futures. Whereas once upon a time you had to be accredited to trade commodities, there were now all sorts of ways that outsiders could get into the market.

Coupled with the new interpretation of prudence—this notion that institutional investors not only could diversify into other types of investments, but *should* or *had to*—there was suddenly a huge inpouring of money into the commodity futures market.

"Once upon a time, you had to be an accredited investor, and commodities weren't considered an asset class," says Pat McHugh, a trader in natural gas futures who has spent upwards of twenty years watching changes in the market. "Now all of a sudden commodities, it was like it was something you had to have."

Now, with all these changes, the massive pools of money sitting around in funds like CalPERS (the California state employees pension funds) and other state-run pension plans were fair game for the salesmen of banks like Goldman Sachs looking to pitch this exciting new class of investment as a way of complying with what Langbein, the Yalie professor, called the "powerful duty to diversify broadly." These plans tended to be guarded by midlevel state employees with substandard salaries and profound cases of financial penis envy who were exquisitely vulnerable to the bullshit sales pitches of the Wall Street whiz kids many of them secretly wanted to be.

When I told Langbein that I was interested in how it came to be that so many institutional investors ended up putting gobs of money into the commodity futures market in the late part of the last decade, he immediately interjected that such investing was not a good idea for everyone. "Just because it is not prohibited does not mean it's prudent for everyone to invest in oil futures," he said. "Because they are very volatile."

Well, I said, given that they are volatile, what would be an example of a situation in which it *would* be prudent for a trust—something, again, that is supposed to be supersafe—to invest in oil futures?

"Well, um . . . ," he began. "Say . . . Well, let's say the trust portfolio owns real estate that contains oil, real estate whose value fluctuates with oil prices. Then you might want to buy oil futures as a hedge."

Sounds like the kind of extremely common eventuality that is worth completely revamping the regulatory environment for.

Anyway, commodity index investing had one more thing going for it. It was about to be the last thing left on the institutional investment menu that Wall Street did not completely fuck up. By the mid-to-late 2000s the stock market, the consumer credit market, and the housing market had all either imploded spectacularly or were about to implode spectacularly. Those big pools of money had to go somewhere, and the key word that everyone was interested in hearing, after all these disasters, was "safety." And "quality," that was another word. And hell, what seemed more solid than oil? Or sugar? Or wheat?

That was the pitch, anyway. And the banks started hitting that theme really hard in the middle part of the decade.

"Going long on index investing has long been popular in the securities markets," wrote a cheerful Will Acworth in the May 2005 issue of *Futures Industry* magazine. "Now it is coming into fashion in the futures world, and bringing a new source of liquidity to commodity futures contracts."

That probably doesn't make much sense to you now, and wouldn't have made much sense to you in 2005. It did, however, make sense, back then, to the people who managed the great pools of money in this world—the pension funds, the funds belonging to trade unions, and the sovereign wealth funds, those utterly gigantic quasi-private pools of money run by foreign potentates, usually Middle Eastern states looking to do something with their oil profits. It meant someone was offering them a new place to put their money. A safe place. A profitable place.

Why not bet on something that people can't do without—like food or gas or oil? What could be safer than that? As if people will *ever* stop buying gasoline! Or wheat! Hell, this is America. Motherfuckers be eating pasta and cran muffins by the metric ton for the next ten centuries! Look at the *asses* on people in this country. Just let them try to cut back on wheat, and sugar, and corn!

At least that's what Goldman Sachs told its institutional investors back in 2005, in a pamphlet entitled *Investing and Trading in the Goldman Sachs Commodities Index,* given out mainly to pension funds and the like. Commodities like oil and gas, Goldman argued, would provide investors with "equity-like returns" while diversifying portfolios and therefore reducing risk. These investors were encouraged to make a "broadly-diversified, long-only, passive investment" in commodity indices.

But there were several major problems with this kind of thinking— i.e., the notion that the prices of oil and gas and wheat and soybeans were something worth investing in for the long term, the same way one might invest in stock.

For one thing, the whole concept of taking money from pension funds and dumping it long-term into the commodities market went completely against the spirit of the delicate physical hedger/speculator balance as envisioned by the 1936 law. The speculator was there, remember, to serve traders on both sides. He was supposed to buy corn from the grower when the cereal company wasn't buying that day and sell corn to the cereal company when the farmer lost his crop to bugs or drought or whatever. In market language, he was supposed to "provide liquidity."

The one thing he was not supposed to do was buy buttloads of corn and sit on it for twenty years at a time. This is not "providing liquidity." This is actually the opposite of that. It's hoarding.

When an investment banker coaxes a pension fund into the commodities markets, he's usually not bringing it in for the short term. "Pension funds and other institutional investors have extremely long time horizons," says Mike Masters of Masters Capital Management, who has been agitating against commodity speculation for years. He notes, for example, that the average duration of a pension fund's portfolio is designed to match the average employee's years until retirement. "Which could be twenty years, or more," says Masters.

The other problem with index investing is that it's "long only." In the stock market, there are people betting both for and against stocks. But in commodities, nobody invests in prices going down. "Index speculators lean only in one direction—long—and they lean with all their might," says Masters. Meaning they push prices only in one direction: up.

The other problem with index investing is that it brings tons of money into a market where people traditionally are extremely sensitive to the prices of individual goods. When you have ten cocoa growers and ten chocolate companies buying and selling back and forth a total of half a million dollars on the commodities markets, you're going to get a pretty accurate price for cocoa. But if you add to the money put in by those twenty real traders $10 million from index speculators, it queers the whole deal. Because the speculators don't really give a shit what the price is. They just want to buy $10 million worth of cocoa contracts and wait to see if the price goes up.

To use an example frequently offered by Masters, imagine if someone continually showed up at car dealerships and asked to buy $500,000 worth of cars. This mystery person doesn't care how *many* cars, mind you, he just wants a half million bucks' worth. Eventually, someone is going to sell that guy one car for $500,000. Put enough of those people out there visiting car dealerships, your car market is going to get very weird very quickly. Soon enough, the people who are coming into the dealership looking to buy cars they actually plan on driving are going to find that they've been priced out of the market.

An interesting side note to all of this: if you think about it logically, there are few reasons why anyone would want to invest in a rise in commodity prices over time. With better technology, the cost of harvesting and transporting commodities like wheat and corn is probably going to go down over time, or at the very least is going to hover near inflation, or below it. There are not many good reasons why prices in valued commodities would rise—and certainly very few reasons to expect that the prices of twenty-four different commodities would all rise over and above the rate of inflation over a certain period of time.

What all this means is that when money from index speculators pours into the commodities markets, it makes prices go up. In the stock markets, where again there is betting both for and against stocks (long and short betting), this would probably be a good thing. But in commodities, where almost all speculative money is betting long, betting on

prices to go up, this is not a good thing—unless you're one of the speculators. But chances are that's not who you are in this drama. You are
far more likely to be Priscilla Carillo or Robert Lukens, dealing with a
sudden price hike for reasons you know nothing about.

"It's one thing if you're getting people to invest in IBM or something," says McHugh, the natural gas futures trader. "But wheat and
corn and soybeans . . . this stuff actually affects people's lives."

Anyway, from 2003 to July 2008, that moment when Priscilla
started living in her car, the amount of money invested in commodity
indices rose from $13 billion to $317 billion—a factor of twenty-five in
a space of a little less than five years.

By an amazing coincidence, the prices of all twenty-five commodities listed on the S&P GSCI and the Dow-AIG indices rose sharply
during that time. Not some of them, not all of them on the aggregate,
but all of them individually and in total as well. The average price increase was 200 percent. Not one of these commodities saw a price decrease. What an extraordinarily lucky time for investors!

In and around Wall Street, there was no doubt what was going on.
Everyone knew that the reason the price of commodities was rising had to
do with all the new investor flows into the market. Citigroup in April
2008 called it a "Tidal Wave of Fund Flow." Greenwich Associates a
month later wrote: "The entry of new financial or speculative investors
into global commodities markets is fueling the dramatic run-up in prices."

And the top oil analyst at Goldman Sachs quietly conceded, in May
2008, that "without question the increased fund flow into commodities
has boosted prices."

One thing we know for sure is that the price increases had nothing to
do with supply or demand. In fact, oil supply was at an all-time high, and
demand was actually falling. In April 2008 the secretary-general of OPEC,
a Libyan named Abdalla El-Badri, said flatly that "oil supply to the market
is enough and high oil prices are not due to a shortage of crude." The U.S.
Energy Information Administration (EIA) agreed: its data showed that
worldwide oil supply rose from 85.3 million barrels a day to 85.6 million
from the first quarter to the second that year, and that world oil demand
dropped from 86.4 million barrels a day to 85.2 million.

Not only that, but people in the business who understood these things knew that the supply of oil worldwide was about to increase. Two new oil fields in Saudi Arabia and another in Brazil were about to start dumping hundreds of thousands more barrels of oil per day into the market. Fadel Gheit, an analyst for Oppenheimer who has testified before Congress on the issue, says that he spoke personally with the secretary-general of OPEC back in 2005, who insisted that oil prices had to be higher for a very simple reason—increased security costs.

"He said to me, if you think that all these disruptions in Iraq and in the region . . . look, we haven't had a single tanker attacked, and there are hundreds of them sailing out every day. That costs money, he said. A lot of money."

So therefore, Gheit says, OPEC felt justified in raising the price of oil. To *45 dollars a barrel*! At the height of the commodities boom, oil was trading for three times that amount.

"I mean, oil shouldn't have been at sixty dollars, let alone a hundred and forty-nine," Gheit says.

This was why there were no lines at the gas stations, no visible evidence of shortages. Despite what we were being told by both Barack Obama and John McCain, there was no actual lack of gasoline. There was nothing wrong with the oil supply.

But despite what Wall Street players were saying amongst themselves, the message to potential investors was very different. In fact, it still is. Banks like Goldman Sachs continually coaxed new investors into the commodities market by arguing that there would be major disruptions to the world oil supply that would cause oil prices to spike. In the beginning of 2008, Goldman's chief oil analyst, Arjun Murti, called an "oracle of oil" by the *New York Times,* predicted a "super spike" in oil prices, forecasting a rise in price to two hundred dollars a barrel.

Despite the fact that there was absolutely no evidence that demand was rising or supply falling, Murti continually warned of disruptions to the world oil supply, even going so far as to broadcast the fact that he owned two hybrid cars, adding with a straight face: "One of the biggest challenges our country faces is its addiction to oil."

This was a continuation of a theme Goldman had shamelessly pimped for years, that high prices were the fault of the piggish American consumer; in 2005 a Goldman analyst even wrote that we wouldn't know when oil prices would fall until we knew "when American consumers will stop buying gas guzzling sport utility vehicles and instead seek fuel efficient alternatives."

"Everything that Goldman cooked up or predicted, by hook or by crook, it happened," Gheit says. "[Goldman and Morgan Stanley] pushed these prices up."

All of these factors contributed to what would become a historic spike in gas prices in the summer of 2008. The press, when it bothered to cover the story at all, invariably attributed it to a smorgasbord of normal economic factors. The two most common culprits cited were the shaky dollar (investors nervous about keeping their holdings in U.S. dollars were, according to some, more likely to want to shift their holdings into commodities) and the increased worldwide demand for oil caused by the booming Chinese economy.

Both of these factors were real. But neither was any more significant than the massive inflow of speculative cash into the market.

The U.S. Department of Energy's own statistics prove this to be the case. It was true, yes, that China was consuming more and more oil every year. The statistics show the Chinese appetite for oil did in fact increase over time:

YEAR	CONSUMPTION (barrels per year)
2002	1,883,660,777
2003	2,036,010,338
2004	2,349,681,577
2005	2,452,800,000
2006	2,654,750,989
2007	2,803,010,200
2008	2,948,835,000

If you add up the total increase between each of those years, i.e., the total increase in Chinese oil consumption over the five and a half years between the start of 2003 and the middle of 2008, it turns out to be just under a billion barrels—992,261,824, to be exact.

During the same time period, however, the increase in index speculator cash pouring into the commodities markets for petroleum products was almost exactly the same—speculators bought 918,966,932 barrels, according to the CFTC.

But it was almost impossible to find mention of this as a cause for the spike in gas prices anywhere in the American media, which at the time was focused on more important things, like the geographical proximity of Bill Ayers to Barack Obama, or whether Geraldine Ferraro was being racist or just stupid when she said that Obama would not be winning the nomination "if he were a white man."

I was out there, covering the campaign, and what I remember was a lot of ginned-up anger between working-class Democrats (who supported Hillary) and yuppie Democrats (who supported Obama), a lot of anger emanating from female Hillary supporters (at a Hillary rally in Washington, DC, I saw two women tear an Obama sign away from a young girl and call her a "traitor"), and in general a lot of noise about things that, in retrospect, had nothing to do with anything at all.

While most of the country was talking about Reverend Wright and superdelegates, media coverage of the soaring gas prices was curiously nonspecific and unconvincing. The *New York Times* ran one of the first stories on high gas prices and specifically blamed the rise on "global oil demand," which it called "the relentless driver behind higher prices." That was at the end of February 2008, when oil hit what was then a record high of $100.88 a barrel.

A CNN story back in March 2008 called "Gasoline Price Spike Has Only Just Begun" told us that the reason for the surge was, well, because this is what always happens in between winter and summer:

> The price of gasoline usually increases this time of year. Several factors contribute to the runup: Low refinery output due to mainte-

nance, a switch from winter to pricier summer blends, and the looming high-demand summer driving season.

Politicians blamed the high prices on a variety of factors—the most ridiculous perhaps being Kentucky senator Mitch McConnell blaming high prices on an automatic gas tax instituted by his electoral opponent, Bruce Lunsford, in the Kentucky state legislature thirty years before.

By late spring and early summer the stories about the gas spike were more common, but quite often they seldom even mentioned a cause for the price disruptions. In most cases it was simply assumed that the high prices were caused by too much consumption, that Americans were going to have to change their habits if they wanted to survive the high costs.

When gas soared to over four dollars a gallon in May, *USA Today* ran a story called "Gas Prices Rattle Americans" that talked about the sobering—perhaps even positive—effect the high prices had had on the national psyche:

> The $4 mark, compounded by a sagging economy, could be a tipping point that spurs people to make permanent lifestyle changes to reduce dependence on foreign oil and help the environment, says Steve Reich, a program director at the Center for Urban Transportation Research at the University of South Florida.
>
> "This is a more significant shift in behavior than I've seen through other fluctuations in gasoline prices," he says. "People are starting to understand that this resource . . . is not something to be taken for granted or wasted."

There is nothing new about the political press in America getting a story wrong, especially a financial story. But what was unique about the gas spike story was that it was an issue that profoundly affected the lives of virtually everyone in the country, was talked about heatedly by both parties and by pundits in the midst of a presidential election year, and yet as far and as wide as you search, you simply will not find much of a mention anywhere about the influx of new commodity index money as a potential cause of this crisis.

And you barely heard it on the Hill. Several different congressional committees decided to hold hearings on the high gas prices, including Joe Lieberman's Homeland Security and Governmental Affairs Committee and the House Agriculture Subcommittee on General Farm Commodities and Risk Management. At these hearings there were some voices, like those of Mike Masters and Fadel Gheit, who tried to talk about the real causes of the crisis, but the headlines generally followed the pronouncements of the CFTC's chief economist, Jeffrey Harris, who said that the whole problem stemmed from normal supply and demand issues.

In written testimony before both committees in May 2008, Harris convincingly dismissed the notion that speculators played any role in the high prices.

"All the data modeling and analysis we have done to date indicates there is little evidence to suggest that prices are being systematically driven by speculators in these markets," he said. "Simply put, the economic data shows that overall commodity price levels . . . are being driven by powerful fundamental economic forces and the laws of supply and demand." He cited, as evidence of "fundamentals," the increased demand from emerging markets, decreased supply due to "weather or geopolitical events," and a weakened dollar.

The government's chief economist on the matter blamed the oil spike on the *weather*!

Even weirder was the fact that Harris was apparently so determined to keep any suggestion that speculation played a role in the problem out of the hearings, he even called up at least one witness to try to get him to change his mind.

"This guy tried to shake me down!" says Gheit, still incredulous at the story. He recounts a bizarre phone call in which Harris called up the Oppenheimer analyst, put him on speakerphone so that another colleague could listen in, and proceeded to tell Gheit that he had no evidence that speculation played a role in the crisis and that maybe he should consider this before he testified.

Gheit, who actually thought the call was coming from a staffer in Senator Carl Levin's office at first, found himself wondering what the hell was going on. "I said, 'Whose side are you on?' " As the phone call progressed, Gheit began to consider other possibilities. "I was sure it was someone from Goldman Sachs or Morgan Stanley. That's how weird it was."

It would be a full year before the CFTC under the Obama administration would admit that Harris's analysis was based on "deeply flawed data" and that speculators played a major role in the crisis.

But by then it was too late to stop what happened in 2008. Oil shot up like a rocket, hitting an incredible high of $149 a barrel in July 2008, taking with it prices of all the other commodities on the various indices. Food prices soared along with energy prices. According to some estimates by international relief agencies—estimates that did not blame commodity speculation for the problem, incidentally—some 100 million people joined the ranks of the hungry that summer worldwide, because of rising food prices.

Then it all went bust, as it had to, eventually. The bubble burst and oil prices plummeted along with the prices of other commodities. By December, oil was trading at $33.

And then the process started all over again.

The oil bubble, taking place as it did smack-dab in the middle of a feverish presidential campaign, was really a textbook example of how our national electoral politics and our media watchdogs are inadequate to address even the most glaring emergencies.

When you have a system with an electorate divided up into two fiercely warring tribes, each determined to blame the country's problems on the other, it will often be next to impossible to get anyone to even pay attention to a problem that is not the fault of one or the other group. Moreover it is incredibly easy to shift blame for the problem to one of those groups, or to both of them, if you know how to play things right—which happened over and over again in this case.

Throughout the spike, America accepted almost without question the notion that our problems were self-inflicted, caused by our obscene consumption of oil. It was a storyline that appealed in different ways to the prejudices of both of the two main political demographics.

It naturally appealed to the left, which for entirely logical reasons saw an evil in America's piggish dependence upon petroleum and had just spent five long years protesting an invasion of Iraq seemingly driven by our political elite's insatiable thirst for oil.

Oil consumption for progressives was, in fact, at the heart of two of their core protest issues: America's rapacious militarism and its environmental irresponsibility. America had bowed out of Kyoto. We had supported dictatorships in Saudi Arabia and Kuwait and (once upon a time) Iran in our hunger for oil and had toppled or tried to topple regimes in oil-rich countries like Iraq and Venezuela for seemingly the same reason.

More to the point, America was the birthplace of the SUV—the evil symbol of American oil gluttony that in one conveniently boxy package tied together all of the symbolic frustrations of the American progressive. It had a vaguely militaristic symbolism (the domestic Hummer was a modified military vehicle). It was driven unashamedly by big-assed conservatives and their teeming white-trash families who openly thumbed their noses at environmental concerns—witness the bumper stickers often seen plastered to the hugest SUV brands, with messages like "I'll Give Up My SUV When Al Gore Gives Up His Limo" and "Hybrids Are for Pussies" and "My SUV Can Beat Up Your Prius."

The last sticker had a particular sting, given that just as driving a big gas-guzzling SUV was a mode of political expression for conservatives, driving hybrids was one of the easiest ways for progressives to "have an impact" on the causes they cared about. The San Francisco political activist Robert Lind in the early part of the decade had encouraged opponents of SUVs and people who drove energy-efficient vehicles to download bumper stickers that read, "I'm Changing the Climate! Ask Me How!" He was followed by the Evangelical Environmental Network, which started its "What Would Jesus Drive?" bumper sticker campaign in 2002, which prompted a *60 Minutes* story about the anti-SUV backlash.

In short, the idea that Americans consumed too much oil had enormous traction with American progressives, among other things because it happened to be true.

So it wasn't at all hard to sell Democratic voters on the notion that the oil spike was related to overconsumption. In fact, the whole consumption issue had enormous symbolic import for Democratic voters, and it wasn't a surprise when presidential candidates started working vague references to overconsumption—divorced, of course, from specific policy proposals—into speeches that were supposedly addressing the gas price issue. When Obama went to Oregon in May 2008, right in the middle of the oil bubble, he specifically referenced SUVs, as I would hear him do over and over again that summer. "We can't drive our SUVs and eat as much as we want and keep our homes on seventy-two degrees at all times" was one of his favorite lines.

He consistently got cheers with that line, and to me it seemed obvious that these were angry cheers, cheers directed at the "other side," who consumed as much as they wanted and thought the Prius was for fags.

Meanwhile conservatives bought the supply-disruption storyline because it fit in seamlessly with the story of capitalist efficiency thwarted by regulators, tree-huggers, and OPEC. An oil spike caused by shortages justified the Iraq invasion and put the blame on environmentalists who blocked drilling in the Alaska National Wildlife Refuge and the outer continental shelf and those other dickwads who were always sacrificing American jobs on the altar of the spotted owl.

Those same SUVs that had once been bedecked with bumper stickers justifying the vehicle itself were, in the summer of 2008, starting to be plastered with new stickers that saw their owners' right to consume as a protest cause. "Drill Here, Drill Now!" was one sticker we saw a lot that summer.

What made this important was the fact that the new Obama administration really changed very little when it came to the problem of index speculation. The public was never focused on it, not really. When Obama nominated the new CFTC chief, Gary Gensler, a former Goldman executive and lieutenant to Bob Rubin who had been partially responsible for deregulating the derivatives market in 2000, few people even blinked.

This was news for specialists and experts in the industry, of course (Gheit compared putting Gensler in charge of the CFTC to "making a former legalization advocate the drug czar"), but America is no longer a country that cares about experts. In fact, it hates experts. If you can't fit a story into the culture-war storyline in ten seconds or less, it dies.

That's what happened to the oil speculation problem. Although the CFTC would finally, in August 2008, admit that speculation was a serious issue, and Gensler himself would demonstrate what appears to be a real conversion on the core problems, the root causes remained basically unchanged—so much so that at this writing, oil prices are once again soaring, once again thanks to prodding from the same old cast of villains.

In a weekly newsletter distributed to its own investors only, given to me by a source in the industry, Goldman Sachs in October 2009 repeated its classic "oil is going up because of the fundamentals" act.

"We believe oil prices are poised to move higher, with the catalyst likely to be evidence of rebounding diesel demand," the company wrote. "The normal Christmas retail seasonal effect suggests we should see a rebound in diesel demand in mid to late October to restock shelves." The newsletter continued later: "Crude oil prices have been both volatile and range bound, but poised to break out."

That particular analysis memo was released on a Monday (October 19), just after oil had crept back above $70 a barrel for the first time in more than a year. By that Wednesday the price of crude had gone up seven whole dollars. By Friday, October 23, it was closing at $81.19 a barrel.

What is interesting about this Goldman memo is not how obviously full of shit it is, but the disclaimer that is hidden in the very back of it.

On the very last page of the newsletter, in tiny print, Goldman wrote, under the heading "General Disclosures," the following:

> Our salespeople, traders, and other professionals may provide oral or written market commentary or trading strategies to our clients and our proprietary trading desks that reflect opinions that are contrary to the opinions reflected in this research. Our asset manage-

ment area, our proprietary trading desks and investing businesses may make investment decisions that are inconsistent with the recommendations or views expressed in this research.

We and our affiliates, officers, directors, and employees, excluding equity and credit analysts, will from time to time have long or short positions in, act as principal in, and buy and sell, the securities or derivatives, if any, referred to in this research.

Translated into English, Goldman can take your investment order and do anything they want with it, no matter how conflicted they might be. They might be recommending that you buy oil futures for "fundamental reasons," like the holiday shopping season or some such bullshit, but in the fine print they admit that, "from time to time," they might have long positions themselves as they make that recommendation.

Here, in this one document, is laid bare the whole basic stratagem behind the oil bubble. The big investment banks convince the ordinary investor that oil prices are going up because of "fundamentals," then they get all that money coming in, at which point their predictions about prices going up actually come true. Then they ride in with their own bets and make a fortune, front-running the massive flows of capital pouring into the market. Meanwhile, we all end up paying $4.50 a gallon for gas, just so these assholes can make a few bucks trading on what amounts to inside information.

"The reality is that if Goldman is successful enough marketing commodity index swaps to institutional clients they can make their research self-fulfilling," says one commodities trader. "Because those money flows that Goldman's marketing efforts create can move prices by themselves."

This story is the ultimate example of America's biggest political problem. We no longer have the attention span to deal with any twenty-first-century crisis. We live in an economy that is immensely complex and we are completely at the mercy of the small group of people who understand it—who incidentally often happen to be the same people who built these wildly complex economic systems. We have to trust these people to do the right thing, but we can't, because, well, they're scum. Which is kind of a big problem, when you think about it.

And here's the punch line: bubbles like the one we saw in 2008 are only one-half of the oil-price scam. Because *taking* your money through the indirect taxation of high energy and food prices, and reducing you to beggary as you struggle to pay for them, is only half of the job. What these clowns did with all that cash they siphoned from you and what they did to take advantage of your newfound desperation is the other end of the story.

5

The Outsourced Highway
Wealth Funds

IN THE SUMMER of 2009 I got a call from an acquaintance who worked in the Middle East. He was a young American who worked for something called a sovereign wealth fund, a giant state-owned pile of money that swims around the world in search of things to buy.

Sovereign wealth funds, or SWFs, are huge in the Middle East. Most of the bigger oil-producing states have massive SWFs that act as cash repositories (with holdings often kept in dollars) for the revenues generated by, for instance, state-owned oil companies. Unlike the central banks of most Western countries, whose main function is to accumulate reserves in an attempt to stabilize the domestic currency, most SWFs have a mission to invest aggressively and generate huge long-term returns. Imagine the biggest and most aggressive hedge fund on Wall Street, then imagine that that same fund is fifty or sixty times bigger and outside the reach of the SEC or any other major regulatory authority, and you've got a pretty good idea of what an SWF is.

My buddy was a young guy who'd come up working on the derivatives desk of one of the more dastardly American investment banks.

After a few years of that he decided to take a step up morally and flee to the Middle East to go to work advising a bunch of sheiks on how to spend their oil billions.

Aside from the hot weather, it wasn't such a bad gig. But on one of his trips home, we met in a restaurant and he mentioned that the work had gotten a little, well, weird.

"I was in a meeting where a bunch of American investment bankers were trying to sell us the Pennsylvania Turnpike," he said. "They even had a slide show. They were showing these Arabs what a nice highway we had for sale, what the toll booths looked like . . ."

I dropped my fork. "The Pennsylvania Turnpike is for sale?"

He nodded. "Yeah," he said. "We didn't do the deal, though. But, you know, there are some other deals that have gotten done. Or didn't you know about this?"

As it turns out, the Pennsylvania Turnpike deal almost went through, only to be killed by the state legislature, but there were others just like it that did go through, most notably the sale of all the parking meters in Chicago to a consortium that included the Abu Dhabi Investment Authority, from the United Arab Emirates.

There were others: A toll highway in Indiana. The Chicago Skyway. A stretch of highway in Florida. Parking meters in Nashville, Pittsburgh, Los Angeles, and other cities. A port in Virginia. And a whole bevy of Californian public infrastructure projects, all either already leased or set to be leased for fifty or seventy-five years or more in exchange for one-off lump sum payments of a few billion bucks at best, usually just to help patch a hole or two in a single budget year.

America is quite literally for sale, at rock-bottom prices, and the buyers increasingly are the very people who scored big in the oil bubble. Thanks to Goldman Sachs and Morgan Stanley and the other investment banks that artificially jacked up the price of gasoline over the course of the last decade, Americans delivered a lot of their excess cash into the coffers of sovereign wealth funds like the Qatar Investment Authority, the Libyan Investment Authority, Saudi Arabia's SAMA Foreign Holdings, and the UAE's Abu Dhabi Investment Authority.

Here's yet another diabolic cycle for ordinary Americans, engineered by the grifter class. A Pennsylvanian like Robert Lukens sees his business decline thanks to soaring oil prices that have been jacked up by a handful of banks that paid off a few politicians to hand them the right to manipulate the market. Lukens has no say in this; he pays what he has to pay. Some of that money of his goes into the pockets of the banks that disenfranchise him politically, and the rest of it goes increasingly into the pockets of Middle Eastern oil companies. And since he's making less money now, Lukens is paying less in taxes to the state of Pennsylvania, leaving the state in a budget shortfall. Next thing you know, Governor Ed Rendell is traveling to the Middle East, trying to sell the Pennsylvania Turnpike to the same oil states who've been pocketing Bob Lukens's gas dollars. It's an almost frictionless machine for stripping wealth out of the heart of the country, one that perfectly encapsulates where we are as a nation.

When you're trying to sell a highway that was once considered one of your nation's great engineering marvels—532 miles of hard-built road that required tons of dynamite, wood, and steel and the labor of thousands to bore seven mighty tunnels through the Allegheny Mountains—when you're offering that up to petro-despots just so you can fight off a single-year budget shortfall, just so you can keep the lights on in the state house into the next fiscal year, you've entered a new stage in your societal development.

You know how you used to have a job, and a house, and a car, and a wife and a family, and there was food in the fridge—and now you're six months into a drug habit and you're carrying toasters and TVs out the front door every morning just to raise the cash to make it through that day? That's where we are. While a lot of this book is about how American banks used bubble schemes to strip the last meat off the bones of America's postwar golden years, the cruelest joke is that American banks now don't even have the buying power needed to finish the job of stripping the country completely clean.

For that last stage we have to look overseas, to more cash-rich countries we now literally have to beg to take our national monuments off our hands at huge discounts, just so that our states don't fall one by one in a domino rush of defaults and bankruptcies. In other words, we're being colonized—of course it's happening in a clever way, with very careful paperwork, so we have the option of pretending that it's not actually happening, right up until the bitter end.

Let's go back in time, to the early seventies. It's 1973, and Richard Nixon's White House makes the fateful decision to resupply the Israelis with military equipment during the 1973 Arab-Israeli War.

This pisses off most of the oil-producing Arab states, and as a result, the Organization of the Petroleum Exporting Countries, or OPEC—a cartel that at the time included Saudi Arabia, Kuwait, the UAE, Libya, Iraq, and Iran, among others—decided to make a move.

For the second time in six years, they instituted an embargo of oil to the United States, and eventually to any country that supported Israel. The embargo included not only bans of exports to the targeted countries, but an overall cut in oil production.

The effect of the 1973 oil embargo was dramatic. OPEC effectively quadrupled prices in a very short period of time, from around three dollars a barrel in October 1973 (the beginning of the boycott) to more than twelve dollars by early 1974. The United States was in the middle of its own stock market disaster at the time, caused in part by the dissolution of the Bretton Woods agreement (the core of which was Nixon's decision to abandon the gold standard, an interesting story in its own right). In retrospect we ought to have known we were in trouble earlier that year because on January 7, 1973, then–private economist Alan Greenspan told the *New York Times,* "It is very rare that you can be as unqualifiedly bullish as you can be now." Four days later, on January 11, the stock market crash of 1973–74 began. Over the course of the next two years or so, the NYSE would lose about 45 percent of its value.

So we're in this bad spot anyway, in the middle of a long period of decline, when on October 6 Egypt and Syria launch an attack on the territories Israel had captured in the 1967 Six-Day War. The attack takes place on the Yom Kippur holiday and the war would become known as the Yom Kippur War.

Six days later, on October 12, Nixon institutes Operation Nickel

Grass, a series of airlifts of weapons and other supplies into Israel. This naturally pisses off the Arab nations, which retort with the start of the oil embargo on October 17.

Oil prices skyrocketed, and without making a judgment about who was right or wrong in the Yom Kippur War, it's important to point out that it only took about two months from the start of the embargo for Nixon and Kissinger to go from bluster and escalation to almost-total surrender.

On January 18, 1974, Kissinger negotiated an Israeli withdrawal from parts of the Sinai. By May, Israel agreed to withdraw from the Golan Heights.

This is from the U.S. State Department's own write-up of the episode:

> Implementation of the embargo, and the changing nature of oil contracts, set off an upward spiral in oil prices that had global implications. The price of oil per barrel doubled, then quadrupled, leading to increased costs for consumers world-wide and to the potential for budgetary collapse in less stable economies . . . The United States, which faced growing oil consumption and dwindling domestic reserves and was more reliant on imported oil than ever before, had to negotiate an end to the embargo from a weaker international position. To complicate the situation, Arab oil producers had linked an end to the embargo to successful U.S. efforts to create peace in the Middle East.

Hilariously, the OPEC states didn't drop the prices back to old levels after the American surrender in the Yom Kippur episode, but just kept them flat at a now escalated price. Prices skyrocketed again during the Carter administration and the turmoil of the deposition of the shah of Iran, leading to the infamous "energy crisis" with its long gas lines that some of us are old enough to remember very well.

Then, after that period, the United States and the Arab world negotiated an uneasy détente that left oil prices at a relatively steady rate for most of the next twenty-five years or so.

So now it's 2004. The United States and George W. Bush have just done an interesting thing, going off the map to launch a lunatic invasion of Iraq in a move that destabilizes the entire region, again pissing off pretty much all the oil-rich Arab nationalist regimes in the Middle East, including the Saudi despots—although, on the other hand, fuck them.

The price of oil pushes above forty dollars a barrel that year and begins a steep ascent. It's also around then that the phenomenon of the sovereign wealth fund began to evolve rapidly. According to the Sovereign Wealth Fund Institute:

> Since 2005, at least 17 sovereign wealth funds have been created. As other countries grow their currency reserves, they will seek greater returns. Their growth has also been skyrocketed by rising commodity prices, especially oil and gas, especially between the years 2003–2008.

Dr. Gal Luft, director of a think tank called the Institute for the Analysis of Global Security, would later testify before the House Foreign Affairs Committee about the rise of the SWFs. This is what he told the committee on May 21, 2008:

> The rise of sovereign wealth funds (SWF) as new power brokers in the world economy should not be looked at as a singular phenomenon but rather as part of what can be defined a new economic world order. This new order has been enabled by several megatrends which operate in a self-reinforcing manner, among them the meteoric rise of developing Asia, accelerated globalization, the rapid flow of information and the sharp increase in the price of oil by a delta of over $100 per barrel in just six years which has enabled Russia and OPEC members to accumulate unprecedented wealth and elevate themselves to the position of supreme economic powers. Oil-rich countries of OPEC and Russia have more than quadrupled their revenues, raking some $1.2 trillion in revenues last year alone. At $125 a barrel oil they are expected to earn close to $2 trillion in 2008.

In fact, oil would go up to $149 that summer. Luft went on:

> SWF are pouring billions into hedge funds, private equity funds, real estate, natural resources and other nodes of the West's economy. No one knows precisely how much money is held by SWFs but it is estimated that they currently own $3.5 trillion in assets, and within one decade they could balloon to $10–15 trillion, equivalent to America's gross domestic product.

Luft's analysis would square with a paper written by the San Francisco branch of the Federal Reserve Bank in 2007, which concluded that "analysts put current sovereign wealth fund assets in the range of $1.5 to 2.5 trillion. This amount is projected to grow sevenfold to $15 trillion in the next ten years, an amount larger than the current global stock of foreign reserves of about $5 trillion."

The San Francisco paper noted that most SWFs avoid anything like full disclosure, and there is little information available about what they may have invested in. One source I know who works at a Middle Eastern SWF explains that this is very much part of their investment strategy.

"They don't want publicity," he says. "They just want to make the money. That's one reason why you almost always see them buying minority stakes, as majority stakes would cause some countries to make issue of foreign ownership of investments. Sometimes it's multiple SWFs buying minority stakes in the same investment. But it's always thirty percent, twenty-five percent, and so on."

We've seen how banks like Goldman Sachs and Morgan Stanley helped engineer an artificial run-up in commodity prices, among other things by pushing big institutional investors like pension funds into the commodities market. Because of this lack of transparency, we can't know exactly how much the SWFs also participated in this bubble by pouring their own money into energy commodities through hedge funds and other avenues.

The CFTC's own analysis in 2008 put the amount of SWF money in commodity index investing at 9 percent overall, but was careful to note that none of them appeared to be Arab-based funds. The oddly specific insistence in the report that all the SWF money is "Western" and not Arab is particularly amusing because it wasn't like the question of Arab ownership was even mentioned in the report—this was just the Bush administration enthusiastically volunteering that info on its own.

Adam White, director of research at White Knight Research and Trading, says not to put too much stock in the CFTC analysis, however.

"I am doubting that result because I think it would be easy for an SWF to set up another company, say in Switzerland, or work through a broker or fund of funds and therefore not have a swap on directly with a bank but through an intermediary," he says. "I think that the banks in complying with the CFTC request followed the letter of the law and not the spirit of the law."

He goes on: "So if a sovereign wealth fund has an investment in a hedge fund—which they have a bunch—and that hedge fund was then invested in commodities, I expect that a bank would report that as a hedge fund to the CFTC and not a sovereign wealth fund. And their argument would be, 'How can we know who the hedge fund's investors are?'—even if they know darn well.

"I think that this is very much a national security issue because the Arab states might be pumping up oil prices and siphoning off huge amounts of money from our economy," he adds. "A rogue state like Iran or Venezuela could use their petrodollars to keep us weak economically."

We know some things about what happened between the start of the Iraq war and 2008 in the commodities market. We know the amount of speculative money in commodities exploded, that between 2003 and 2008 the amount of money in commodities overall went from $13 billion to $317 billion, and that because virtually all investment in commodities is long investment, that nearly twenty-five-fold increase necessarily drove oil prices up around the world, putting great gobs of money into the coffers of the SWFs.

There is absolutely nothing wrong with oil-producing Arab states accumulating money, particularly money from the production of oil, a resource that naturally belongs to those countries and ought rightly to contribute to those states' prosperity. But for a variety of reasons the United States's relationship to many Arab countries is complicated and at times hostile, and the phenomenon of the wealth funds of these states buying up American infrastructure is something that should probably not happen in secret.

But more to the point, the origin of these SWFs is not even relevant, necessarily. What is relevant is that these funds are foreign and that thanks to a remarkable series of events in the middle part of the last decade, they rapidly became owners of big chunks of American infrastructure. This is a process of a country systematically divesting itself of bits and pieces of its own sovereignty, and it's taking place without really anyone noticing it happening—often not even the people asked to vote formally on the issue.

What was that process?

The explosion of energy prices—thanks to a bubble that Western banks and perhaps some foreign SWFs had a big hand in creating—led to Americans everywhere feeling increased financial strain. Tax revenue went down in virtually every state in the country. In fact, the correlation between the rising prices from the commodities bubble and declining tax revenues is remarkable.

According to the Rockefeller Institute, which tracks state revenue collection, the rate of growth for state taxes hit its lowest point in five years in the first quarter of 2008, which is when oil began its surge from around $75 to $149 a barrel.

In the second quarter the institute reported continued slowdowns, and in the third quarter, the quarter in which oil reached that high of $149, overall tax growth was more or less flat, at 0.1 percent, the lowest rate since the bursting of the tech bubble in 2001–2.

Obviously the collapse of the housing market around that time was a major factor in all of this, but surging energy prices impacting the entire economy—forcing business and consumer spending alike to retract—also had to be crucial.

Around this time, state and municipal executives began putting their infrastructure assets up to lease—essentially for sale, since the proposed leases in some cases were seventy-five years or longer. And in virtually every case that I've been able to find, the local legislature was never informed who the true owners of these leases were. Probably the best example of this is the notorious Chicago parking meter deal, a deal that would have been a hideous betrayal even without the foreign ownership angle. It was a blitzkrieg rip-off that would provide the blueprint for increasingly broke-ass America to carry lots of these prized toasters to the proverbial pawnshop.

"I was in my office on a Monday," says Rey Colon, an alderman from Chicago's Thirty-fifth Ward, "when I got a call that there was going to be a special meeting of the Finance Committee. I didn't know what it was about."

It was December 1, 2008. That morning would be the first time that the Chicago City Council would be formally notified that Mayor Richard Daley had struck a deal with Morgan Stanley to lease all of Chicago's parking meters for seventy-five years. The final amount of the bid was $1,156,500,000, a lump sum to be paid to the city of Chicago for seventy-five years' worth of parking meter revenue.

Finance Committee chairman Ed Burke had the job of informing the other aldermen about the timetable of the deal. Early that morning he called for a special meeting of the Finance Committee that Wednesday, to discuss the deal. That afternoon the mayor's office submitted paperwork calling for a meeting of the whole City Council the day after the Finance Committee meeting, on December 4, "for the sole purpose" of approving the agreement.

"I mean, they told us about this on a Monday, and it's like we had to vote on a Wednesday or a Thursday," says Colon.

"We basically had three days to consider the deal," says fellow alderman Leslie Hairston.

On that Tuesday, December 2, Daley held a press conference and said the deal was happening "just at the right time" because the city was in a budget crunch and needed to pay for social services.

He then gave them the details: he had arranged a lease deal with Morgan Stanley, which put together a consortium of investors which in turn put a newly created company called Chicago Parking Meters LLC in charge of the city's meters. There was no mention of who the investors were or who the other bidders might have been.

The next day the Finance Committee met to review the deal, and ten minutes into the meeting some aldermen began to protest that they hadn't even seen copies of the agreement. Copies were hastily made of a very short document giving almost nothing in the way of detail.

"It was like an eight-page paper," says Colon.

The *Chicago Reader*'s write-up of the meeting describes the commotion that followed:

> "We're rushing through this," says Alderman Robert Fioretti. "Why?"
>
> "We've been working on this for the better part of a year, so we haven't been hasty," [city chief financial officer Paul] Volpe insists.
>
> "You had a year, but you're giving us two days," says Alderman Ike Carothers.
>
> To help aldermen understand some of the terms, Jim McDonald, a lawyer for the city, reads some legalese from the proposed agreement.
>
> [Alderman Billy] Ocasio bellows: "What does that all mean?"

The aldermen are told by CFO Volpe that the reason the deal has to be rushed is that a sudden change in interest rates could cost the city later on, which makes one wonder about Volpe's qualifications for the CFO job—this was in the wake of the financial crash, and interest rates were at rock bottom, meaning the city stood only to lose money by hurrying. Higher interest rates would have allowed them to use the interest on the lump payment to fill their budget gaps, rather than the principal of the payment itself.

"I hear that excuse a lot whenever the mayor wants to pass something fast," says Colon. "As far as I'm concerned, I'll take that risk."

Again, the council at this time has no idea who's actually behind the deal. "We were never informed," says Hairston. "Not even later."

Nonetheless, the measure ended up passing 40–5, with Hairston and Colon being among the votes against. I contacted virtually all of the aldermen who voted yes on the deal, and none of them would speak with me.

Mayor Daley, who had already signed similar lease deals for the Chicago Skyway and a series of city-owned parking garages, had been working on this deal for more than a year. He approached a series of investment banks and companies and invited them to submit bids on seventy-five years' worth of revenue on the city's 36,000 parking meters. Morgan Stanley was one of those companies.

Here's where it gets interesting. What Morgan Stanley has to do from there is two things. One, it has to raise a shitload of money. And two, it has to find a public face for those investors, a "management company" that will be presented to the public as the lessee in the deal.

Part one of that process involved the bank's Infrastructure group going on a road tour to ask people with lots of cash to pony up. It was these guys from Morgan's Infrastructure desk who took their presentation to the Middle East and pitched Chicago's parking meters to a room full of bankers and analysts in Abu Dhabi, the Abu Dhabi Investment Authority, who ultimately agreed to purchase a large stake.

Here's how they pulled off the paperwork in this deal. It's really brilliant.

At the time the deal was voted on in December 2008, an "Abu Dhabi entity," according to the mayor's office, had just a 6 percent stake in the deal. Spokesman Peter Scales of the Chicago mayor's office has declined to date to identify which entity that was, but by sifting through the disclosure documents, we can find a few possibilities, including a group called Cavendish Limited that is headquartered in Abu Dhabi.

Apart from that, most of the investors in the parking meter deal at the time it was voted on look like they were either American or from nations with relatively uncomplicated relationships with America. The Teacher Retirement System of Texas had a significant stake in one of the Morgan Stanley funds at the time of the sale, as did the Victorian Funds Management Corporation of Australia and Morgan Stanley itself. A Mitsubishi fund called Mitsubishi UFJ Financial Group also had a stake. There were a variety of other German and Australian investors.

All of these companies together put up the $1.2 billion or so to win the bid, and once they secured the deal, they created Chicago Parking Meters LLC, a new entity, which in turn hired an existing parking management company called LAZ to run the meter system in place of city-run parking police. The press stories about the deal invariably reported only that the city of Chicago had leased its parking meters to some combination of Morgan Stanley, Chicago Parking Meters LLC, and LAZ. A *Chicago Sun-Times* piece at the time read:

> Under questioning from Finance Committee Chairman Edward M. Burke (14th), top mayoral aides acknowledged that the partnership that includes Morgan Stanley Infrastructure Partners and LAZ Parking recently formed a limited liability corporation in Delaware, but never bothered to register in Illinois.

But two months after the deal, in February 2009, the ownership structure completely changed. According to Scales in the mayor's press office:

> In this case, after the Morgan Stanley investor group's $1.15 billion bid was accepted and approved by the City in December 2008, Morgan Stanley sought new investors to provide additional capital and reduce their investment exposure—again, not an unusual move.
>
> So, while a group of several Morgan Stanley infrastructure funds owned 100% of Chicago Parking Meters, LLC in December 2008, by February 2009, they had located a minority investor— Deeside Investments, Inc.—to accept 49.9% ownership. Tannadice Investments, a subsidiary of the government-owned Abu Dhabi Investment Authority, owns a 49.9% interest in Deeside.

So basically Morgan Stanley found a bunch of investors, including themselves, to put up over a billion dollars in December 2008; a big chunk of those investors then bailed out to make way in February 2009 for this Deeside Investments, which was 49.9 percent owned by Abu Dhabi and 50.1 percent owned by a company called Redoma SARL, about which nothing was known except that it had an address in Luxembourg.

Scales added that after this bait and switch, the original 6 percent Abu Dhabi "entity" reduced its stake by roughly half after Tannadice got involved. According to my math, that still makes Abu Dhabi–based investors at least 30 percent owners of Chicago's parking meters. God knows who the other real owners are.

Now comes the really fun part—how crappy the deal was for other reasons.

To start with something simple, it changed some basic traditions of local Chicago politics. Aldermen who used to have the power to close streets for fairs and festivals or change meter schedules now cannot— or if they do, they have to compensate Chicago Parking Meters LLC for its loss of revenue.

So, for example, when the new ownership told Alderman Scott Waguespack that it wanted to change the meter schedule from 9 a.m. to 6 p.m. Monday through Saturday to 8 a.m. to 9 p.m. seven days a week, the alderman balked and said he'd rather keep the old schedule, at least for 270 of his meters. Chicago Parking Meters then informed him that if he wanted to do that, he would have to pay the company $608,000 over three years.

The bigger problem was that Chicago sold out way too cheap. Daley and Co. got roughly $1.2 billion for seventy-five years' worth of revenue from 36,000 parking meters. But by hook or crook various aldermen began to find out that Daley had vastly undervalued the meter revenue.

When Waguespack did the math on that $608,000 he was going to be charged, he discovered that the company valued the meters at about 39¢ an hour, which for 36,000 meters works out to $66 million a year, or about $5 billion over the life of the contract.

"When it comes to finding a figure for the citizens of Chicago, they say the meters are worth $1.16 billion," Waguespack said shortly after the deal. "But when it comes to finding a figure to cover Morgan Stanley, they say they're worth, what, $5 billion? Who are they looking out for, the residents or Morgan Stanley?"

The city inspector at the time, David Hoffman, subsequently did a study of the meter deal and concluded that Daley sold the meters for at least $974 million too little. "The city failed to make a calculation of what the value of the parking meter system was to the city," Hoffman said.

What's even worse is this—if they really needed the up-front cash, why sell the meters at all? Why not just issue a bond to borrow money against future revenue collection, so that the city can maintain possession of the rights to park on its own streets?

"There's no reason they had to do it this way," says Clint Krislov, who's suing the city and the state on the grounds that the deal is unconstitutional.

When they asked why the city didn't just do a bond issue, some of the aldermen say they never got an answer.

"You'd have to ask the mayor that," says Colon.

But the most obnoxious part of the deal is that the city is now forced to cede control of their streets to a virtually unaccountable private and at least partially foreign-owned company. Written into the original deal were drastic price increases. In Hairston's and Colon's neighborhoods, meter rates went from 25¢ an hour to $1.00 an hour the first year, and to $1.20 an hour the year after that. And again, the city has no power to close streets, remove or move meters, or really do anything without asking the permission of Chicago Parking Meters LLC.

Colon, whose neighborhood had an arts festival last year, will probably avoid festivals in the future that involve street closings.

"It's just something that's going to be hard from now on," he says.

In the first year of the deal, Alderman Hairston went to a dinner on Wacker Drive near the Sears Tower (now the Willis Tower, renamed after a London-based insurer), parked her car, and pressed the "max" button on a meter, indicating she wanted to stay until the end of that night's meter period. She got a bill for $32.50, as Chicago Parking Meters LLC charged her for parking overnight.

"There are so many problems—I've had so many problems with them," says Hairston. "It tells you you've got eight minutes left, you get back in seven, and it charges you for the extra hour. Or you don't get a receipt. It's crazy."

But to me, the absolute best detail in this whole deal is the end of holidays. No more free parking on Sunday. No more free parking on Christmas or Easter. And even in Illinois, no free parking on days celebrating, let's say, a certain *local* hero.

"Not even on Lincoln's birthday," laughs Krislov.

"Not even on Lincoln's birthday," sighs Colon.

Wanna take Lincoln's birthday off? Sorry, America—*fuck you, pay me!*

And here's the last very funny detail in this whole business. It was the grand plan of CFO Volpe to patch the budget hole with the interest earned on that big pile of cash. But interest rates stayed in the tank, and so the city was forced to raid the actual principal. In a few years, the money will probably be gone.

"We did have a big hole in the budget," admits Colon. "But this didn't fix the problem. We might still have the same hole next year, and then where will the money come from?"

Bizarrely, a month and a half or so after this deal was done, a gloating Mayor Daley decided to offer some advice to the newly inaugurated President Obama, also an Illinois native. He told Obama he needed to "think outside the box" to solve the country's revenue problems.

"If they start leasing public assets—every city, every county, every state, and the federal government—you would not have to raise any taxes whatsoever," he says. "You would have more infrastructure money that way than any other way in the nation."

And America is taking Daley's advice. At this writing Nashville and Pittsburgh are speeding ahead with their own parking meter deals, as is L.A. New York has considered it, and the city of Miami just announced its own plans for a leasing deal. There are now highways, airports, parking garages, toll roads—almost everything you can think of that isn't nailed down and some things that are—for sale, to bidders unknown, around the world.

When I told Pennsylvania state representative Joseph Markosek that someone had been pitching the Pennsylvania Turnpike to Middle Eastern investors, he laughed.

"No kidding," he said. "That's interesting."

Markosek was one of the leading figures in killing Governor Ed Rendell's deal to sell off the turnpike, but even he didn't know who the buyers were going to be. He knew that Morgan Stanley was involved, but that was about it. Mostly he just thought it was a bad idea on general principle. "It would have been a bad deal for Pennsylvania," says Markosek. "There's a lot of speculation that the governor would have just taken that lump sum and used it to balance the budget this year, because he has a significant problem with the budget this year. But that would have left us with seventy-four more years on the lease."

The reason these lease deals happen is the same reason the investment banks made bad investments in mortgage-backed crap that was sure to blow up later, but provided big bonuses today—because the politicians making these deals, the Rendells and Daleys, are going to be long gone into retirement by the time the real bill comes due.

Welcome to life in the Grifter Archipelago.

6

The Trillion-Dollar Band-Aid
Health Care Reform

ON JANUARY 21, 2010, just a couple of days after a dingbat cookie-cutter right-wing automaton named Scott Brown defeated a hapless historical footnote named Martha Coakley in the Massachusetts Senate race, Mississippi Democratic congressman Gene Taylor stood up at a meeting of the House Democratic Caucus and through a deliberate Gulf Coast drawl tried to put things in perspective.

Speaker of the House Nancy Pelosi was trying to buck up her caucus and convince them that President Obama's health care bill was not actually dead yet, that the loss of the Democrats' so-called supermajority in the Senate thanks to Brown's upset win didn't mean the jig was up, that this thing could still get done. Pelosi was talking about using the reconciliation process—a parliamentary maneuver allowing a bill to pass with a simple majority instead of the usual way requiring a filibuster-proof sixty votes—to get some defaced version of whatever would be left of the bill passed. This was ironic because the Democrats probably should have gone that route all along but were reverting to it now in desperation just so they could pass *something* they could call health care reform. Taylor, whose Fourth Mississippi District covers Biloxi and other parts of Mississippi's Katrina-ravaged coastline, wasn't so sure it was going to work.

"This is a flashback, for me, to Katrina," Taylor told the Democrats.

He then told a story about how he and his family had evacuated from the coastline during Katrina to a spot some twenty miles inland. And after the wind and the storm had died down a bit, he went back to his neighborhood to take a look at what was left.

"I drive down, take a boat, go back to Bay St. Louis," he said. "And I go around the bend, to where there used to be a big ol' concrete bridge. And at the foot of the bridge, that's where the yacht club used to be. And a little bit up from the yacht club, well, there's my house.

"I go around the bend, there's no bridge. No yacht club. And no house."

Taylor then told the story of going back inland and telling his neighbors, who are waiting for a report: "It's all gone."

And they say, "What do you mean, it's gone?"

"They're just gone," he said.

Then he told the story of one particular woman who refused to believe Taylor's report: "But not *mah* house," she said. "Mah house cain't be gone. You cain't see mah house from your house, because *mah* house behind Corky house."

To which Taylor answered, "My house is gone. Corky's house is gone. And *your* house is gone."

He went on: "And this woman, she tried to ask: 'You mean, just the roof is gone?' And I said, 'No, ma'am. It's *all* gone.' "

He paused, to let the story sink in for the Democratic Caucus.

"And that," he said, "is where this health care bill is right now."

When the bill miraculously revived and passed, Barack Obama evaded what would've gone down as one of the most awesome blows to the American democratic process in the whole history of our country. It would've been a blow to democracy not because it was a good bill— it wasn't. In fact, it might very well have been the *worst* bill ever to make its way through both houses of Congress. No, what the near failure of Obamacare represented instead was a colossally depressing truth about the American political system, which is that our government is so dysfunctional that it can no longer even efficiently sell out to the private interests that actually run things in this country. Taylor was wrong about the bill. But he was right, too. *Something* was long gone.

Obamacare had been designed as a coldly cynical political deal: massive giveaways to Big Pharma in the form of monster subsidies, and an equally lucrative handout to big insurance in the form of an individual mandate granting a few already-wealthy companies 25–30 million new customers who would be forced to buy their products at artificially inflated, federally protected prices.

The essence of Obamacare was two ruthless power plays fused at the hip. It was the federal government seizing control of a sector of America's private industry worth about 16 percent of GDP. And it was that same sector of private industry in turn seizing permanent control of about 8 percent of America's taxable income, for converting to private profit. What was little understood by the public, even after more than a year of near-constant media blathering and manufactured talk-radio controversies, is that the Obama administration tried to pay for the first power play by green-lighting the other.

The admittedly ingenious plan devised by our freshman president and his indomitable chief of staff—an overconfident and immensely unlikable neo-Svengali named Rahm Emanuel, who resembled Karl Rove, only more driven, with better hair, and without the distantly validating sense of humor—was to buy the insurance and pharmaceutical industries' acquiescence to the gentlest of regulatory regimes by giving them back the one thing they had to trade: the power to tax the public.

The result was a new law that will radically remake the faces of both the federal government and the private economy and also ratify the worst paranoid fears of both ends of the political spectrum.

The right-wing teabagger crowd spent all of 2009 protesting Obamacare as a radical socialist redistribution, and you know what? They weren't all wrong, although the people who wrote this bill were about as far from being socialists as people can be.

Meanwhile the castrated left wing, the constituency that worked so hard to get Barack Obama elected in the first place, suddenly perceived Obamacare as a crypto-fascist fusing of state and private power, an absurdly expensive capitulation of democratically elected officials to concentrated private interests. And *they* weren't wrong, although whatever negative ideology they thought they were protesting in the bill was mostly in there by accident.

Really Obamacare was designed as a straight money trade. The administration meant to deal away those billions in subsidies and the premiums from millions of involuntary customers in exchange for the relevant industries' campaign contributions for a few election cycles going forward. It was almost the perfect example of politics in the Bubble Era, where the time horizon for anyone with any real power is always close to zero, long-term thinking is an alien concept, and even the most massive and ambitious undertakings are motivated entirely by short-term rewards. A radical reshaping of the entire economy, for two election cycles' worth of campaign cash—that was what this bill meant. It sounds absurdly reductive to say so, but there's no other explanation that makes any sense.

That the bill was a grotesque giveaway was, by the end, a secret to almost nobody in Washington. If you wanted proof of that, all you had to do was look at who wrote one of the bill's early drafts—a Senate aide named Liz Fowler who had joined Senator Max Baucus's staff in February 2009 after a few lucrative years away from government, working for the insurance giant WellPoint. Here's something that Liz Fowler said out loud a few years back, during her brief but lucrative hiatus from government service:

"People used to love me when I worked on the Hill," she said, "because I wrote bills that gave away money."

And she outdid herself this time, but the public perception of the thing was almost exactly the opposite. "It was . . . I guess the word is just *weird*," said a sort of dazed-sounding Dennis Kucinich a day after the Taylor speech about the health care house being gone with the flood.

"There was this conscious effort to try to make this into a left versus right thing when that was in fact a nonsensical interpretation. It was a backroom deal that had nothing to do with the public perception. There's a book in this somewhere, about how the public debate around this thing was crafted."

The epic struggle to pass health care reform was at once a shameless betrayal of the public trust of historic proportions and proof that a nation that perceives itself as being divided into red and blue should start paying attention to a third color that rules the day in Washington—a sort of puke-colored politics that puts together deals like this one and succeeds largely through its mastery of the capital city's bureaucracy. The defining characteristic of puke politics is that if it must have government at all, the government should be purposefully ineffectual almost across the board in terms of the functions we usually ascribe to the state and really only competent in one area, and that's giving away taxpayer money in return for campaign contributions.

In the summer of 2009 I visited a hospital that was embroiled in a losing battle with an insurer. The plight of the Bayonne, New Jersey, Medical Center exactly symbolized the comical levels of cruelty, inefficiency, and unnecessary expense handcuffing the American health care system—and it was the almost universal exposure of the American public to exactly the sorts of problems Bayonne was experiencing that made radical health care reform such a winning rallying cry during the 2008 presidential election.

On a muggy afternoon in August in Bayonne I walked into a modest conference room at the medical center, an unassuming little hospital in a middle-class neighborhood surrounded by the ambiguous smells of the nearby Hudson River. The hospital president, Dan Kane, accompanied by a PR spokesman named John Dinsmore, sat with folded hands looking at me nervously—I got the feeling they had been through this ritual, unsuccessfully, with many other reporters.

"So we had this one patient," Kane began. "It wasn't such a serious problem that he had, but he was on Coumadin."

This patient, he said, was being treated at home for a chronic illness, one that required him to take that common blood thinner. But he had a complication and had to come in to his local hospital for surgery. So he came in and the doctors slowly weaned him off the Coumadin before operating. "We didn't do anything to him, just gave him some time to get off the Coumadin," Kane said. "Once we were clear, we did the procedure, and everything worked out great."

Shortly thereafter the word came back from the insurer: it would not be paying the bill for this procedure, because the operation had not been conducted "in a timely fashion."

Of course, had the hospital operated on the patient "in a timely fashion," he would have bled to death on the operating table, because you can't operate on a patient taking blood thinners.

The Bayonne doctors in New Jersey—a state that had seen ten hospitals close since 2007, and another six file for bankruptcy, a little slice of the national hospital network that might easily be described as the front lines of the death of American health care—pointed this little issue out to the insurer, Horizon Blue Cross Blue Shield. No soap.

"We explained it, said, you know, we would have killed the guy if we'd operated. But their physician's assistant upheld the denial," Eileen Popola, the hospital's case manager later explained.

Popola estimates that she spends roughly half her time chasing claims from just this one insurer, the dominant insurer in New Jersey; her hospital estimates that fully half of its administrative staff is employed solely to try to collect payment from insurers.

This backs up the one thing we know for sure about health care in America: a great deal of the costs come from the one part of this whole equation that absolutely nobody gives a fuck about, that has no natural support in the Congress or anywhere else—the paperwork.

Because we have no single-payer system, because we have 1,300 different insurance companies that all require different forms to be filled out and have different methods for judging claims, the great bulk of nonmedical personnel at hospitals and clinics are assigned to chasing claims. The half of the Bayonne administrative staff devoted to claims is not at all unusual.

American health care, to employ a seriously overused term, is a Kafkaesque parody of corporate inefficiency, with urgently necessary procedures approved at split-second speed by doctors standing over living patients at one end, balanced out on the other end by a huge Space Mountain of corporate denials that must later on be negotiated in the dark by helpless underpaid clerks in order to extract payment for those same procedures.

Studies have backed up the notion that paperwork is where most of the excess cost in the U.S. health care system comes from. By now almost everyone knows that American health care costs more than health care anywhere else in the world: the most recent studies show that American health care costs more than 16 percent of GDP, compared with notoriously socialistic states like France (its next-closest competitor) at around 11 percent, Sweden at 9.1 percent, and England at 8.4 percent.

Americans spend an average of about $7,200 a year on health care, compared with the roughly $2,900 average for the other market economies that make up the OECD (Organization for Economic Cooperation and Development), and for that greatly increased outlay we get higher infant mortality, higher obesity rates, lower longevity, fewer doctors per 1,000 people (just 2.4 per 1,000 in the United States, compared with 3.1 in OECD states), and fewer acute care hospital beds (2.7 per 1,000, compared to 3.8 per 1,000 in the OECD countries).

Moreover, private insurance provides almost nothing in the way of financial protection for those who have it. A full 50 percent of all bankruptcies in America are related to health care costs, and of those, three-fourths involve people who actually have health insurance.

So where does all that added expense come from? Among other things, from the added paperwork from the nonstandardized insurance company system. A 2003 *New England Journal of Medicine* study found that administrative costs make up a full 31 percent of all health care spending in the United States. That's compared to 16.7 percent in Canada. Moreover, the administrative costs in the United States are not only growing but skyrocketing: they were $450 per capita in 1991, but were up to $1,059 per capita in 2003. All that extra money is going to the one part of this whole deal that adds nothing to patient care: clerks fighting over claims.

Bayonne had been one of the six facilities in New Jersey bankrupted since 2007. It was in reorganization now, and by the time the Obama administration sent Congress to work reforming the health care system in the summer of 2009, it was slowly getting back on its feet financially.

But it was in a war with Horizon Blue Cross, which was miffed that the hospital had been insolent enough to drop out of its network earlier in the year, imperiling its revenue stream as it prepared for an IPO in the next year that would make its executives an instant fortune.

The current American health care system is not regulated at the federal level and instead relies upon a tight network of powerful state-level insurers and plugged-in state regulatory officials, with whom the relevant companies have close relationships. Jack Byrne, who served as the CEO of the insurance giant GEICO for decades, described it to me as a "cartel" system and said that at the state level, the relationship with the state regulator is crucial.

"I probably spent ten to fifteen percent of my career in meetings with state regulators," Byrne, seven years retired, recalls now. "That was so much of how this business works."

In any case, Horizon Blue Cross was the poster child for local health insurance cartels—it dominated the state of New Jersey, operating like a Mafia gang that insisted on its protection money, and it was a dangerous thing for any hospital to buck its power. In this case, Bayonne's decision to drop out of the network inspired a serious reprisal: the insurer drowned Bayonne in paper and denials.

It denied repayment in one case involving a patient who had come in to the hospital and received IV antibiotics; the grounds were that the patient had been a nurse twenty years earlier and should have been able to administer that care herself, in her own home.

"I guess if your father's a surgeon and your mother's an anesthesiologist, lie down on the kitchen table and get your heart fixed there," Kane quipped.

Routine requests for approval for an ambulance ride to rest homes and other secondary care facilities were often held up until the end of business hours or the next morning, or just long enough to stick the hospital with the cost of caring for the patient for one more day. Popola was flooded with requests for more clinical information before payments were approved: send copies of this, of that, we'll get back to you. Meanwhile, the costs piled up.

And worst of all, patients who were brought to Bayonne for emergencies were systematically sought out and pressured to move to member hospitals—sometimes by couriers sent by Horizon, who snuck past hospital security and warned still-woozy patients in their beds that if they stayed, they might incur massive bills of tens of thousands of dollars or more.

And if Horizon couldn't get couriers through, they'd pepper the patient's family with phone calls, or call the patient himself. They did this to patients after heart attacks, after accidents and trauma—the hospital even had a frightened patient get up and walk out of the hospital on his own two feet *one day* after going into atrial fibrillation, which is very often a fatal event.

The Bayonne doctor (who also didn't give his name, depending heavily as he does on Horizon customers) who told me about watching his atrial fibrillation patient walk out the front door recounted the story like a man describing a fantastic dream—"I literally couldn't believe my eyes."

One patient, who also declined to give her name, had checked herself into the hospital with pneumonia and within three days was getting phone calls from Horizon and being told to pull out her IV drips, get up, and leave. "Horizon told me I was well enough to move, to get dressed and walk out of the hospital," she says. "I panicked. I was having trouble breathing. So I did what they said."

One would think that hospitals would have some sort of recourse against these kinds of tactics, but in point of fact the behavior of Horizon Blue Cross is exactly in line with the way the American health care system was drawn up. The system is *designed* to give regional insurers the power to coerce and intimidate customers in exactly this manner, and also to force them to pay inflated rates.

This is thanks to one of the worst pieces of legislation in American history, a monster called the McCarran-Ferguson Act that just might be a more shameful chapter in our legal history than the Jim Crow laws—and you won't understand exactly how bad a deal Obamacare is until you can grasp the subtext of the whole so-called health care reform effort, which was to pass a "health care reform bill" without touching McCarran-Ferguson.

Almost everyone in America is familiar with the Sherman Antitrust Act, and most people have a fairly good idea of why it was enacted. The law was passed in 1890 (sponsored, ironically, by a predecessor of Max

Baucus, a Senate Finance Committee chairman named John Sherman) and was designed to curtail the power of the monopolistic supercompanies that were beginning to dominate American business.

The original law grew out of an investigation into the practices of the insurance, coal, railroad, and oil industries in Ohio, where state officials had begun to see evidence of collusion and price-fixing among those firms, one of which was John D. Rockefeller's Standard Oil. The truly amusing thing about the Sherman Antitrust Act (and the related state vanguard legislation, Ohio's Valentine Antitrust Act of 1898) is that most modern Americans look back at the period when powerful companies routinely got together and colluded to constrict supply and jack up prices as something out of the Stone Age, impossible to conceive of in the modern United States.

In the case of Rockefeller in Ohio, the old buzzard had arranged things leading up to the turn of the century so that his control over the oil supply into Ohio was almost absolute; he could therefore contract the oil supply on demand and escalate prices as he pleased. He was actually tried once in the Hancock County courthouse under the Valentine Act and in that case one of the jurors, a Mr. C. J. Myers, was twice offered a bribe of five hundred dollars to hang the jury, which was hot to convict Rockefeller. Unlike our modern congressmen, who would have taken the money without blinking, Myers refused the bribe and instead ratted out Rockefeller's henchmen, leading to new charges.

The Sherman and Valentine acts were mostly ineffective at first but ultimately were used to break up all of the famous monopolies: Standard Oil, which became Exxon, Mobil, Chevron, and Amoco, among others; American Tobacco, which became R. J. Reynolds and Liggett and Myers; and the American Railway Union, which had forced the government into its business thanks to the Pullman fiasco of 1893.

George Pullman, the millionaire owner of the Pullman Palace Car Company, had decided to execute numerous wage cuts. The thing is, most of his employees lived in Pullman, Illinois, a town he virtually owned, meaning his employees were forced to buy from his stores, rent his houses, and so on. When he cut wages repeatedly without cutting other prices in Pullman, the workers flipped and, led by Eugene Debs, went on strike.

So Pullman did a brilliant thing and decided to attach U.S. Mail cars to his Pullman trains. Without workers servicing the mail cars, the mail stopped operating and the strikers were suddenly criminals guilty of interfering with the delivery of the U.S. Mail. Grover Cleveland sent twenty thousand troops to break up the strike and get the trains running, and Debs got six months in jail.

On the flip side, however, the Sherman Act was shortly thereafter used to break up Pullman's authority. This was the sort of thing Congress used to have to do to make sure revered businessmen didn't act like antebellum plantation owners, and the fact that both Congress and a few presidents (most notably Teddy Roosevelt) fought hard to give these laws teeth and break up these companies provides a sharp contrast between what government used to be like and what government is like, well, now.

However, the Sherman story wasn't entirely rosy. It seems there was one important exception to the Sherman Act, and that was the insurance business, which by custom and in many cases by statute was simply not regarded as "commerce" under the trust-busting laws designed to regulate interstate commerce.

And for decades insurance companies basically had carte blanche to behave exactly as Rockefeller and Pullman did, until in the early forties a southern cartel of insurance firms went a little too far and got themselves dragged into the Supreme Court.

The case involved a group of insurance firms headquartered primarily in Georgia called the South-Eastern Underwriters Association, which were basically pulling all the same old shit Rockefeller pulled in Ohio, creating an impenetrable local cartel that dominated the whole market and then not only fixing prices but intimidating vendors and customers by threatening to walk away entirely if their price demands were not met (hold on to that thought—that theme will resurface in a moment).

The SEUA's lawyers in this case somewhat nonsensically argued that the federal government did not have the authority to regulate insurance as interstate commerce because insurance was somehow not commerce.

These appellants were backed by decades of congressional decisions affirming, if not always directly, their contention that the Sherman Act was not intended to apply to insurance companies. Hugo Black and a majority of other justices disagreed and threw *U.S. v. South-Eastern Underwriters Association* back in their faces, announcing once and for all that insurance companies operating across state lines were interstate commerce and therefore could be regulated by the federal government.

The Supreme Court had spoken, but the insurance companies weren't giving up. They immediately turned to the Senate, where they had an ally in an unbelievable asshole of a Nevada senator named Pat McCarran.

McCarran might have been the Joe McCarthy of his era if McCarthy hadn't been more of a press hound, though he did achieve another sort of fame. He was the model for the horny extortionist character Senator Pat Geary in *The Godfather: Part II,* whose great onscreen moment came when he tried to shake down Michael Corleone for a gaming license, saying: "I despise the way you pose yourself. You and your whole fucking family."

To which Al Pacino offered the classic reply: "Senator, you can have my answer now, if you like. My final offer is this: nothing. Not even the fee for the gaming license, which I would appreciate if you would put up personally."

In any case, in addition to being the inspiration for one of the great iconic corrupt politicians in the history of cinema, McCarran spent much of his career tilting at communist conspiracy windmills and with great fanfare got passed the McCarran-Walter Act, which imposed quotas on certain types of immigrants. He also passed the McCarran Internal Security Act, which forced political parties like the American Communist Party to register with the federal government.

Despite his fetish for wielding federal power, McCarran had a very different opinion about its purview over business and worked feverishly to keep the government off the backs of the insurance companies. In 1944 he teamed up with Homer Ferguson, a Michigan senator who also had a flair for the anticompetitive, to pass the McCarran-Ferguson Act.

Hilariously, Ferguson too was the inspiration for a corrupt senator of cinema yore. If you've seen the underrated Jeff Bridges movie *Tucker,* the

Ferguson character is played by Lloyd Bridges; he's the federal heavy working with the big automakers to make sure the upstart automaker/inventor Preston Tucker spent his days battling phantom federal investigations instead of making cheap, efficient cars that might have challenged the big three, which incidentally are basically all bankrupt now.

Working together, these two dumbasses McCarran and Ferguson passed their law, which essentially invalidated the *U.S. v. South-Eastern Underwriters Association* Supreme Court decision and established the ground rules for decades of insurance robbery.

Even the way this unseemly mess of a bill was passed was an embarrassment to the whole concept of democracy. The bill that McCarran and Ferguson introduced to the Senate and which also passed in the House was originally written to maintain the authority of the states over the insurance industry, but it also expressly included a provision maintaining that the Sherman Act would apply if and when the state laws proved inadequate.

The original McCarran-Ferguson Act was also intended, quite explicitly, to be temporary, and according to the original text was supposed to expire in 1947. Because the bill as written did not seem all that controversial, and would in any case be temporary, it sailed through both the House (where it was passed by the Judiciary Committee without a debate) and the Senate with very limited discussion, to say nothing of opposition. Even Franklin Roosevelt, when he signed the bill into law, was absolutely explicit that it was designed to expire in the near future.

"After a moratorium period, the antitrust laws," Roosevelt said at the signing ceremony, "will be applicable in full force and effect to the business of insurance."

But here's the thing about Congress. No matter how much any bill is debated in either the House or the Senate, it can always be rewritten, even written to have an opposite meaning, in the conference committee process, which takes place after bills have been passed in both houses.

In this case, the McCarran-Ferguson Act emerged from conference with an important new clause added: it said that after January 1, 1948, the Sherman, Clayton, and Federal Trade Commission acts "shall be applicable to the business of insurance to the extent that such business is not regulated by State law."

In other words, instead of being a temporary moratorium designed to explicitly allow the Sherman Act to come into play when state laws proved inadequate, the law *now* was a permanent act that explicitly *excluded* the application of the Sherman Act, the Clayton Antitrust Act (an extension of Sherman that prohibited other forms of collusion and intimidation), and the FTC Act in any case where there were already existing state laws.

Thus the insurance industry was given a permanent license to steal. There were all sorts of ways in which insurance companies, freed of federal regulatory authority, could collude to manipulate prices. Among other things, they pooled loss information and were allowed legally to set prices through cartel-like organizations such as the Insurance Services Office (ISO).

The same sorts of corporate-crime activities that are outlined in great cloak-and-dagger detail in books like Kurt Eichenwald's *The Informant*—which described the high-stakes efforts of a group of agricultural conglomerates to evade the FBI and foreign police agencies while they surreptitiously colluded to set the prices of a feed product called lysine—are done openly and legally in the insurance world.

"If a bunch of construction contractors got together and decided to set the prices of bricks and mortar, they'd all go to prison," says Robert Hunter of the Consumer Federation of America, who served as a federal insurance administrator under President Ford. "But in insurance, it's all legal."

Insurance companies could also collude to threaten boycotts or worse, depending on (a) how big their market share was or (b) how small a state they were dealing with, meaning how totally they had the local population by the balls.

A great example of the kind of bullshit that goes on all the time in insurance is the state of Mississippi, which became famous as one of the racketeering capitals of America even before Katrina.

Back in 2003 there was a much-ballyhooed malpractice crisis in which newspaper and TV reporters flooded the state to describe a tort system run amok, where patients in pursuit of big malpractice claims—

what was called "jackpot justice" by groups like the U.S. Chamber of Commerce and repeated by their stooges in the media and Congress—hit up doctors for bogus settlements. While some of this undeniably went on, what was far less publicized was the insurance industry's unique response to this crisis.

"We had a malpractice crisis in Mississippi," says Brian Martin, an aide to Congressman Gene Taylor. "The insurance companies basically said, 'We're going to stop issuing malpractice insurance to ob-gyns, neurosurgeons, and emergency room doctors, unless Mississippi passes tort reform.'"

Crucially, this wasn't one company making the threat, and the threat wasn't to pull insurance for doctors who'd been sued. This was a whole group of supposed competitors acting in concert, threatening to abandon whole classes of doctors, regardless of their records.

Taylor had been a state senator in Mississippi and in that capacity had actually supported tort reform to rein in excessive settlement awards, which he believed were a real problem. But once he reached Congress he started to notice a pattern.

"As soon as the stock market started going in the tank and insurance companies weren't making enough money, suddenly there was always a tort reform crisis," explains his aide Martin.

Then in 2005 Katrina happened, and that's where we really saw the fangs of the antitrust exemption. Government agencies determined that there were at least four hours of hurricane-force winds during the storm surge, and it was obvious to everyone in the area that wind accounted for much of the damage—I myself was in the Biloxi area shortly after the storm and saw houses miles inland simply blown down.

"You had people who were standing in their houses when the wind blew them down," Marvin Koury, a real estate adviser in Gulfport, Mississippi, told me back then, "and the insurance companies were trying to tell them it was flood."

Despite that fact and despite the fact that in larger, better-regulated states like Louisiana insurance companies paid out huge claims to homeowners for wind damage, in Mississippi the local insurance cartel—in this case an ad hoc union of State Farm, Allstate, Nationwide, USAA, and many others—decided en masse to deny all claims for wind damage except for those that the homeowner could demonstrate took place separate from flood damage.

State Farm's statement right after Katrina went as follows:

> Where wind acts concurrently with flooding to cause damage to the insured property, coverage for the loss exists only under flood coverage, if available.

Nationwide issued a similar statement, telling adjusters that "if loss is caused by wind and flood there is no coverage."

Why pass the buck from wind to flood? That's easy—there was a federal, taxpayer-backed program to cover flood damage! In this case the National Flood Insurance Program issued many ruined homeowners checks from Uncle Sam to repair their flooded houses. And in a supreme bit of irony, the federal government contracted out to private companies to issue those rewards, even as some of those same companies were denying their own wind coverage.

"So here's State Farm," explains Martin, "running around, saying, here's your $250,000 from the government for your flood damage, but oh, by the way, we don't see any wind damage."

Taylor's home was one of the ones State Farm decided not to cover, which was bad enough—messing with a U.S. congressman. But the insurers were so brazen they denied coverage to *Trent fucking Lott,* who at the time was not very far removed from being the Senate majority leader, undoubtedly one of the most powerful men in America (to say nothing of Mississippi).

What was State Farm's final offer to Trent Lott, who wanted this out-of-state insurer to pay the claim on his home? Its final answer was:

> Nothing. Not even the fee for the gaming license, which I would appreciate if you would put up personally . . .

And that's not even a joke. Lott ultimately was forced to sue State Farm for refusing to pay up for wind damage to his home. He later issued a statement:

Today I have joined in a lawsuit against my longtime insurance company because it will not honor my policy, nor those of thousands of other South Mississippians, for coverage against wind damage due to Hurricane Katrina.

The thing of it was, neither Lott nor anyone else could do a damn thing, legally, about these sorts of moves by insurance companies. Way back in 1980, an amendment to the Federal Trade Commission Act had been passed making it basically illegal for the federal government not only to investigate the insurance industry but even to conduct studies in that area.

That change had come about when the FTC had begun making noise about investigating the industry's practice of charging higher property and casualty insurance premiums based on credit scores. Almost immediately the industry had lobbied to preempt this investigation, and section 6 amending the FTC Act was passed.

In the report accompanying the amendment it was written that "under the amendment, the FTC's *investigative and reporting powers* [emphasis mine] are made explicitly inapplicable to the business of insurance."

Any industry that basically has government license to (a) fix prices and (b) refuse to uphold legal contracts is going to make money almost without regard to the economic climate.

That helps explain why in 2005, despite the fact that it was blindsided by Katrina, one of the biggest natural disasters in American history, the property/casualty industry made an after-tax profit of $48.8 billion—a new record, beating out the previous year's record of $40.5 billion.

In 2006, with no hurricane to muddy the waters, the industry made a whopping after-tax profit of $68.1 billion. They were able to get away with this despite taking a dump on two sitting members of Congress, who found themselves with absolutely no way to successfully fight back.

The only way to get at this sort of crap was to overturn the entire McCarran-Ferguson Act. Fortunately, that crazy episode in 2005 in which the insurers decided to fuck with Trent Lott led to an unprecedented left-right coalition in Congress that was bent on repealing those antitrust laws. In 2007 Taylor teamed up with Oregon's Pete DeFazio and Louisiana Republican Bobby Jindal to propose a repeal of McCarran-Ferguson. In the Senate, Lott teamed up with Mary Landrieu of Louisiana and Pat Leahy of Vermont to go after McCarran-Ferguson.

They failed. Not even the specter of poor Trent Lott getting up and personally telling his sob story about getting fucked around by State Farm could move the Senate to do something about the situation, not even out of corporate loyalty.* In fact, neither the House nor the Senate bill ever made it out of committee. The bill was opposed by basically every single insurance industry lobbying arm in the country. The insurance industry that cycle spent more than $46 million in political contributions. Notably, Pat Leahy, chair of the Judiciary Committee at the time, received a grand total of $4,500, in contrast to the $287,000 they gave to fellow committee member John Cornyn, who came out in opposition to the gambit.

Then Barack Obama got elected, with a strong mandate to reform American health care. Surely something could be done this time, right? After all, how was it even possible—theoretically—to pass a massive new federal health care bill giving the federal government regulatory authority over the health insurance industry without touching the insurance industry's antitrust exemption? Leaving aside for a moment the obvious point that including anything less than a full repeal of McCarran-Ferguson in a health care bill would be pointless, how could such an insane move even be accomplished logistically?

Well, Barack Obama and the Democrats figured out a way. And how they handled this issue perfectly symbolized what this whole thing was about, from the start.

At the very beginning of the process, there was a meeting on the House side for staffers of the three committees that would be crafting health

---

*Lott's weepy *My house! They took my fucking house!* speech on March 7, 2007: "It wasn't until after Hurricane Katrina that I gained a true understanding of the fact that the insurance industry had a blanket exemption from our antitrust law. And as I witnessed the reprehensible behavior of the insurance industry in their response to Katrina, I became curious about the history, rationale, and wisdom of such a broad exemption from federal oversight."

bills—Energy and Commerce, Ways and Means, and Education and Labor. And at that conference, the subject of the insurance industry's antitrust exemption came up. At first, the Democrats had no plan whatsoever to take on the exemption.

Taylor's aide Martin was there, and he explains what the leadership's thinking was.

"Well, first of all, their thinking was, this is a Judiciary Committee issue, and here we are, Ways and Means and Energy and Commerce and whatnot, so it's not our problem," he says. "That was one thing. The other thing was, they thought there was going to be a strong public option, so that was their way of guaranteeing competition."

There probably isn't a better example of how the Democratic Party thinks, or nonthinks as it were, than this. Instead of repealing a grossly anticompetitive law that was passed basically by mistake sixty years ago, the party decided to try to ensure private competition in the health insurance industry by creating a state-run insurance plan. "They basically didn't want to pick another fight," says Martin.

Dumb as this idea was, it didn't hold. The heads of both the House and the Senate Judiciary committees—John Conyers in the House and Pat Leahy in the Senate—decided to introduce amendments to the various health care bills (which did not address the issue originally) that would have repealed one tiny little slice of McCarran-Ferguson.

"Both amendments only pertained to the health insurance industry and the medical malpractice insurance industry," says Erica Chabot, an aide to Senator Leahy.

"And not only that," says Martin. "Not only did they not repeal the exemption for all other types of insurance, but they also included a provision that said, basically, that this repeal only applies to price-fixing, bid-rigging, and market allocation. Anything that didn't fall into those categories, those were still legal."

So, really, Leahy and Conyers were trying to score one small victory: instead of establishing primacy over the entire insurance industry, they merely wanted to pass laws making it illegal for health or medical malpractice insurers to fix prices, rig bids for contracts, or divide up markets among themselves. They didn't even attempt to broadly outlaw unfair anticompetitive practices.

"But what if, for instance, an insurer says, 'You can't buy this product unless you also buy this other product'? Is that covered or not covered?" says Martin.

If you're wondering why a law like that would even be necessary, since there are all sorts of federal laws that broadly outlaw fraud and unfair practices, here's the problem: even though those laws exist, there's no federal agency that legally has jurisdiction over the insurance industry, again thanks to that FTC law.

So, to recap: none of the five congressional committees that originally put together health care bills (the three in the House, and then in the Senate Max Baucus's Finance Committee and Tom Harkin's Health, Education, Labor, and Pensions, or HELP, Committee) even tried at the start to do anything about the antitrust exemption enjoyed by the health insurance industry.

Here you have a cartel system in which individual customers, hospitals, and doctors alike are at the mercy of an unaccountable industry that can deny coverage or fix prices as it pleases, resulting in the crappy or even openly threatening service and ballooning costs that necessitated the call for health care reform in the first place. And all that is because of one law, and this law is the one that none of the five reigning Democratic committee chairmen thought prudent to touch as they "took on" the problem of health care reform.

So after these five committees whiff on the issue, in step Leahy and Conyers with amendments that address the problem in, to put it politely, the least aggressive way possible. They offer mini-repeals of the exemption, little rubber rafts they then attempt to tack on to the great tanker-bills moving their way through the process. In the first version of the first attempt to merge the three different bills from the different House committees (called the manager's amendment), the watered-down Conyers amendment was in there.

But in the House, some members fought back. After a tough August in which the teabagger movement forced Democratic members to go home and deal with pitchfork-wielding wingers in furious town hall meetings where the representatives were attacked as socialist brigands, a few more aggressive members were emboldened. In a meeting with the Democratic Caucus, DeFazio made one last play for a stronger bill.

"I came back and said to everyone, hey, we've all had a pretty trau-
matic August here," he says now. "But I told them, 'I did fourteen town
halls, with eight thousand people, and there was one thing, one thing,
that the people from the teabag rebellion to the single-payer people
agreed on, and that was ending the antitrust exemption for the insurance industry.' "

That speech drew applause at the House caucus meeting, and from
there, with the support of other members like Louise Slaughter, who
was writing the manager's amendment, a real, almost full-blown repeal
of McCarran-Ferguson was attached to the bill, and it passed. In other
words, an actual repeal of the antitrust exemption went before the full
Congress and was approved by democratically elected representatives of
the people.

In the Senate, Leahy pushed for his much weaker amendment
throughout the autumn, with the support of Majority Leader Harry
Reid, who incidentally had been a cosponsor of an earlier Leahy bill that
was much more aggressive in its attempt to repeal the exemption. And
after much prodding Reid finally allowed Leahy on December 1 to file
the amendment and tack it on to an early version of the Senate health
bill that had been voted on over the Thanksgiving holiday. And then . . .

"Well, that's sort of the end of the story," says Chabot.

It was the end because somewhere between Reid giving Leahy the
okay to file his amendment on December 1 and the Christmas holiday,
when the Senate actually voted on the final version of the health care
bill, the Leahy amendment was stripped from the whole effort. And
since it was known all along that the Senate version of health care was
the one that actually mattered, that really meant the antitrust exemption had survived, again.

What happened? At least three members of Congress I spoke to
said that a deal had been cut—that the White House bought the vote
of Nebraska senator Ben Nelson, a former CEO of the Central National Insurance Group, by agreeing to drop even a modest cutback of
the antitrust exemption. And Nelson is one of the all-time leaders in insurance company largesse—no other industry has given him more
money in his career, a total that currently stands at over $1,259,000.

"Nelson goes way back with the insurance industry," said one

House member. "He was the insurance commissioner for Nebraska, remember. So this was part of his price."

Remember also, this wasn't the only bribe that Nelson extracted for his vote. The Democratic leadership also gave Nelson $100 million and allowed Nebraska to have its Medicaid payments subsidized almost entirely by other states.

But more importantly, this was a White House deal, a Democratic Party deal all the way. The whole style of Obama's health care "initiative" was to try to smooth the bill's passage by neutralizing the opposition of the relevant industries by giving way on key issues. With the health insurance industry, the White House was clearly willing to give way on the antitrust exemption at the outset, in exchange for the health insurance industry not beating up on Obama with an ad blitz, the way they beat up Clinton all those years ago.

"This was a deal," says Kucinich. "They promised PhRMA"—the Pharmaceutical Research and Manufacturers of America—"they wouldn't back reimportation and bulk negotiating for Medicare purchases of drugs. And this is what they gave the health insurance industry. They backed off the antitrust exemption."

"The weird thing is, it's not like they were buying the support of these industries by doing this stuff," says an aide to one Democratic House member. "They thought they were neutralizing them. They weren't neutralizing them. They were just surrendering completely as an opening strategy in the long war. It was like that Monty Python movie about the crack suicide squad, that was their way of doing things."

DeFazio says he spoke with Obama personally at a Democratic Caucus meeting in early 2010, around the time of Brown's victory in Massachusetts, and asked him about his position on the antitrust exemption.

"What he told me," DeFazio says, "is that he always thought it was 'weird' that the insurance industry had this exemption. But what he also said is, he needed his sixty votes."

The reason the Democrats pursued the strategy they did was based almost entirely on their perception of the political playing field. This was a party leadership that was not really interested in actually *fixing* the health care problem; what they were much more concerned with was passing something they could call "health care reform" while at the same time doing it in a way that kept campaign contributions from the insurance and pharmaceutical industries away from the Republicans.

This was Rahm Emanuel's political unified field theory: score a monster political win with the electorate and a massive takeaway of campaign funds at the same time, a great interconnected loop of deals that would keep them in office for two terms at the least. And to achieve this, all they had to do was sell out just enough to buy the acquiescence of the relevant businesses.

That would be a straight business deal, a backroom calculation of the sort the modern Democrats are quite good at. But the other half of the deal, managing the internal dynamics of their own party, that was less predictable, and from the outset it was clearly the problem that troubled the party leadership the most.

The setup for all of this started when George W. Bush pissed away the stratospheric approval ratings and virtually unlimited political capital of the post-9/11 period in just seven short years of radical incompetence. Bush's record of reckless spending, bumbling foreign policy disasters, and monstrous tax giveaways to the rich set the stage for the Democrats to seize full control of the state, reducing the Republican Party to a sideshow role in the health care fiasco. Once the Democrats rode Bush's unpopularity to within striking distance of those filibuster-proof sixty Senate votes, the real obstacle to Obamacare was suddenly not where it was before.

With impenetrable majorities in both houses, the Democrats now mainly needed to worry not about conquering anti-entitlement sentiment on the right, but about keeping their own troops in line. And in practice the only real ideological opposition along the whole spectrum of Democrats would come from the progressive side, which not only had high hopes for real health care reform but would likely renounce any bill perceived as a giveaway to private industry.

Thus with Republicans effectively sidelined by their own incompetence and the Clintonian mainstream Democrats likely to be the authors of the bill and hence not opposed to it, the real problem in getting health care passed was always about finding a way to keep the Democratic Party's left/progressive flank on board with the program. And

Barack Obama achieved this in a number of ways, with the first and most important being an old political standby: he lied.

Toward the end of Obama's first year in office, when certain pundits and journalists (myself included) began going after him for breaking an alarming number of campaign promises, a small public relations campaign gurgled up in the nation's editorial pages in response. It was suggested that it's unreasonable to criticize a politician for breaking campaign promises, apparently because expecting a candidate to avoid lying during an election campaign is unrealistic.

A White House spokesman even expressed that idea in graphic terms to a *New York Times* reporter, in response to a question about activists harping on Obama's broken promises. These critics, he said, "need to take off their pajamas, get dressed, and realize that governing a closely divided country is complicated."

But in the case of Barack Obama, complaints about broken promises—particularly with regard to those he made on health care—were, for two key reasons, not just a matter of weepy pajama-wearing teenage idealists failing to grasp how the hard, hard adult world works.

For one thing, Obama won a furious primary campaign over Hillary Clinton by the slimmest conceivable margin thanks in large part to his successful conquest of the party's liberal/progressive flank. It's very safe to say that Barack Obama would not have been enjoying that difficult challenge of governing such a closely divided country if he hadn't managed two winters ago to convince large numbers of Democratic primary voters in traditionally liberal states like Oregon, Minnesota, and Washington that he was more real than Hillary on domestic policy issues in general, and health care in particular.

As a reporter who covered Obama on the campaign trail I can report that Barack Obama was at his oratorical best when he was talking about nothing at all, but his second-best subject at the campaign lectern was health care. Candidate Obama was remarkably frank and eloquent about the problems of the current system, and some of his best applause lines came when he went after politicians who talked the talk on health care only to change their minds after election.

"We are tired of watching as year after year, candidates offer up detailed health care plans with great fanfare and promise, only to see them crushed under the weight of Washington politics, and drug and insurance lobbying, once the campaign is over," Obama told a campaign audience in Newport News, Virginia, in 2008.

Lines like that bring out the second important point about Obama's broken promises: these weren't just occasional minor fibs. Obama's campaign deceptions on health care were both incredibly specific and grossly serial in nature, and are suggestive not of an idealistic politician who was forced to change course once reality set in but of one who spearheaded a comprehensive, *intentional* campaign strategy to buy votes with empty promises.

In the age of insta-polling and focus groups it is hard to imagine that the Obama campaign did not know exactly what it was doing when it promised on the one hand to support drug reimportation, televise all negotiations on C-SPAN, and push for bulk pharmaceutical purchases for Medicare, and on the other swore it would never tax health care benefits, push for an individual mandate, or support any health care bill that did not have a public option in it. He would completely reverse himself on all those positions and more.

Obama made a lot of these policy promises sound like they weren't particularly tough decisions for him, either. My personal favorite was his take on the individual mandate, offered in February 2008 in an interview on CNN. Obama is *laughing* when he's asked about mandates. "If a mandate was the solution," he chuckles, "we could try that to solve homelessness by mandating everybody buy a house." Roughly a year later, Obama would be ramming a sweeping mandate to buy insurance down the throats of the entire U.S. population.

Candidate Obama similarly laughed at the notion that reimporting cheap drugs from Canada was unsafe, but when he became president his administration ultimately rejected reimportation over safety issues. His campaign take on taxing "Cadillac" health plans (a major McCain campaign idea) was just as eloquent; candidate Obama was one of the few politicians to grasp that a lot of these so-called Cadillac plans were union benefits that had been negotiated up in exchange for concessions on salary in collective bargaining.

"John McCain calls these plans 'Cadillac plans,' " Obama said in October 2008. "Now in some cases, it may be that a corporate CEO is getting too good a deal. But what if you're a line worker making a good American car like the Cadillac? What if you're one of the steelworkers . . . and you've given up wage increases in exchange for better health care?"

It wasn't just the promise, it was the candidate's nuanced understanding of issues like this, added to a seemingly rare willingness to educate the public about these matters, that impressed voters like me before the election. Obama clearly understood that taxing Cadillac plans would disproportionately punish union members, but then as president he turned around and pushed for exactly that tax as health care moved toward the finish line, eschewing a genuinely progressive millionaire's tax as an alternative.

Probably the most cynical reversal of all was Obama's extremely sudden change of heart when it came to Billy Tauzin, the former Louisiana congressman who was the principal author of the Bush-era prescription drug benefit bill of 2003—a massive giveaway to the pharmaceutical industry that barred the government from negotiating bulk rates for Medicare purchases of drugs. Here is the text of an Obama campaign ad called "Billy" that showed Obama talking to a small group of seniors:

> The pharmaceutical industry wrote into the prescription drug plan that Medicare could not negotiate with drug companies. And you know what, the chairman of the committee who pushed the law through went to work for the pharmaceutical industry making two million dollars a year. Imagine that. That's an example of the same old game playing in Washington. I don't want to learn how to play the game better. I want to put an end to the game playing.

Well, guess what? Billy Tauzin turned out to be one of the very first people Obama invited to the White House, and he became one of his most frequent visitors. Between February 4 and July 22, 2009, Tauzin visited the White House eleven times, an average of once every fifteen days or so, in the process making his notorious deal to pay for a few pro-Obama commercials in exchange for billions in subsidies.

Rahm Emanuel's decision to crawl up the ass of Tauzin's pharmaceutical lobby in the political back room is almost exactly reminiscent of Dick Cheney's subpoena-proofed relationship with the energy industry.

In a similar aping of Bush-era corruption, the Obama administration served up an almost exact answer to the Armstrong Williams scandal (in which a conservative pundit was paid $240,000 via a Department of Education grant in exchange for his public promotion of George Bush's No Child Left Behind Act) by repeatedly citing the work of an MIT economist named Jonathan Gruber in its propagandizing of health care reform. The administration failed to disclose that Gruber, who was extremely enthusiastic about Obamacare all year, had received some $780,000 in taxpayer money via a consulting contract with the Department of Health and Human Services.

"If this had been George Bush, liberals would have been screaming bloody murder," says author and activist David Sirota. "But they were silent."

Why were they silent? Well, among other things, because the White House carefully disciplined virtually the entire universe of liberal activist groups through regular contact, instruction, and intimidation. One of the chief forums here was the little-publicized meetings of a group called Common Purpose, run by former Dick-Gephardt-aide-turned-lobbyist Erik Smith and held once a week at the Capitol Hilton.

At these weekly meetings, liberal activist groups like Change to Win, Rock the Vote, and MoveOn would show up and receive guidance—some would say marching orders—from a White House representative, typically former Max Baucus aide and legendary Washington hardass Jim Messina.

It says a lot that the White House would choose as its liaison to the liberal activist community a former aide to ultraconservative Max Baucus. Messina, incidentally, once authored a gay-baiting attack ad against a Montana state senator who happened to be a former hairdresser (the ad showed the candidate working in a hairdressing salon, massaging a man's temples, with the voice-over: "Mike Taylor: not the way we do business here in Montana").

"[Messina] was a strange choice," says Mike Lux, who served as the White House's liaison to progressives during Obama's transition.

The operating dynamic here is important to understand. At these meetings the White House representative would sometimes be flanked by important donors, and in any case the White House influence over major funding sources like the Democracy Alliance network was implicitly understood by all.

"There's a group of donors in the Democracy Alliance who collectively come together to make investments, and those folks certainly talk regularly with the White House about who the good [activist] groups are," says one former Obama aide. "That's one of the reasons why some people are afraid to cross the White House."

Again, the White House would often stand literally side by side with the donor. This was even spelled out explicitly in one e-mail circulated to Common Purpose attendees, in which the incipient arrival of Larry Summers deputy Diana Farrell and Assistant Treasury Secretary Michael Barr was paraded alongside news of a "potentially significant" donor:

> All:
> A reminder of the Common Purpose meeting on Tuesday afternoon at 3:30, and encouragement to attend.
> We expect that a potentially significant funder . . . will be at the meeting this week, and that Michael Barr and or Diana Farrell will be there, and available for updates on the full range of issues.

But the threat here wasn't always merely implicit. Sometimes it was literally screamed at the attendees—the most famous instance being when Rahm Emanuel himself showed up and roared at group members who were planning to run ads targeting conservative Blue Dog Democrats. He screamed at the members, calling them "fucking retards" and telling them they weren't going to derail a legislative winning streak Rahm apparently was proud of. "We're thirteen and zero going into health care," he yelled. "We're not going to be thirteen and one!"

The bizarre tirade exploded by word of mouth within the gossipy Beltway ("I heard about it within five minutes," says the former Obama aide), yet it somehow managed to avoid appearing in most of the media. One of the few stories was a sanitized Politico version in which Rahm's actual words were excised in favor of a more general report:

"White House chief of staff Rahm Emanuel warned liberal groups this week to stop running ads against Democratic members of Congress."

That the direction was coming from Emanuel was hardly surprising, since the health care business seemed to confirm what a lot of DC observers had begun to suspect, which is that the Obama presidency was basically run out of the chief of staff's office. Emanuel in a short period of time had amassed tremendous power, thanks in large part to certain quirks of Barack Obama's personality. One former Obama aide compared him to another Democratic president he worked for, Bill Clinton.

"Clinton and his lifestyle . . . well, he knew a lot of people, and he actually listened to a lot of people," he says. "Obama is different. He basically takes his marching orders from Rahm. He doesn't talk to all sorts of people at four a.m. that Rahm doesn't know about."

In any case, Emanuel's open bullying of Obama fan-club groups like MoveOn and Unity '09 explains in large part why throughout 2009 there was virtually no left flank in the health care debate educating the public about the ramifications of things like the individual mandate.

"One of the big reasons there was no public outcry about a lot of this stuff is that people didn't hear about it. People aren't getting the e-mails from those groups, so they don't know anything's wrong," says Firedoglake blogger Jane Hamsher, who herself was involved with a March 2009 ad campaign against "obstructionist" Democrats that the White House largely succeeded in spiking.

That particular movement, led by the Campaign for America's Future, had originally targeted that caucus of conservative Democrats, led by Indiana senator Evan Bayh, who were arguing against their own right to use the reconciliation process.

The CAF originally opposed those Democrats' positions on a variety of issues, including their stance on reconciliation and also their stance against cramdown legislation (which would have allowed mortgage holders in bankruptcy to negotiate to keep their homes).

They announced the campaign on the morning of Tuesday, March 24. By that same afternoon, after hearing objection from the White House, the CAF had backed down and scaled it back.

The largely successful muffling of the progressive opposition meant there was never an organized grassroots protest run to match the amazingly energetic antisocialist yell-off whipped up by the right-wing talk-radio crowd, who that summer proved once again that unlike a lot of Democrats, politics for them isn't just about wearing a T-shirt.

That absence of popular protests from their base certainly made it easier for Democrats to vote for the bill—but even so, some members needed one last push to bite the bullet. On both ends of the spectrum, wavering Democratic Caucus members took historically massive pork payouts and other concessions in exchange for their votes for H.R. 3590. The craziest of these involved Nelson and the aforementioned Mary Landrieu, who each agreed to vote for the bill in exchange for, respectively, a $100 million exemption from Medicaid payments and $300 million in extra federal spending.

Deals like this increased the obligation of the average taxpayer under Obamacare to a triple ultimatum: many of us would now have to (1) buy our own private health insurance, (2) pay taxes to subsidize the insurance of low-income citizens across the country, and (3) pay still more taxes to subsidize the ordinary Medicaid payments for the citizens of the state of Nebraska, which thanks to Nelson and the White House would not have to pay its own share. That was the original deal, anyway.

Some of these pork bribes were of a type analysts had never seen before: David Williams of Citizens Against Government Waste calls the people behind these deals "pork entrepreneurs."

"In the past what we've seen is silly little projects—a teapot museum, the Tiger Woods Foundation, and so on," says Williams. "But what we're seeing here is the government tweaking the Medicaid rate to the tune of hundreds of millions or billions of dollars. It has the same corrupting influence as the pork we're used to seeing every day, but it's on a scale we've never seen before."

A hundred million dollars appeared to be the going rate for the vote. Nelson got his $100 million in Medicaid exemptions; Daniel Inouye got the same amount in aid for Hawaiian hospitals. And somebody in Connecticut got $100 million for a "Health Care Facility . . . at a Public Research University in the United States That Contains a State's Sole Public Academic Medical and Dental School."

"We don't even know if it was for Dodd or for Lieberman," says Williams. "It might have been for both."

Thus in the end the health care drama played out almost entirely within the Democratic Party. It was a multistage process.

Stage one involved the election campaign of a magnetic, personable intellectual named Barack Obama who corralled millions of voters into his camp by promising health care reform with a public option that would reduce costs without being an open giveaway to the drug and insurance industries.

Stage two: after getting elected, Obama invited said industries to the White House early on in the process and cut a private deal to reverse virtually all of his campaign promises in exchange for their support of the bill.

Stage three then involved pretending the deal hadn't been made (the White House to this day denies that the PhRMA deal that Tauzin admitted to took place) and insisting instead that the bill Obama supported was not an industry giveaway but simply good policy—and to prove it, they moved to stage four, which was repeatedly citing the research of an MIT economist who received nearly a million dollars from the federal government.

Stage five involved bullying their own ranks to lay off conservative Democrats and get in line behind a public relations campaign against a totally idiotic and irrelevant Republican-led protest movement.

Stages six through eight were blaming the Senate for taking all the good stuff out of the bill, buying off the remaining recalcitrant members for $100 million apiece, and then sauntering off into the sunset atop a multitrillion-dollar corporate welfare program that might further wreck an already wrecked system for a generation, but will keep Rahm Emanuel rolling in campaign contributions for, well, the next two electoral cycles.

And then of course there was stage nine—losing Ted Kennedy's seat and having to use the reconciliation process after all, but not taking advantage of that process to improve the bill in any significant way.

To say that this monstrous bill was all the work of the Democrats is not entirely accurate, of course. The truth is that a scam on this scale required the negative assistance from all ends of the DC zoo, with the seemingly irrelevant Republicans playing an important part.

The moronic and absurdly hypocritical objections of stammering jerks like John Boehner and Mitch McConnell about Obamacare ultimately served to discredit any progressive criticism of the legislation and helped further soil this historically corrupt bill by ensuring that the *Congressional Record* will forever show that it was passed in a romper room of overgrown children seemingly barely old enough to keep from peeing on themselves.

Instead of spearheading a real cogent opposition to the genuine and obvious flaws in the bill, in particular those areas that corrupt their fetishized free-market principles, the Republicans disgraced themselves by spitting out one easily debunked lie after another and in the final hours reducing congressional procedure to something very like a breath-holding contest.

Despite the fact that the bill's passage seemed a foregone conclusion and the Democrats had their sixty votes wrapped up, McConnell and Co. tried to rerun *Mr. Smith Goes to Washington* live on C-SPAN by attempting one filibuster after another and then insisting on the full thirty hours of debate each time their filibusters were broken.

These pointless stall tactics resulted in five consecutive days of post-midnight votes in the week before Christmas, with two sessions ending at dawn, one at midnight, and two at 1:00 a.m., including the final vote on Christmas Eve. With the Christmas holidays of virtually every staffer in Washington thus ruined, the Republicans then turned around and wailed to the media about how the Democrats were trying to do dirt in the middle of the night.

"It's obvious why the majority has cooked up this amendment in secret, has introduced it in the middle of a snowstorm, has scheduled the Senate to come in session at midnight, has scheduled a vote for one a.m., is insisting that it be passed before Christmas—because they don't want the American people to know what's in it," said Tennessee's Lamar Alexander.

And once that drum started being beaten, the inevitable Fox/Murdoch idiot parade chimed in, with junior-Goebbels-in-heels Michelle Malkin railing against the Democrats' "Vampire Congress"—apparently forgetting that that term was originally invented to describe the Republican-run Congresses of Tom DeLay and David Dreier, who one year pushed 78 of 191 bills through the Rules Committee after 8:00 p.m., with 21 coming in as late as seven in the morning.

Thus in the end this awful bill not only threatened to screw us all out of billions a year for decades to come, it treated us to the spectacle of our elected representatives behaving at their very best, reducing the Senate chamber to a screeching apeararium on Christmas and ensuring at least a few years more of pointless deadlock and legislative pissing contests as our nation bumbles its way through a cratering economy and two losing wars.

There will be a lot to say about health care for years to come, but the most important thing about it is that it proved the government's utter helplessness to police whole sectors of society. Forget about *fixing* the health care industry; what President Obama proved to America is that his government couldn't even win back the right to truly regulate this massive industry, even with a historic mandate at his back and after giving away everything he had to trade, conceding even the power to tax. There is a universe under which the passage of Obamacare leads to future legislative tinkering that drives prices down and chips away at the industry's antitrust exemption. But it's equally possible that the passage of the bill presages a revolutionary new vision for America's industrial economy—one in which companies compete not on price and quality but in political influence, and earn profits not by attracting customers with good service, but by using the power of the state to protect markets and force customers into the fold.

The mistake our politicians so often make with these industry leaders is in thinking they are interested in, or respectful of, the power of government. All they want is to keep stealing. If you can offer them the government's seal of approval on that, they'll take it. But if you can't, well, they'll take that too.

7

The Great American Bubble Machine

During the winter of 2008–9, when I was just feeling my way through the first story I was writing for Rolling Stone *about the financial crisis, I started to notice something amusing. One of the keys to talking to sources about any subject is clicking with their sense of humor, and I was noticing that with a lot of the financial people I was calling, I was missing laugh cues whenever anyone mentioned the investment bank Goldman Sachs. No one ever just referenced "Goldman"; they would say, "those motherfuckers" or "those cocksuckers" or "those motherfucking cocksucking assholes at Goldman Sachs." It was a name spoken with such contempt that you could almost hear people holding the phone away from their faces as they talked, the way you do with the baggie you have to pick up curbing your dog on the streets of New York.*

After a few months I also started to notice that every time someone wanted to provide an example of some sordid scam the investment banking community was into, they used Goldman as an example. The bank was also continually held up as a model for how certain firms used their connections with government to buffer business risk—Goldman, I was told, was expert at using campaign contributions as a kind of market insurance to hedge their investments. Many of the people I talked to were from firms that didn't get particularly advantageous treatment from the government during the bailout season, and so I assumed their take on the crisis, and Goldman, was colored by that.

After writing one story on the crisis that was mostly about AIG, I suggested to my editors at the Stone *that we do a piece on Goldman that we could use as a window into the whole world of investment banking and what it's been up to for the past few decades. We did the story; in retrospect we left out quite a lot, a problem I've tried to rectify here by adding some to the original text.*

But perhaps as interesting as the actual material in the original piece was what happened after we ran it, as the magazine and I got sucked into a public relations firestorm that was both bizarre and educational. My initial reaction to being blasted in the media by commentators from CNBC ("Stop Blaming Goldman Sachs!" read Charlie Gasparino's rant; another on-air talent called me a "lunatic"), the Atlantic, *and other outlets was that this was just typical media turf-war stuff: a bunch of insiders angrily piling on someone who didn't have any background in their area of expertise (which I did not) and yet was not-so-subtly indicting them for falling asleep on the job.*

That was part of the story. If Goldman Sachs really was, as we'd described, little more than an upscale version of a boiler-room pump-and-dump operation, then that definitely was an indictment of the financial press, which almost universally praised the bank as a pillar of economic genius. If financial journalists like the Charlie Gasparinos and Megan McArdles out there took it that way, good—I meant it that way.

But when the uproar continued for more than a month—an eternity in news cycle time—it was clear that there was something else at work. Looking back now, what I experienced in the wake of the Goldman piece was a lesson in a subtle truth about class politics in this country.

Which is this: you can pick on the rich in an ironic, Arrested Development *sort of way, you can muss Donald Trump's hair, you can even talk abstractly about class economics using clinical terms like "income disparity." But in our media you're not allowed to just kick the rich in the balls and use class-warfare language. The taboo isn't so much the subject matter, the taboo is the tone. You're allowed to grimace and shake your head at their shenanigans, but you can't call them crooks and imply that they haven't earned their money by being better or smarter than everyone else, at least not until they've been indicted or gone bankrupt.*

Goldman was the ultimate embodiment of this media privilege. The most valuable item in all the bank's holdings was its undeserved reputation for brilliance and efficiency. The narrative that Goldman had always enjoyed was a sort of ongoing validation of the Ayn Rand/Alan Greenspan fairy tale, in which their riches and power sufficed as testimony to their social value. They made lots of money, they were good at whatever it is they did, therefore they were "producers" and should be given the benefit of the doubt. This fairy tale was deeply ingrained in the financial press, to the point where any suggestion to the contrary had to be attacked, regardless of the substance of that suggestion.

The abuse I was taking after my Goldman story came out wasn't so much a media turf war as a defense of The Narrative. I believe now that there's real fear of what happens once The Narrative blows up—because once we've ripped the rich to shreds, what we're left with is a whole bunch of broke people wondering where the hell their money went, without even a soothing fairy tale to help them get to sleep at night.

People in the financial community who actually worked in that world, the traders and the bankers themselves who joked with me about "those motherfuckers," did not have these illusions. You're not going to be good at making money if you need there to be a halo around the moneymaking process. The only people who really clung to those illusions were the financial commentators, right up to the point where those illusions became completely unsustainable. Within six months after this article came out, it was de rigueur even for wire services to reference Goldman's "vampire squid" reputation. But by then the executives at Goldman weren't worrying all that much about their plummeting reputation—and that, in the end, turned out to be the most interesting part of this story. But more on that at the end of this updated version of the original piece,* which I've saved for last in this book because the history of Goldman—a company that has developed a reputation as the smartest and nimblest of corporate enterprises—is the story of the great

---

*The original story, "The Great American Bubble Machine," appeared in *Rolling Stone* 1082–83, July 9–23, 2009.

lie at the center of our political and economic life. Goldman is not a com-
pany of geniuses, it's a company of criminals. And far from being the best
fruit of a democratic, capitalist society, it's the apotheosis of the Grifter Era, a
parasitic enterprise that has attached itself to the American government and
taxpayer and shamelessly engorged itself on us all.

THE FIRST THING you need to know about Goldman Sachs is that it's everywhere. The world's most powerful investment bank is a great vampire squid wrapped around the face of humanity, relentlessly jamming its blood funnel into anything that smells like money. In fact, the history of the recent financial crisis, which doubles as a history of the rapid decline and fall of the suddenly swindled-dry American empire, reads like a Who's Who of Goldman Sachs graduates.

Most of us know the major players: Henry Paulson, George Bush's last Treasury secretary, who used to run Goldman and was the architect of a suspiciously self-serving plan to funnel trillions from the Treasury to a small list of his old friends on Wall Street. Bob Rubin, Bill Clinton's former Treasury secretary, spent twenty-six years at Goldman and later went on to become chairman of Citigroup—which in turn got a $300 billion taxpayer bailout from Paulson.

There's John Thain, the asshole chief of Merrill Lynch who bought a $28,000 set of curtains and an $87,000 area rug for his office as his company was going broke; this former Goldman banker got a multibillion-dollar handout from Paulson, who used billions in taxpayer funds to help Bank of America rescue Thain's sorry company. And Robert Steel, Goldmanite former head of Wachovia, who scored himself and his fellow executives $225 million in golden parachute payments as the company was imploding. The heads of the Canadian and Italian national banks are Goldman alums, as is the head of the World Bank, the head of the New York Stock Exchange, the current chief of staff of the Treasury, the last two heads of the New York Federal Reserve Bank (which incidentally is now in charge of regulating Goldman), and on and on.

But any attempt to construct a narrative around all the former Goldmanites in influential positions quickly becomes an absurd and pointless exercise, like trying to make a list of everything. So what you need to know is the big picture: if America is circling the drain, Goldman Sachs found a way to be that drain—an extremely unfortunate loophole in the system of Western democratic capitalism, which never foresaw that in a society governed passively by free markets and free elections, organized greed always defeats disorganized democracy.

The bank's unprecedented reach and power has enabled it to manipulate whole economic sectors for years at a time, moving the dice game as this or that market collapses, and all the time gorging itself on the unseen costs that are breaking families everywhere—high gas prices, rising consumer credit rates, half-eaten pension funds, mass layoffs, future taxes to pay off bailouts. All that money that you're losing, it's *going* somewhere, and in both a literal and a figurative sense Goldman Sachs is where it's going: the bank is a huge, highly sophisticated engine for converting the useful, deployed wealth of society into the least useful, most wasteful and insoluble substance on earth, pure profit for rich individuals.

It achieves this using the same playbook over and over again. What it does is position itself in the middle of horrific bubble manias that function like giant lottery schemes, hoovering vast sums from the middle and lower floors of society with the aid of a government that lets it rewrite the rules, in exchange for the relative pennies the bank throws at political patronage. This dynamic allows the bank to suck wealth out of the economy and vitality out of the democracy at the same time, resulting in a snowballingly regressive phenomenon that pushes us closer to penury and oligarchy at the same time.

They have been pulling this same stunt for decades, and they're preparing to do it again. If you want to understand how we got into this crisis, you first have to understand where all the money went—and in order to understand that, you first need to understand what Goldman has already gotten away with, a history exactly three bubbles long.

Goldman wasn't always a too-big-to-fail Wall Street behemoth and the ruthless, bluntly unapologetic face of kill-or-be-killed capitalism on steroids—just almost always. The bank was actually founded in 1882 by a German Jewish immigrant named Marcus Goldman, who built it up with his son-in-law, Samuel Sachs. They were pioneers in the use of commercial paper, which is just a fancy way of saying they made money lending out short-term IOUs to small-time vendors in downtown Manhattan.

You can probably guess the basic plotline of Goldman's first one hundred years in business: plucky immigrant-led investment bank beats the odds, pulls itself up by its bootstraps, makes shitloads of money. In that ancient history there's only one episode that bears real scrutiny now, in light of more recent events: Goldman's disastrous foray into the speculative mania of precrash Wall Street in the late 1920s and the launch of now-infamous "investment trusts" like the Goldman Sachs Trading Corporation, the Shenandoah Corporation, and the Blue Ridge Corporation.

It's probably not worth getting into the arcane details of these great Hindenburgs of financial history too much, but they had some features that might sound familiar. Similar to modern mutual funds, investment trusts were companies that took the cash of investors large and small and (theoretically at least) invested it in a smorgasbord of Wall Street securities, though which securities and in which amounts were often kept hidden from the public. So a regular guy could invest ten bucks or a hundred bucks in a trust and pretend he was a big player. Much as in the 1990s, when new vehicles like day trading and e-trading attracted reams of new suckers from the sticks who wanted to be big shots, investment trusts roped in a generation of regular-guy investors to the speculation game.

Beginning a pattern that would repeat itself over and over again, Goldman got into the investment trust game slightly late, then jumped in with both feet and went absolutely hog wild. The first effort was the Goldman Sachs Trading Corporation; the bank issued a million shares at $100 apiece, bought all those shares with its own money, and then sold 90 percent of the fund to the hungry public at $104.

GSTC then relentlessly bought shares in itself, bidding the price up further and further. Eventually it dumped part of its holdings and sponsored a new trust, Shenandoah, and issued millions more in shares in that fund—which in turn later sponsored yet another trust called Blue Ridge. The last trust was really just another front for an endless investment pyramid, Goldman hiding behind Goldman hiding behind Goldman. Of the 7,250,000 initial shares of Blue Ridge, 6,250,000 were actually owned by Shenandoah, which of course was in large part owned by Goldman Trading.

The end result (ask yourself if this sounds familiar) was a daisy chain of borrowed money exquisitely vulnerable to any decline in performance anywhere along the line. It sounds complicated, but the basic idea isn't hard to follow. You take a dollar and borrow nine against it; then you take that ten-dollar fund and borrow ninety; then you take your hundred-dollar fund and, so long as the public is still lending, borrow and invest nine hundred. If the last fund in the line starts to lose value, you no longer have the money to pay everyone back, and everyone gets massacred.

The famed economist John Kenneth Galbraith wrote up the Blue Ridge/Shenandoah incidents as a classic example of the insanity of leverage-based investment; in today's dollars, the losses the bank suffered through trusts like Blue Ridge and Shenandoah totaled about $485 billion and were a major cause of the 1929 crash.

Fast-forward about sixty-five years. Goldman had survived the crash and, thanks largely to its legendary senior partner Sidney Weinberg (famous for having moved from being a janitor's assistant to being the head of the company), gone on to prosper and become the underwriting king of Wall Street. Through the seventies and eighties Goldman was not quite the planet-eating Death Star of indomitable political influence it is today, but it was a top-drawer firm that had a reputation for attracting the very smartest talent on the Street.

It also, oddly enough, had a reputation for relatively solid ethics and long-term thinking, as its executives were trained to adopt the firm's mantra, "Long-term greedy." One former Goldman banker who left the firm in the early nineties recalls seeing his superiors give up a very profitable deal on the grounds that it was a long-term loser. "We gave back money to 'grown-up' corporate clients who had made [for them] bad deals with us," he says. "Everything we did was legal and fair . . . but 'long-term greedy' said we didn't want to make such a profit at the clients' collective expense that we spoiled the marketplace."

But then something happened. It's hard to say what it was exactly;

it might have been the fact that its CEO in the early nineties, Robert Rubin, followed Bill Clinton to the White House, where he was the director of Clinton's new National Economic Council and eventually became Treasury secretary. While the American media fell in love with the storyline of a pair of baby-boomer, sixties-child, Fleetwood Mac–fan yuppies nesting in the White House, it also nursed an undisguised crush on the obnoxious Rubin, who was hyped as the smartest person ever to walk the face of the earth.

Rubin was the prototypical Goldman banker. He was probably born in a four-thousand-dollar suit, he had a face that seemed permanently frozen just short of an apology for being so much smarter than you, and he maintained a Spocklike, emotion-neutral exterior; the only human feeling you could imagine him experiencing was a nightmare about being forced to fly coach. The press went batshit over him and it became almost a national cliché that whatever Rubin thought was probably the correct economic policy, a phenomenon that reached its nadir in 1999, when Rubin appeared on that famous *Time* magazine cover with Alan Greenspan and then–Treasury chief Larry Summers under the headline "The Committee to Save the World."

And "what Rubin thought," mostly, was that the American economy, and in particular the financial markets, were overregulated and needed to be set free. During his tenure the Clinton White House made a series of moves that would have drastic consequences. The specific changes Rubin made to the regulatory environment would have their most profound impact on the economy in the years after he left the Clinton White House, in particular during the housing, credit, and commodities bubbles. But another part of his legacy was his complete and total inattention to and failure to regulate Wall Street during Goldman's first mad dash for obscene short-term profits, in the Internet years.

The basic scam in the Internet age is pretty easy even for the financially illiterate to grasp. It was as if banks like Goldman were wrapping ribbons around watermelons, tossing them out fiftieth-story windows, and opening the phones for bids. In this game you were a winner only if you took your money out before the melon hit the pavement.

It sounds obvious now, but what the average investor didn't know at the time was that the banks had changed the rules of the game, making the deals look better than they were, setting up what was in reality a two-tiered investment system—one for bankers and insiders who knew the real numbers, and another for the lay investor, who was invited to chase soaring prices the banks themselves knew were irrational. While Goldman's later pattern would be to capitalize on changes in the regulatory environment, its key innovation in the Internet years was its executives' abandonment of their own industry's quality control standards.

"What people don't realize is that the banks had adopted strict underwriting standards after the Depression," says one prominent hedge fund manager. "For decades, no bank would take a company public unless it met certain conditions. It had to have existed for at least five years. It had to have been profitable for at least three years in a row. It had to be making money at the time of the IPO.

"Goldman took these rules and just threw them out the window. They'd sign up Worthless.com and take it public five minutes into its existence. The public mostly had no idea. They assumed these companies met the banks' standards."

Jay Ritter, a professor at the University of Florida, says the decline in underwriting standards began in the eighties. "In the early eighties the major underwriters insisted on three years of profitability. Then it was one year, then it was a quarter. By the time of the Internet bubble things had declined to the point where not only was profitability not required next year, they were not requiring profitability in the foreseeable future."

Goldman has repeatedly denied that it changed its underwriting standards during the Internet years, but the statistics belie the bank's claims. Just like it did with the investment trust phenomenon, Goldman in the Internet years started slow and finished crazy.

After it took a little-known company with weak financials called Yahoo! public in 1996, it quickly became the IPO king of the Internet era. Of the twenty-four Internet companies it took public in 1997 for which data are available, a third were losing money at the time of the IPO. In the next year, 1998, the height of the Net boom, it took eighteen companies public in the first four months, and fourteen of them were money losers at the time of the IPO.

By the following April, the number of Internet IPOs on Wall Street had shot up ninefold compared to the first four months of 1998, and the overall amount of money raised by IPOs had jumped to more than $45 billion, topping the tally for the entire calendar year 1996. Goldman by then was underwriting a fifth of all Internet IPOs and went on to underwrite forty-seven new offerings in 1999.

Of those 1999 IPOs, a full four-fifths were Internet companies (including stillborns like Webvan and eToys), making Goldman the leading underwriter of Internet IPOs during the boom. The company's IPOs were consistently more volatile than those of their competitors: the average Goldman IPO in 1999 leapt 281 percent above its offering price that year, compared to the Wall Street average of 183 percent.

How did they manage such extraordinary results? One answer was that they used a practice called laddering, which is just a fancy way of saying they manipulated the share price of new offerings. Here's how it works: Say you're Goldman Sachs and Worthless.com comes to you and asks you to take their company public. You agree on the usual terms: you'll price the stock, determine how many shares should be released, and take the Worthless.com CEO on a "road tour" to meet and schmooze investors, in exchange for a substantial fee (typically 6–7 percent of the amount raised, which added up to enormous sums in the tens if not hundreds of millions).

You then promise your best clients the right to buy big chunks of the IPO at the low offering price—let's say Worthless.com's starting share price is 15—in exchange for a promise to reenter the bidding later, buying the shares on the open market. Now you've got inside knowledge of the IPO's future, knowledge that wasn't disclosed to the day-trader schmucks who only had the prospectus to go by: you know that certain of your clients who bought X amount of shares at 15 are also going to buy Y more shares at 20 or 25, virtually guaranteeing that the price is going to go past 25 and beyond. In this way the bank could artificially jack up the new company's price, which of course was to the bank's benefit—a 6 percent fee of a $500 million or $750 million IPO was serious money.

Goldman was repeatedly sued for engaging in these laddering practices by shareholders of a variety of Net IPOs, including Webvan and NetZero. Moreover, they were outed by one Nicholas Maier, the former syndicate manager of Cramer & Co., the hedge fund then run by the now-famous chattering television asshole Jim Cramer, himself a Goldman alum. While working for Cramer between 1996 and 1998, Maier contends that he was repeatedly forced to engage in the laddering practice in IPO deals with Goldman.

"Goldman, from what I witnessed, they were the worst perpetrator," Maier said later. "They totally fueled the bubble. And it's specifically that kind of behavior that has caused the market crash. They built these stocks upon an illegal foundation—manipulated up, and ultimately, it really was the small person who ended up buying in."

In what would become a pattern of somehow managing to escape responsibility and legal problems by paying absurdly small fines, Goldman eventually agreed to pay a mere $40 million fine in 2005 to the SEC for its laddering violations, a fine that was obviously beyond puny relative to the sums involved. Also in line with the bank's incredible pattern of general impunity, it managed to get off on its laddering offenses without a formal admission of wrongdoing.

Another practice Goldman engaged in during the Net boom and managed to escape serious punishment for was "spinning." Here the investment bank would offer the executives of the newly public company shares at advantageous prices in exchange for promises of future underwriting business. Typically investment banks that engaged in spinning undervalued the initial offering price so that those "hot" opening-price shares would be more likely to rise quickly and therefore offer bigger first-day rewards.

In one example, Goldman allegedly gave multimillion-dollar special offerings to eBay CEO Meg Whitman (she was also a director at Goldman) and eBay founder Pierre Omidyar in exchange for a promise that eBay would use Goldman for future i-banking business.

And this wasn't the only example: a 2002 House Financial Services Committee report showed that in twenty-one different instances, Goldman gave top executives in companies they took public special stock offerings that in most cases were quickly sold at a huge profit. According to the report, executives who received this preferential treatment from Goldman included Yahoo! founder Jerry Yang and two of the great Oil Can Harrys of the financial scandal age—Tyco's Dennis Kozlowski and Enron's Ken Lay.

Goldman was furious about the report and blasted back at then–committee chair Mike Oxley and the rest of Congress. "This is an egregious distortion of the facts," said Lucas van Praag, a spokesman for Goldman Sachs. "The suggestion that Goldman Sachs was involved in spinning or other inappropriate practices around IPO allocations is simply wrong."

And yet: at the end of that same year Goldman agreed to settle with not-yet-disgraced New York attorney general Eliot Spitzer, who accused Goldman, along with eleven other companies, of spinning and issuing bogus buy ratings of stocks. Here Goldman again got off easy, paying just $50 million. It also agreed, as part of the settlement, to no longer engage in spinning; in return, Goldman again got to avoid formally pleading guilty to any charges, and regulators agreed to forgo charges against its chief executives, who at the time included Hank Paulson.

Well, who cares about all this, right? Why begrudge a few rich guys a few advantageous stock offerings? There are actually many reasons. One, it's bribery. Two, practices like spinning not only artificially lowered the initial offering price but deprived ordinary investors of critical information; they had no way of knowing that Goldman was playing around with the price of newly public companies in order to secure other business.

Beyond that, the House Committee concluded that Goldman's analysts had kept on issuing "buy" recommendations long after the value of the stocks had fallen, in some cases doing so in exchange for promises of future business. Ritter, the Florida professor, concluded that companies whose IPOs were "spun" were deprived of about a fifth of what they could have made, on average. "We compute what the offer price would have been on each IPO to result in a first-day return that would have been 22.68 percent less," he says. In other words, a company that took its company public in a "spun" IPO might lose $20 million on a $100 million offering.

Even worse was the practice of "soft dollar commissions." Here Goldman would approach large institutional investment clients—insurance companies, pension funds, mutual funds, thrifts, and so on—and tell them that their access to hot Internet IPO shares would be contingent upon how much underwriting business they threw the bank's way over time. Again, this artificially drove the initial offering price down, induced more investors to chase first-day gains, and generally fucked with the market by hiding pertinent information from investors on the outside.

"Basically the way this worked is that the investment banker would call up the investor and say, 'We're taking this company public, here's the offering price—I'm your buddy, would you be willing to take ten thousand shares?' " says Tony Perkins, author of *The Internet Bubble*. "Then he'd say, 'But since I'm your buddy, if I give you ten thousand shares, next time you have some underwriting business, you've got to be my buddy.' "

The SEC "investigated" the problem in 1998 but in the end basically blew the issue off. "The SEC basically turned a blind eye to this," says Ritter. "The code word for investment bankers and regulators was 'Relationships are okay.' That was the word for bribery—'relationships.' "

All of these factors conspired to turn the Internet bubble into one of the greatest financial disasters in world history. More than $5 trillion of wealth was wiped out on the NASDAQ alone—an amount that doesn't seem like an incomprehensible disaster only in light of recent developments. But despite the enormous evaporation of public wealth and similarly large job losses that without a shadow of a doubt were due in significant part to the bank's indifferent IPO ethics, Goldman's employees—in what again would be a pattern with the bank—managed to do just fine throughout the crash.

The bank paid out $6.4 billion in compensation and benefits to 15,361 employees in 1999 (an average of close to $420K per employee), paid $7.7 billion to 22,627 employees in 2000 (an average of $340K), and stayed at $7.7 billion, paid out to 22,677 employees ($339K), in 2001. Even in 2002, the year the bank was most affected by the crash, employee compensation barely moved: the total payout was $6.7 billion to 19,739 employees, an average of $341K per person—virtually the same as in the precrash years.

Those numbers are important because the key legacy of the Internet boom years was that the economy was now driven in large part by the pursuit by individual bankers of the enormous personal bonuses the bubble made possible. The notion of "long-term greedy" vanished into thin air as the game became about getting your check before the melon hit the pavement.

Now, if you laddered and spun fifty Internet IPOs and forty-five of them went bust within a year, and besides that you got caught by the SEC and your firm was forced to pay a $40 million fine, well, so what? By the time the SEC got around to fining your firm, the yacht you bought with your IPO bonuses was already five or six years old. Besides, you were probably out of Goldman by then, running the Treasury or maybe the state of New Jersey. (One of the truly comic moments in the history of America's recent financial collapse came when Jersey governor Jon Corzine, who ran Goldman from 1997 to 1999 and left with $320 million in IPO-fattened Goldman stock, said in 2002 that "I've never even heard of 'laddering.' ")

Thus, once the Internet bubble burst Goldman didn't bother to reassess its strategy; it just searched around for a new bubble. As it happens, it had one ready, thanks in large part to Rubin.

Goldman's role in the sweeping global disaster that was the housing bubble is not hard to trace. By the peak of the housing boom, 2006, Goldman was issuing $44.5 billion worth of mortgage-based investment vehicles annually (mainly CDOs), a lot of it to institutional investors like pensions and insurance companies. Of course, as we've seen, within this massive issue was loads of pure crap, loans underwritten according to a pyramid of lies and fraudulent information. How does a bank make money selling gigantic packages of grade-D horseshit? Easy: it bets against the stuff as it's selling it! What was truly amazing about Goldman was the sheer balls it showed during its handling of the housing business. First it had the gall to take all this hideous, completely irresponsible mortgage lending from beneath-gangster-status firms like Countrywide and sell it to pensioners and municipalities, old people for God's sake, and pretend the whole time that it wasn't toxic waste. But at the same time, it took short positions in the same market, in essence betting against the same crap it was selling. And worse than that, it bragged about it in public.

"The problem I have with Goldman as opposed to all these other banks is that all the other banks, they were just stupid," says a hedge fund CEO. "They bought this stuff and they actually believed it. But Goldman knew it was crap."

Indeed, Goldman CFO David Viniar in 2007 boasted that Goldman was covered in the mortgage area because it had shorted the market. "The mortgage sector continues to be challenged," he said. "As a result, we took significant write-downs on our long inventory positions . . . *However, our risk bias in that market was to be short and that net short position was profitable.*"

I asked the hedge fund CEO how it could be that selling something to customers that you're actually betting against, particularly when you know more about the weaknesses of those products than the customer, how that isn't securities fraud.

"It's absolutely securities fraud," he said. "It's the heart of securities fraud."

Eventually, lots of aggrieved investors would agree. In a virtual repeat of the IPO craze, Goldman after the collapse of the housing bubble was hit with a wave of shareholder lawsuits, many of which accused the bank of withholding pertinent information about the quality (or lack thereof) of the mortgages in their CDO issues.

In 2009, for instance, the New York City and State comptrollers sued Goldman for selling bundles of crappy Countrywide mortgages to the city and state pension funds, which lost as much as $100 million in the investments. The suit alleges that Goldman misled investors by "falsely representing that Countrywide had strict and selective underwriting . . . ample liquidity . . . and a conservative approach."

When Viniar bragged about being short on mortgages, he was probably referring to credit default swaps the bank held with firms like AIG. This is part of the reason that the AIG bailout is so troubling: when at least $13 billion worth of taxpayer money given to AIG in the bailout ultimately went to Goldman, some of that money was doubtless going to cover the bets Goldman had made against the stuff the bank itself was selling to old people and cities and states. In other words, Goldman made out on the housing bubble twice: it fucked the investors who bought their horseshit CDOs by betting against its own crappy product, then it turned around and fucked the taxpayer by making him pay off those same bets.

Again, while the world crashed down all around the bank in 2006, gross employee pay went up to $16.5 billion that year for 26,000 employees, an average of $634,000 per employee. A Goldman spokesman explained: "We work very hard here."

Fall 2008. After the bursting of the commodities bubble, which, as we've seen, was another largely Goldman-engineered scam, there was no new bubble to keep things humming—this time the money seems really to be gone, like worldwide depression gone. Then–Treasury secretary and former Goldman chief Paulson makes a momentous series of decisions. Although he has already engineered a rescue of Bear Stearns that same spring, and helped bail out quasi-private lenders Fannie Mae and Freddie Mac, Paulson elects to let Lehman Brothers—one of Goldman's last real competitors—collapse without intervention.

That same weekend, he green-lights a massive $80 billion bailout of AIG, a crippled insurance giant that just happens to owe Goldman Sachs about $20 billion. Paulson's decision to intervene selectively in the market would radically reshape the competitive dynamic on Wall Street. Goldman's main competitor, Lehman Brothers, was wiped out, as was Merrill Lynch, which was bought by Bank of America in a Treasury-brokered shotgun wedding. Bear Stearns had died six months earlier. So when the dust settles after the AIG wreck, only two of the top five investment banks on Wall Street are left standing: Goldman and Morgan Stanley.

Meanwhile, after the AIG bailout, Paulson announces his federal bailout for the financial industry, a $700 billion plan called the Troubled Asset Relief Program (or TARP), and immediately puts a heretofore unknown thirty-five-year-old Goldman banker named Neel Kashkari in charge of administering the funds. In order to qualify for bailout monies, Goldman announces that it will be converting from an investment bank to a bank holding company—a move that allows it access not only to $10 billion in TARP funds but to a whole galaxy of less conspicuous publicly backed funding sources, most notably lending from the discount window of the Federal Reserve Bank. Its chief remaining competitor, Morgan Stanley, announces the same move on the same day.

No one knows how much either bank borrows from the Fed, but by the end of the year upwards of $3 trillion will have been lent out by the Fed under a series of new bailout programs—and thanks to an obscure law allowing the Fed to block most congressional audits, both the amounts and the recipients of these monies remain almost entirely secret.

Moreover, serendipitously from Goldman's point of view, its conversion to a bank holding company means that its primary regulator is now the New York Federal Reserve Bank, whose chairman at the time is one Stephen Friedman, a former managing director of, well, you know.

Friedman is technically in violation of Federal Reserve policy by remaining on the board of Goldman Sachs even as he supposedly is regulating the bank; in order to rectify the problem, he applies for, and of course gets, a conflict-of-interest waiver from Thomas Baxter, the Federal Reserve's general counsel.

Friedman, in addition, is supposed to divest himself of his Goldman stock after Goldman becomes a bank holding company, but he not only doesn't dump his holdings, he goes out and buys 37,000 *additional* shares in December 2008, leaving him with almost 100,000 shares in his old bank, worth upwards of $13 million at the time.

Throughout that crisis period Goldman can't move an inch without getting a hand job from a government agency. In that same period, in late September 2008, both Goldman CEO Lloyd Blankfein and Morgan Stanley CEO John Mack lobby the government to impose restrictions on short sellers who were attacking their companies—and they get them, thanks to a decision by the SEC on September 21 to ban bets against some eight hundred financial stocks. Goldman's share price rises some 30 percent in the first week of the ban.

The short-selling ban was galling for obvious reasons: the same bank that just a year before had bragged about the fortune it had made shorting others in the housing market was now getting its buddies in the government to protect it from short sellers in a time of need.

The collective message of all of this—the AIG bailout, the swift approval for its conversion to bank holding company status, the TARP funds, and the short-selling ban—was that when it came to Goldman Sachs, there wasn't a free market at all. The government might let other players on the market die, but it simply would not allow Goldman Sachs to fail under any circumstances. Its implicit market advantage suddenly became an open declaration of supreme privilege.

"It wasn't even an implicit assumption anymore," says Simon Johnson, an economics professor at MIT and former International Monetary Fund official who compared the bailouts to the crony capitalism he had seen in the underdeveloped world. "It became an explicit assumption that the government would always rescue Goldman."

All of this government aid belies the myth of Goldman as a collection of the smartest cats in the world. All of this stuff sounds complicated, but when you get right down to it, it isn't. Ask yourself how hard it would be for you to make money if someone fronted you a billion free dollars a week, and you get a rough idea of how Goldman's relationship to the government pays off.

"It takes skill to borrow money at three percent and lend it at five and make a profit," says Peter Morici, a professor at the University of Maryland. "It takes less skill to borrow at two percent and lend at five and make a profit. And that's what's going on."

Morici adds that these programs allow Goldman and other banks to make money on the backs of unsuspecting ordinary consumers. With so much cheap government money available, for instance, banks no longer need to pay a premium to attract money from private depositors, which (among other things) has driven interest rates on certificates of deposit (CDs) way down. Many elderly people rely on CD interest for their income, but they're shit out of luck in an era when the government chooses to bail out rich bankers, not poor old people. "It's taxing Grandma to pay Goldman," says Morici.

Here's the real punch line. After playing an intimate role in three historic bubble catastrophes, after helping $5 trillion in wealth disappear from the NASDAQ in the early part of the 2000s, after pawning off thousands of toxic mortgages on pensioners and cities, after helping drive the price of gas up above $4.60 a gallon for half a year, and helping 100 million new people around the world join the ranks of the hungry, and securing tens of billions of taxpayer dollars through a series of bailouts, what did Goldman Sachs give back to the people of the United States in the year 2008?

Fourteen million dollars.

That is what the firm paid in taxes in 2008: an effective tax rate of exactly 1, read it, *one,* percent. The bank paid out $10 billion in compensation and bonuses that year and made a profit above $2 billion, and yet it paid the government less than a third of what it paid Lloyd Blankfein, who made $42.9 million in 2008.

How is this possible? According to its annual report, the low taxes are due in large part to changes in the bank's "geographic earnings mix." In other words, the bank moved its money around so that all of its earnings took place in foreign countries with low tax rates. Thanks to our completely fucked corporate tax system, companies like Goldman can ship their revenues offshore and defer taxes on those revenues indefinitely, even while they claim deductions up front on that same untaxed income. This is why any corporation with an at least occasionally sober accountant can usually find a way to pay no taxes at all. A Government Accountability Office report, in fact, found that between 1998 and 2005, two-thirds of all corporations operating in the United States paid no taxes at all.

This should be a pitchfork-level outrage—but somehow, when Goldman released its postbailout tax profile, barely anyone said a word: Congressman Lloyd Doggett of Texas was one of the few to remark upon the obscenity. "With the right hand begging for bailout money," he said, "the left is hiding it offshore."

Once the bleeding of the black summer of 2008 stopped, Goldman went right back to business as usual, immediately dreaming up new schemes despite the very recent glimpse of the abyss of bankruptcy its last run of bubble-manic Hamburglaring had provided. The bank was like a drug addict who wakes up from a near OD and, first thing, runs out of the ER in a hospital johnny to go cop again.

One of its first moves of the post-AIG era was to surreptitiously push forward its reporting calendar a month. For years Goldman had called its first quarter the three-month period beginning on December 1 and ending on February 28. In 2009, however, it started its first quarter on January 1 and ended it on March 31. The only problem was, its fourth quarter of the *previous* year had ended on November 30, 2008.

So what happened to that one-month period, December 1 to December 31, 2008? Goldman "orphaned" it, not counting it in either fiscal year. Included in that "orphaned" month were $1.3 billion in pretax losses and $780 million in after-tax losses; the bank's accountants simply waved a wand and the losses were gone, disappeared Enron style down the wormhole of the nonexistent month. This is the accounting equivalent of kicking the ball forward ten yards between plays to get a first down, and they did it right out in the open.

At the same time it was orphaning more than a billion dollars in losses, the bank announced a highly suspicious $1.8 billion profit for the first quarter of 2009, with a large chunk of that money seemingly coming from money funneled to it by taxpayers via the AIG bailout (although the bank cryptically claims in its first-quarter report that the "total AIG impact on earnings, in round numbers, was zero"). "They cooked those first-quarter results six ways from Sunday," says the hedge fund manager. "They hid the losses in the orphan month and called the bailout money profit."

Two more numbers stood out from that stunning first-quarter turnaround: one, the bank paid out an astonishing $4.7 billion in bonuses and compensation in that quarter, an 18 percent increase over the first quarter of 2008. The other number was $5 billion—the amount of money it raised in a new share issue almost immediately after releasing its first-quarter result. Taken altogether, what these numbers meant was this: Goldman essentially borrowed a $5 billion salary bump for its executives in the middle of a crisis, using half-baked accounting to reel in investors, just months after receiving billions in a taxpayer bailout.

Moreover, despite being instructed by the feds not to give any public indication of what the results of a government "stress test" of bailed-out banks might be, Goldman made its $5 billion share offering right before its test results were announced. The $5 billion offering came on April 15, 2008, and was later bumped up to $5.75 billion; Goldman also issued $2 billion in bonds two weeks later, on April 30. By the end of the first week in May, the stress test results had been announced and Goldman had passed with flying colors.

Doing the share offering and the bond when it did was more or less an open signal to the market that Goldman knew it was going to pass its test. It was a brazen announcement of insider privilege, and everybody on Wall Street knew what it meant. In a Bloomberg story on April 30 you could almost see the smirk emanating from the bank's public relations department:

> April 30 (Bloomberg)—Goldman Sachs Group Inc., by selling bonds and stock yesterday, may be signaling that there won't be any surprises next week when the results of government stress tests are revealed . . .
>
> Securities laws require the company to reveal material nonpublic information before selling any stock or bonds. Lucas van Praag, a spokesman for New York–based Goldman Sachs, declined to comment.

Beyond that, the bank somehow seemed to know exactly what the Federal Reserve's conditions would be before it would be allowed by the government to repay its TARP debt, which was supposed to be a carefully managed process—the government, at least theoretically, did not want any of the TARP recipients paying the money back too soon, as this might reflect poorly on those banks that were still unable to pay.

So on June 1, the Fed outlined its criteria for repayment: banks hoping to pay money back would have to do so by issuing non-FDIC-backed debt and meet a series of other conditions, all of which Goldman appeared to know in advance.

"They seemed to know everything that they needed to do before the stress test came out, unlike everyone else, who had to wait until after," says Michael Hecht of JMP Securities. "[The government] came out as part of the stress test and said, If you want to be able to pay back TARP eventually, you have to issue five-year or greater, non-FDIC-insured debt—which Goldman Sachs already had, a week or two before."

Unlike Morgan Stanley, which didn't orphan its losses in a phantom December and didn't show a house-of-cards profit in the first quarter of 2009, Goldman was pronounced healthy enough to start repaying TARP. "We would like to get out from under [TARP]," said Goldman CFO David Viniar, who described repayment of TARP as the bank's patriotic "duty."

Which it might have been, but it also happened to be the last necessary step to ending the compensation restrictions that went with the bailout money. Once the bank fulfilled its "duty," its executives would be free once again to pay themselves truly obscene salaries without government interference.

And that's exactly what happened: Goldman announced a stunning second-quarter profit of $3.44 billion. Less than a year removed from its near-death experience after the AIG implosion—when the bank needed an overnight conversion to bank holding company status because it apparently couldn't last through the mandatory five-day waiting period to borrow money—it was posting the richest quarterly profit in its 140-year history. It simultaneously announced that it had already set aside $11.4 billion for bonuses and compensation for 2009, a staggering amount that was hard to interpret as anything other than a giant "fuck you" to anyone who might suggest that more moderation was in order after the crisis.

That second-quarter profit number would prove to be the high-water mark for Goldman assholedom. From that point forward they would enter new territory, becoming involuntary characters in a media narrative they had little control over. The popular perception is that when the bank was forced to make its debut as a mainstream media pariah, it did a terrible job of it, with its executives proving themselves to be almost comically tone-deaf to public outrage over the bubble thievery they had come to represent.

That's one take on what happened. Since I personally had a role in this I'll offer my own take: Goldman's late-2009 media coming-out party wasn't nearly the disaster many people make it out to be. True, when forced to come out into the light a little, people like Lloyd Blankfein proved to be jaw-droppingly obnoxious douchebags who made you want to drive a fist through your TV set.

But they never really apologized and never renounced their Randian belief system, and despite all the criticism ended the year with $13 billion in profits that they got to keep every last dime of. Which sent a powerful message to the rest of the country: public sentiment, it turns out, is a financial irrelevancy.

Goldman's run of bad luck that summer really began with a *Wall Street Journal* exposé on Stephen Friedman's stock purchases. The *WSJ* story came out in the first week of May 2009, virtually simultaneously with the release of the stress test results. Friedman, at the time still the chairman of the New York Federal Reserve Bank, the most powerful of all the Fed branches and the primary regulator of Wall Street, resigned just days after the *Journal* story broke.

Right around that same time, there were three media stories that helped focus a swirl of seriously negative attention on the bank. My piece was one, *New York* magazine's Joe Hagan wrote another, and the third was a series of stories by a heretofore little-known blogger who went by the nom de plume of "Tyler Durden" on a blog called Zero Hedge.

Durden's blog was written in impenetrable Wall Street jargon, and the man himself—later outed by nosy reporters as an Eastern European trader who had been sanctioned by FINRA, the financial services industry regulator—was intimidating even to Wall Street insiders. "Zero Hedge, man, he makes my head hurt" was a typical comment from my Wall Street sources.

Beginning in early 2009 Durden had been on a jihad about Goldman, having sifted through trading data to make what he insisted was an airtight case proving that the bank's high-frequency or "flash" trading desk was engaged in some sort of large-scale manipulation of the New York Stock Exchange. Durden drew his conclusions by scrupulously analyzing trading data the NYSE released each week. So what happened? Naturally, the NYSE on June 24 changed its rules and stopped releasing the data, seemingly to protect Goldman from Zero Hedge's meddling. The NYSE memo reads:

The purpose of this Information Memo is to advise all member organizations that the New York Stock Exchange LLC ("NYSE") will be decommissioning the requirement to report program trading activity via the Daily Program Trading Report ("DPTR"), which was previously approved by the Securities and Exchange Commission (the "Commission").

The Zero Hedge war on Goldman became legend when his seemingly far-fetched conspiracy theories came sensationally true that summer. That's when a Russian Goldman employee named Sergey Aleynikov was alleged to have stolen the bank's computerized trading code. Aleynikov worked at precisely the desk Zero Hedge had accused of being involved in large-scale manipulations.

And indeed, in a court proceeding after Aleynikov's arrest, Assistant U.S. Attorney Joseph Facciponti reported that "the bank has raised the possibility that there is a danger that somebody who knew how to use this program could use it to manipulate markets in unfair ways." Yes, indeed, it could.

Hagan's piece, meanwhile, was damaging in other ways. Most notably, it reported that Goldman had very nearly gone out of business in the wake of the AIG disaster:

As the market continued to plunge and Goldman's stock price nose-dived, people inside the firm "were freaking out," says a former Goldman executive who maintains close ties to the company.

Many of the partners had borrowed against their Goldman stock in order to afford Park Avenue apartments, Hamptons vacation homes, and other accoutrements of the Goldman lifestyle. Margin calls were hitting staffers up and down the offices. The panic was so intense that when the stock dipped to $47 in intraday trading, Blankfein and Gary Cohn, the chief operating officer, came out of the executive suite to hover over traders on the floor, shocking people who'd rarely seen them there. They didn't want staffers cashing out of their stock holdings and further destroying the share price. (Even so, many did, with $700 million in employee stock liquidated in the first nine months of the crisis.)

Among other things, the significance of the Hagan piece was that it underscored just how completely Goldman's recent success was dependent upon taxpayers. Less than a year before, its executives had been panic selling their beach estates; now they were rolling in billions in profits, all thanks to you, me, and every other taxpayer in the country.

My contribution to this was to launch a debate over whether or not it was appropriate for a reputable mainstream media organization to publicly call Lloyd Blankfein a motherfucker. This was really what most of the "vampire squid" uproar boiled down to. The substance of most of the freak-outs by mainstream financial reporters and the bank itself over the *Rolling Stone* piece was oddly nonspecific. Goldman spokesman Lucas van Praag called the piece "vaguely entertaining" and "an hysterical compilation of conspiracy theories." Van Praag even made an attempt at humor, saying, "Notable ones missing are Goldman Sachs as the third shooter [in John F. Kennedy's assassination] and faking the first lunar landing."

But at no time did the bank ever deny any of the information in the piece. Their only real factual quibble was with the assertion that they were a major player in the mortgage market—the bank somewhat gleefully noted that its "former competitors," like the since-vaporized Bear Stearns, were much bigger players.

The bank didn't really bother with me at all—why would it need to?—but other financial reporters surely did. Overwhelmingly the theme of the criticism was not that my reporting was factually wrong, but that I'd missed the larger, meta-Randian truth, which is that while Goldman might be corrupt and might have used government influence to bail itself out, this was necessary for the country, because our best and our brightest must be saved at all costs. Otherwise, who would put bread on our tables? Gasparino, the CNBC tool, put it best:

> And thank God Paulson and Bernanke turned to Blankfein and not the editors at *Rolling Stone* for help. I hate to break it to everyone out there in a class-warfare mood, but if AIG is imploding and you're the government and you need help restructuring the company or figuring out ways the government can fix the problem, Goldman is a good place to start.

Gasparino said this in the midst of an article that was filled with an extraordinary series of concessions; he ended up agreeing with almost everything I wrote. Some examples:

> Was Blankfein in the room when they discussed this and how to save the system? Of course he was. Was Goldman saved from extinction in the process? Undoubtedly . . . Say what you want about the bailout—it was fast and dirty, but it was necessary . . . Of course the firm had conflicts of interest—given its exposure to AIG insured debt and all its connections in government—but so did just about everyone else in this sordid mess . . . No rational person can deny the fact that Goldman is benefiting from its status as a government protected bank, as it makes big bucks ($3 billion in just the second quarter alone), acting like a hedge fund just after getting bailed out by the feds, and using its status as a commercial bank to borrow cheaply and make huge bond market bets . . . Is Goldman too powerful? Maybe. Was it too big to fail back in September? Given the size of its balance sheet, Goldman's demise would have made Lehman's look insignificant.

There was a lot of stuff like this, where the people who were whaling away at me and *Rolling Stone* were continually conceding the factual parts of the argument but insisting that the wrongness was in the conclusions I was drawing. Megan McArdle of the *Atlantic* put it this way:

> No, [Taibbi's] facts are wrong, his conclusions are wrong, and only his discomfort with Goldman Sachs' role in our public life is correct . . . Or perhaps a better way to say it is that his facts are right, but the mini narratives are ludicrously wrong, which makes the meta narrative suspect.

And what I missed in the meta narrative, of course, is that Goldman Sachs, while perhaps corrupt, and too closely tied to government, and the recipient of far too much taxpayer support, was nonetheless not an appropriate target for anger because we just need them so badly to keep our ship afloat. Once this argument was out there it was only a matter of time before it was institutionalized in the *New York Times* in a column by the archpriest of American conventional wisdom, David Brooks. Brooks argued that the problem with critiques like mine was that while the financial crisis had many causes (including, he insisted with a straight face, the economic rise of China), we were just taking the easy way out—"with the populist narrative, you can just blame Goldman Sachs."

Again, Brooks never at any time took issue with any of the facts in the case against Goldman Sachs. In fact, he conceded them and insisted that this was actually the point, that it's precisely despite the ugly facts that we must indulge the Goldmans of the world. He summed up this point of view in an extraordinary passage:

> Political populists . . . can't seem to grasp that a politics based on punishing the elites won't produce a better-educated work force, more investment, more innovation or any of the other things required for progress and growth . . .
>
> Hamilton championed capital markets and Lincoln championed banks, not because they loved traders and bankers. They did it because they knew a vibrant capitalist economy would maximize opportunity for poor boys like themselves. They were willing to tolerate the excesses of traders because they understood that no institution is more likely to channel opportunity to new groups and new people than vigorous financial markets.

And that's basically what this argument came down to, in the end. It came down to an argument about class privilege. Yes, Goldman might be guilty of many things, they may even have stolen billions of your hard-earned tax dollars to buy themselves yachts and blowjobs, but we can't throw out the baby with the bathwater!

But things did shift a bit. The Narrative was wounded. The mainstream media act just like in the classic studies of herd animals: at the exact instant more than half of the herd makes a move to bolt, they all move. That's what happened in the summer of 2009: for a variety of reasons, including the Friedman and Aleynikov scandals, the tide of public opinion turned against Goldman. The same on-their-knees/at-your-throat media reversal that George Bush felt at the end of his term was now being experienced by the bank. And from there, the next year or so was like one long chorus of exposés about Goldman's behavior. Among the stories that came out:

- In August 2009, the *New York Times* reported that Treasury Secretary Paulson and Lloyd Blankfein were in regular telephone contact throughout the period of the AIG bailout, bolstering the case that Goldman had used its access to its former chief, Paulson, to secure the $13 billion it ultimately got through the AIG bailout. Humorously, the *Times* piece came out just weeks after Gasparino had derided as "the mother of all conspiracy theories" the notion that "during those dark days of 2008, right after the Lehman collapse, and with AIG on the verge of death, Blankfein picked up the phone and called his old partner, then–Treasury Secretary Hank Paulson, and asked to be bailed out."

- The financial services industry was faced with yet another potential catastrophe in early 2010 when some of the interest rate swaps Goldman had created for the nation of Greece blew up. The Greece scandal was a variation on a predatory scam that banks like Goldman and JPMorgan had been using to fleece municipalities in the United States for years; the swaps essentially allowed cities, counties, and countries to refinance their debt in a scheme that was very similar to the mortgage-refi schemes used by predatory lenders in the mid-2000s. The idea behind an interest rate swap, which is yet another type of unregulated derivative instrument, goes like this: a debtor who is paying variable-rate interest pays a bank like Goldman a fee in exchange for the security of fixed interest. In a simplified example, if you're paying a variable rate on a home loan, you go to Goldman and pay them to accept the variable risk; in return, they *swap* you a new fixed interest rate. The scheme allows politicians to kick their debts down the road years, and in some cases (e.g., in the case of Greece) to actually receive cash up front for doing the swap. Unbeknownst to its citizens, Greece had also traded away rights to airport and highway revenue to Goldman in exchange for its cash up front. In this case the Nostradamus was McArdle, who a half year before Greece blew up was reaming me for being too general in my description of Goldman's aggressive forays into the unregulated derivatives market. "At any rate," she wrote, "none of these derivatives have much to do with CDOs or CDSs; you might as well conflate stocks and bonds because they're both 'securities.' *No one, as far as I know, is now proposing that we need to curtail the use of interest rate swaps* [emphasis mine]."

- An earlier example of an interest rate swap disaster had been Jefferson County, Alabama, which in 2008 had been virtually bankrupted by a series of swap deals it entered into with JPMorgan, deals that forced the county to institute mass lay-offs and unpaid leave and left its residents facing a generation of massively inflated sewer bills. In a rare instance of restraint, Goldman was not actually involved with the JeffCo swap deals—but only because it had accepted a $3 million payment from JPMorgan to back off the kill and allow Morgan to do the deals all by itself. The revelations about Goldman's payoff in the Alabama disaster did not raise much public furor but were a classic example of what the bank was all about. "An open-and-shut case of anticompetitive behavior" is how Christopher "Kit" Taylor, the former chief regulator of the municipal bond industry, put it.

Finally, and most importantly, Goldman in the spring of 2010 was sued by the SEC in a hugely publicized case that sent shock waves rippling across Wall Street. The CliffsNotes version of the scandal: Back in 2007, a Harvard-educated hedge fund king named John Paulson (no relation to former Goldman CEO Hank Paulson) decided the housing boom was a mirage and looked for ways to bet against it. So he asked Goldman to work with him to put together a billion-dollar basket of crappy subprime investments he could bet against. Goldman complied, taking a $15 million fee to do the deal and letting Paulson choose some of the toxic mortgages in the portfolio, which would come to be called ABACUS.

Paulson specifically chose to jam into ABACUS adjustable-rate mortgages, mortgages lent to borrowers with low credit ratings, and mortgages from states like Florida, Arizona, Nevada, and California that had recently seen wild home price spikes. In metaphorical terms, Paulson was choosing, as sexual partners for future visitors to the Goldman bordello, a gang of IV drug users and hemophiliacs.

Then Goldman turned around and sold this same poisonous mortgage-backed stuff as good and healthy investments to its customers, in particular a pair of foreign banks—a German bank called IKB and a Dutch bank called ABN-AMRO.

Where Goldman broke the rules, according to the SEC, was in failing to disclose to these two customers the full nature of Paulson's involvement with the deal. Neither investor knew that the deal they were buying into had essentially been put together by a financial arsonist who was rooting for it all to burn down.

One quick humorous side note: the new revelations on ABACUS also helped to underscore Charlie Gasparino's Nostradamus act—he ridiculed the assertion in my piece that "Goldman likely committed 'securities fraud' because it later shorted the same mortgage bonds tied to subprime loans after it knew that billions it underwrote all those years were going bad." He scoffed: "Try proving that one."

Anyway, the SEC suit for the first time gave the general public a villain with a face. It was a wonderfully serendipitous thing that it ended up being the face of a Frenchman named Fabrice Tourre, the Goldman banker who had put together the ABACUS deal, who in almost every way was like a cartoon caricature of an entitled rich dickhead. With his styled hair, his neat, ferretlike manner, his expensive suits, and, well, his Frenchness, Tourre was a personage almost guaranteed to make all of America recoil in disgust, as from rotting cheese, once introduced to him. And introduced to him they would be, as the U.S. Senate called hearings on the ABACUS deal and dragged Tourre and other Goldman employees up on stage to be tele-tarred and feathered for the viewing public.

Through these hearings America got to hear a lot about how Goldman employees behaved in their own environment. They got to hear about Tourre bragging in an e-mail about how much money he was going to make on a deal that he knew was about to blow up and leave a huge omelet in the face of customers like the Dutch bank ABN-AMRO. "More and more leverage in the system. The whole building is about to collapse anytime now," he wrote. "Only potential survivor, the fabulous Fab . . . standing in the middle of all these complex, highly leveraged, exotic trades he created!"

They got to hear about e-mails between Goldman employees talking about other deals like ABACUS that they'd successfully dumped on unwitting clients—including a deal full of subprime trash called Timberwolf that the higher-ups in Goldman had instructed its sales force to unload with gusto. In one e-mail dated June 22, 2007, a Goldman executive named Tom Montag wrote to Daniel Sparks, head of the bank's mortgage division, and said, "Boy, that Timberwolf is one shitty deal."

Remarkably, just one week later, the Goldman sales staff was instructed to make selling the shitty Timberwolf deal a "top priority."

This whole exchange was aired out in the Senate permanent subcommittee on investigations, where chairman Carl Levin, in what was to become a defining moment in the history of Goldman, continually hammered Sparks about selling that "shitty deal."

"You knew it was a shitty deal and that's what your e-mails show," Levin barked. "How much of this shitty deal did you continue to sell to your clients?"

Sparks, like most of the Goldman witnesses who appeared during the hearings, was blatantly evasive and refused to answer. He kept interrupting Levin—whose famed comb-over was practically shaking with anger as he repeated the word "shitty" twelve times, certainly a first for the Senate—and trying to soften the impact of these revelations by asking the senator to consider "some context."

"Some context might be helpful . . . ," Sparks muttered.

Even the audience in the Senate hall twittered at Sparks's continual niggling about context. In fact, the audience literally giggled when Levin read off the July 1, 2007, e-mail instructing the Goldman sales team to make selling Timberwolf a "top priority." The laugh was notable because a year before it would have been unthinkable to imagine a gallery of reporters and observers in a Senate committee hearing being tuned in to Wall Street practices enough to *laugh* at the outrageousness of a bank pushing its sales staff to unload exotic mortgage-backed securities just a week after its executives were e-joking to each other about what a "shitty" product they'd created. At that moment, on some level, the truth about what Goldman and banks like it do to make their money became mainstream.

Goldman survived the initial uproar over the scandal; in fact, although its share price dipped 12.8 percent on the day the SEC filed its suit, the share price jumped back up on the next trading day. A few days after that, Goldman announced a first-quarter profit of $3.46 billion. The bank was still cruising, although its reputation had clearly taken a hit. Over the next months investors gradually began to flee the company, which had been outed not for screwing the taxpayer or mom-and-pop investors, but its own *clients*. Goldman ended up losing nearly $8 billion in share value between the date the suit was announced and the date that it ultimately settled with the SEC later in the summer of 2010 for $550 million—a record fine, but one that nonetheless represented just a fraction even of Goldman's first-quarter profits that year. In fact, news that the SEC fine wasn't larger (many analysts expected it to be over a billion dollars) sent Goldman's stock price soaring back up 9 percent in one day; the bank recovered over $550 million in share value the day the fine was announced.

Nonetheless, the bank's image took such a hit that during the debate on the Senate floor over the Financial Regulatory Reform bill, senators from both parties were invoking the firm's name as a way of disparaging the bill. I was in the Senate chamber one day listening as ant-brained Wyoming Republican Mike Enzi was (incorrectly, I should point out) railing against the regulatory bill on the grounds that it was something Wall Street banks wanted. "Why, Goldman Sachs *likes* this bill!" he boomed. A year or two before, it would have been impossible to imagine a Republican senator saying that something Goldman Sachs wanted had to be a bad thing.

All of these revelations helped solidify Goldman's status as the ultimate symbol of the devious, pompous, entitled criminality of the Bubble Era. Its pop-culture status was formalized when a new Michael Moore movie, *Capitalism: A Love Story,* featured a scene in which Moore wrapped Goldman's 85 Broad Street offices in crime scene tape.

Goldman's response to all of this was remarkable in its tone-deafness. At first it contented itself with mocking dismissals of the various attacks, but as time wore on it gradually became clear that some executives were genuinely wounded by the criticism. They didn't understand it; they really thought they were doing the right thing by rapaciously lunging after every buck within breathing distance.

The Senate testimony of its leading executives after the ABACUS deal was a remarkable demonstration of how insulated and clueless a group of people can become when they make too much money too quickly. In the most important public relations moment in the history of the firm, Blankfein stood up in the Senate and actually said, out loud, that he didn't think his company was obligated to tell his customers that they were being sold a defective product. "I don't think there is a disclosure obligation," Blankfein said, looking incredulous that the question was even being asked.

Even worse was the response of the mortgage chief Sparks, when asked by Carl Levin if he had any regrets. "Regret to me means something that you feel like you did wrong, and I don't have that," Sparks said. Asked a similar question, the French twit Tourre thought for a moment before replying, "I regret these e-mails. They reflect very bad on the firm and on myself. And, um, you know—I wish I hadn't sent those."

They were like a bunch of husbands caught bonking thousand-dollar hookers who, under questioning later on by their wives, could only admit to being sorry they got caught. Now, obviously for legal reasons alone the Goldman executives couldn't stand before the Senate and just admit to being sorry, to knowing they were wrong, to seeing the problem with selling "shitty deals" to clients without telling them.

So no one was surprised that they didn't make admissions; that would have been tantamount to surrendering in the lawsuit. But it was the tone that startled most people. If your wife catches you with another woman, every man knows, even if you're not sorry, you have to *act* sorry. You can't just stare back at her and say, "I don't get what you're so upset about."

And that's exactly how the Goldman executives behaved. It wasn't so much that they lied, it was that they seemed to think they were telling the truth. They seemed to really believe they were right. One Senate aide I talked to after the hearings was still laughing about it weeks later. "It's sort of like someone who goes outside with his fly open and then just walks all the way down the street with his balls hanging out," he said. "You think to yourself: doesn't this person have friends, a wife, *somebody* to tell him how bad he looks? It's like these guys really don't know."

Even before the Senate hearing, there was plenty of evidence of that. Goldman Sachs international adviser Brian Griffiths reached a new low in late 2009 when he told an audience at St. Paul's Cathedral in London that "the injunction of Jesus to love others as ourselves is an endorsement of self-interest" and "We have to tolerate the inequality as a way to achieving greater prosperity and opportunity for all."

Griffiths was followed in very short order by Lloyd Blankfein himself, who in a remarkable interview with the *Times* (London) doled out perhaps the quote of the year. From that piece:

Is it possible to make too much money? "Is it possible to have too much ambition? Is it possible to be too successful?" Blankfein shoots back. "I don't want people in this firm to think that they have accomplished as much for themselves as they can and go on vacation. As the guardian of the interests of the shareholders and, by the way, for the purposes of society, I'd like them to continue to do what they are doing. I don't want to put a cap on their ambition. It's hard for me to argue for a cap on their compensation."

So, it's business as usual, then, regardless of whether it makes most people howl at the moon with rage? Goldman Sachs, this pillar of the free market, breeder of super-citizens, object of envy and awe will go on raking it in, getting richer than God? An impish grin spreads across Blankfein's face. Call him a fat cat who mocks the public. Call him wicked. Call him what you will. He is, he says, just a banker "doing God's work."

The now-notorious "God's work" interview might have been the last straw, the thing that caused Goldman to forfeit for at least the near future any hope at rehabilitating its name with the general public, but here's the interesting thing. From their point of view: so what?

In retrospect the Brookses of the world were right about one thing: it is extremely easy just to point a finger at Goldman Sachs. At this point, it's easy to win a public relations fight with the bank, the same way it's easy to win the public relations battle against Stalin, Charlie Manson, Union Carbide, and syphilis—because what the bank does is indefensible. They're criminals. And if you put what they do in front of enough eyes, even Americans can't miss it.

So we know that now. So what? Now all our cards are on the table, and America and Wall Street are staring at each other like a married couple that has few secrets left between them. But knowing about something and being able to do anything about it are two different things.

Banks like Goldman remain largely shielded from the impact of public opinion because while the public's only link to power is through the clumsy and highly imperfect avenue of elections, a bank of this size has a whole network of intimate connections with direct access to policy. In many cases, their people are sitting in the relevant positions themselves. And while the public at best is left to press their elected representatives (who inevitably are heavily funded by these banks) for investigations or prosecutions to remedy offenses committed years ago, the bank has already moved on to five, six, seven new schemes since then, each shrouded in a layer of complexity that will take years for the public consciousness to even begin to penetrate.

But at least the mystique is gone. The drivers of the Great American Bubble Machine aren't producers, but takers, and we know that now—the only question is, what do we do about it?

EPILOGUE

Summer 2010: more financial crisis hearings in Washington, this time on the role of derivatives in causing the crash. It's almost a packed house in the cavernous fifth-floor Senate conference hall in the Dirksen building, but the crowd is very lobbyist-heavy—not much press. The Gulf oil spill is the big disaster drama now, as the world has mostly moved on from the finance story. A year ago, I was seeing a lot of campaign-trail types at financial hearings on the Hill; now I'm the only political reporter I recognize in the crowd.

The witness before the Financial Crisis Inquiry Commission is one Steve Kohlhagen, a former Cal-Berkeley professor. Back in the nineties and the first years of the 2000s, he headed the derivatives and risk management desk at First Union, the predecessor to Wachovia—a megabank that, thanks in no small part to the failure of its mortgage-backed derivative holdings, disappeared from the face of the earth two years ago.

A Wachovia guy. I wonder what *he'll* have to say about this mess.

The Wells Fargo–Wachovia merger was formally announced on October 12, 2008, the same day that Barack Obama had his infamous encounter with Samuel "Joe the Plumber" Wurzelbacher in Ohio. When the last McCain-Obama debate took place three days later in Hempstead, New York, there was plenty of talk about which candidate was a bigger buddy to middle America's plumbers, but neither man bothered to mention that week's sudden disappearance of the country's fourth-largest commercial bank. In fact, the Wachovia deal was one of many gigantic crisis stories the public never heard much about—the bank was a perfect symbol of the third-world-style oligarchical backroom mergers of public and private interests that became common after the crash.

When Wachovia's portfolio started to go up in smoke in the fall of 2008 thanks to the collapse of the housing boom, depositors started to pull money out of the bank. Seeing this, government officials like future Obama Treasury secretary Tim Geithner (then heading the New York Fed) and FDIC chief Sheila Bair declared the bank a "systemically important" institution, and started frantically searching for a buyer to rescue the firm.

Just like the JPMorgan Chase–Bear Stearns deal and the Bank of America–Merrill Lynch deal, in which taxpayers ended up subsidizing megamergers that left the banking sector even *more* concentrated and dangerous than before, in the Wachovia mess regulators like Geithner and Bair scrambled to find ways to use taxpayer money to bribe would-be buyers like Citigroup and Wells Fargo into swallowing up the troubled bank. They initially settled on a plan to use FDIC funds to subsidize a Citigroup rescue, but in early October backroom negotiations shifted and Wells Fargo announced that it was coming to Wachovia's rescue.

Wells Fargo had originally balked at rescuing Wachovia. But two things happened that changed the bank's mind. First, then–Treasury secretary Hank Paulson made a change in the tax code that promised to mean an almost $25 billion tax break for Wells Fargo. Then Congress passed the TARP bailout, which gave Wells Fargo a $25 billion cash injection. On October 3, the very same day the bailout passed, Wells Fargo decided it would help out the government and buy Wachovia after all, for a bargain price of $12.7 billion. The deal was formally announced a week or so later. "This is of course a very exciting moment in the long history of Wachovia and Wells Fargo," said Wells Fargo's chairman, Richard Kovacevich.

To recap: America's fourth-largest bank goes broke gambling on mortgages, then gets sold to Wells Fargo for $12.7 billion after the latter receives $50 billion in bailout cash and tax breaks from the government. The resulting postmerger bank is now the second-largest commercial bank in the country, and, presumably, significantly more "systemically important" than even Wachovia was. Fattened by all this bailout cash, incidentally, postmerger Wells Fargo would end up paying out $977 million in bonuses for 2008.

Steve Kohlhagen, the witness at the FCIC hearing, has nothing to do with any of this, of course—he left First Union way back in George W. Bush's first term. But as the former derivatives chief of one of the largest derivatives merchants in the country, he'll certainly be worth listening to. Even if he isn't directly guilty, I think, maybe Kohlhagen will break down weeping and confessing anyway, admitting that he sent Wachovia down the road to ruin by cramming its books full of deadly mortgage-backed CDOs. Or maybe he'll apologize on behalf of Wachovia for forcing the American taxpayer to have to pay off Wells Fargo by the tens of billions to take flat-broke, disfigured Wachovia to the altar.

Or maybe not. After FCIC chairman Phil Angelides stumbles while introducing Kohlhagen—he forgets to call him "Doctor"—the former Wachovia chief leans forward and shakes his head generously. " 'Mister' is fine," he says.

Then he starts in about the causes of the financial crisis. Kohlhagen's first point is that over-the-counter derivatives like the mortgage-backed CDOs that sank Wachovia and the credit default swaps that killed AIG had "absolutely no role whatsoever in causing the financial crisis."

Uh-huh. He's entitled to his opinion, I guess. But then he goes on:

"The cause of the financial crisis," he says, "was quite simply the commitment by the United States government to bring home ownership to the next group of people who previously had not been able to own their own homes."

There it is. The financial crisis, you see, had nothing to do with huge aggrandized financial institutions borrowing vast fuckloads of money and gambling it all away, knowing that the government would have to swoop in and rescue them if they failed. No, what sank the economy was poor black people who were pushed into buying houses they couldn't afford by the government.

You have to have truly giant balls to stand up in a senatorial hearing room after your old bank was rescued by a $50 billion government bailout effort and blame the financial crisis on poor people on welfare, which is essentially what Kohlhagen was doing.

A few minutes later, the next witness, Albert "Pete" Kyle, a professor of finance at the University of Maryland, offered his analysis of the crisis. He cited as one of the chief causes "government mandates for home ownership," and said that, in the way of a solution, we "need less emphasis on home ownership as an intrinsically desirable social goal undertaken for its own sake."

After a few hours of this—multiple witnesses and even some of the commissioners sounded similar themes—I started laughing a little. In America, every political issue, no matter how complicated, ultimately takes the same silly ride down the same rhetorical water slide. Complex social and economic phenomena are chopped up into pairs of easy-to-digest sound bites, with one T-shirt slogan for the Fox News crowd and one for the Democrats. And here in this FCIC hearing, two years after the crisis, it struck me that the two sides had finally settled on their T-shirt interpretations of the crash era.

The Republicans were going with this goofy story the Kohlhagens of the world were dumping on the public, that the financial crisis was caused by lazy poor people living in too much house. If you scratched the surface of Republican rhetoric two years later, that's really all it was—a lot of whining about the Community Reinvestment Act of 1977 and Fannie and Freddie, with *social engineering* being the dog-whistle code words describing government aid to minorities. "Private enterprise mixed with social engineering" was how Alabama senator Richard Shelby put it.

The Democrats' line was a little more complicated. They had no problem publicly pointing the finger at companies like Goldman Sachs as culprits in the mess, although behind closed doors, of course, it was Democratic officials like Geithner who were carrying water for Wall Street all along, arranging sweetheart deals like the Wachovia rescue and the Citigroup bailout (notable because Geithner's ex-boss, former Clinton Treasury secretary Bob Rubin, was a big Citi exec). Barack Obama talked a big game about Wall Street, but after he got elected he hired scads of Goldman and Citi executives to run economic policy out of his White House, and his reform bill ended up being a Swiss cheese shot through with preposterous loopholes. The Democrats' response to Wall Street excess was similar to their attitude toward the Iraq War—they were against it in theory, but in practice, they weren't going to do much about it.

A few weeks after that FCIC hearing, there were a few more punctuation-mark moments in the history of the financial crisis. The aforementioned Dodd-Frank financial reform bill, a fiasco that would do nothing to stop too-big-to-fail companies from gambling with America's money, passed and became law. And the SEC settled with Goldman Sachs for $550 million in the infamous ABACUS case, a move that was widely interpreted by Wall Street as the final shoe to be dropped in the area of postcrisis enforcement and punishment. The market had been down 100 points on the day the settlement was announced; it scrambled back to a loss of just 7 by the end of the day, buoyed by the Street-wide sense that there were no more enforcement actions coming. We were going back to business as usual.

Everyone, it seemed, wanted this story to be over. The reason was obvious. The financial crisis had been far too complicated and messy to fit into the usual left-right sound bites. It was a story that for a short but definite period of time had forced the monster of American oligarchy out from below the ocean surface and onto the beach, for everyone to see.

When the economy imploded, the country had for a time been treated to the rare spectacle of a perfectly bipartisan political disaster, with both Republicans and Democrats sharing equally in the decades-long effort at deregulation that opened the door to the Grifter era. And the crisis forced a nation of people accustomed to thinking that their only political decisions came once every four years to consider, for really the first time, the political import of regular or even daily items like interest rates, gasoline prices, ATM fees, and FICO scores.

The powers that be don't want people thinking about any of these things. If the people must politick, then let them do it in the proper arena, in elections between Wall Street–sponsored Democrats and Wall Street–sponsored Republicans. They want half the country lined up like the Tea Partiers against overweening government power, and the other half, the Huffington Post crowd, railing against corporate excess. But don't let the two sides start thinking about the bigger picture and wondering if the real problem might be a combination of the two.

Americans like their politics simple, but Griftopia is as hard as it gets—a huge labyrinth of financial rules and bylaws within which a few thousand bankers and operators bleed millions of customers dry using financial instruments that are far too complex to explain on the evening news. Navigating this mess requires a hell of a lot of effort and attention, and few politicians in either party have any appetite at all for helping ordinary people make that journey. In fact, the situation is just the opposite: they'd rather we latched on to transparently stupid Band-Aid explanations for what happened in 2008, blaming it on black homeowners or bad luck or a few very bad apples in companies like AIG.

By the time this book hits the shelves, the 2010 midterm elections will be upon us, at which time this dumbing-down process with regard to the public perception of the financial catastrophe should be more or less complete. The Tea Party and its ilk will have found a way to push the national conversation in the desired idiotic direction. Instead of talking about what to do about the fact that, after all the mergers in the crisis, just four banks now account for half of the country's mortgages and two-thirds of its credit card accounts, we'll be debating whether or not we should still automatically grant citizenship to the American-born children of illegal immigrants, or should let Arizona institute a pass-law regime, or some such thing.

Meanwhile, half a world away, in little-advertised meetings of international bankers in Basel, Switzerland, the financial services industry will be settling on new capital standards for the world's banks. And here at home, bodies like the CFTC and the Treasury will be slowly, agonizingly making supertechnical decisions on regulatory questions like "Who exactly will be subject to the new Consumer Financial Protection Bureau?" and "What kinds of activities will be covered by the partial ban on proprietary trading?"

On these real meat-and-potatoes questions about how to set the rules for modern business, most ordinary people won't have a voice at all; they won't even be aware that these decisions are being made. But industry lobbyists are already positioning themselves to have a behind-the-scenes impact on the new rules. While the rest of us argue about Mexican babies before the midterms, hotshot DC law firms like Skadden, Arps, Slate, Meagher & Flom may have as many as a hundred lawyers working on the unresolved questions in the Dodd-Frank bill. And that's just one firm. Thousands of lobbyists will be employed; millions of lobbying dollars will be spent.

This is how America works. Our real government is mostly kept hidden from view, and the truly weighty decisions about where our society is going and what rules it is going to live by are made mostly in private, by groups of anonymous lawyers and bureaucrats and lobbyists, government officials and industry reps alike.

As the crisis fades even further from public memory, it seems more and more likely that a whole range of monstrous and disturbing questions raised by the events of the last few years will go unanswered. The Wachovia deal was just one of a handful of massive interventions in the so-called private economy that were seemingly executed, in the proverbial smoke-filled back room, by a few dozen state officials in conjunction with a few counterparts on the private business side.

A few brief months in 2008 saw the following, among other things:

1. In March 2008, Treasury Secretary Henry Paulson put a shotgun to the head of dying Bear Stearns and forced it to sell out to JPMorgan Chase at the absurdly low price of $2 a share (later raised to $10 a share). Chase also got $30 billion in federal guarantees to take the deal. The $2-a-share number was so low that Morgan Stanley CEO John Mack, when he heard the news, publicly wondered aloud if it was a typo and the real number was $20 a share. A few months later, the FDIC seized failing commercial bank Washington Mutual, Inc., and immediately sold it to Chase for the comparably ridiculous price of $1.9 billion; Washington Mutual would later sue, claiming that the FDIC and Morgan conspired to lower WMI's sale price for Morgan.

2. Paulson, a former Goldman Sachs employee, was in
   constant telephone contact with Goldman's new CEO,
   Lloyd Blankfein, during a period in which Paulson was
   negotiating the AIG bailout, which of course led to at least
   $13 billion being transferred directly to Goldman Sachs, a
   major AIG counterparty.
3. Around the same time as the September AIG deal, Bank of
   America entered into a state-aided agreement to buy
   foundering Merrill Lynch, a company run by yet another
   ex-Goldmanite, the notorious asshole John Thain, who had
   become famous for buying an $87,000 rug for his office as
   his company quickly went broke thanks to its reckless
   mortgage gambling.

   A few months later, in December 2008, B of A chief
   Ken Lewis discovered that Merrill had billions in
   previously unreported losses and tried to back out of the
   deal. He then went to Washington and had a discussion
   with Paulson, who apparently threatened to remove both
   the company's management and its board if he didn't do
   the deal. Lewis, whose bank had gotten some $25 billion
   in cash via the TARP bailout, emerged from that meeting
   with Paulson suddenly determined once again to go
   through with the shotgun wedding. A month or so later,
   Bank of America shareholders learned for the first time
   about the billions in losses and about the millions in last-
   minute bonuses paid out by Thain after shareholders
   voted—in one case, Thain paid former Goldman
   executive Peter Kraus a $25 million bonus on Merrill's
   last days even though Kraus had only been at Merrill for
   a few months.

   Lewis had since been placed under investigation, with
   New York attorney general Andrew Cuomo alleging that
   Lewis withheld information about the Merrill losses from
   shareholders at the direction of Paulson and Fed chief Ben
   Bernanke. "I was instructed that 'we do not want a public
   disclosure,'" Lewis said.

There were other stories. The seemingly fortuitous late September 2008 coincidence of Warren Buffett deciding to pledge $5 billion to a then-foundering Goldman Sachs during the same week that the bank was miraculously rescued from possible bankruptcy by Geithner's decision to allow it to convert overnight to bank holding company status—a decision that allowed Goldman to borrow mountains of free cash from the Fed. Or how about Barack Obama putting a sitting Citigroup official (Michael Froman) in charge of his economic transition team right at the time a ridiculously generous federal bailout of Citigroup was being negotiated by Geithner—whose appointment as Treasury secretary was announced the very day the Citi bailout was concluded?

You put all of these stories together and what you get is a bizarre snapshot of a national economy in which the old Adam Smith capitalist notion of companies succeeding or failing on their merits, with the price of their assets determined entirely by the market, was tossed out the window. In its place was a system in which mergers and bankruptcies were brokered not by the market, but by government officials like Paulson and Geithner and Bernanke, and prices of assets were determined not by what investors were willing to pay, but by the level of political influence of the company's leaders.

At the outset of 2008, the five biggest investment banks in America were Morgan Stanley, Goldman, Bear Stearns, Lehman Brothers, and Merrill Lynch; by the end of the year, Morgan and Goldman had been rescued by late-night conversions to commercial bank status, Bear Stearns had been hand-delivered to JPMorgan Chase, bastard child Merrill Lynch and its billions in gambling losses had been forced on sorry-ass Bank of America, and Lehman Brothers had been allowed to die by Hank Paulson. The resulting financial landscape was far more concentrated than before, in both the investment banking sector (where the collapse of Bear, Merrill, and Lehman left Morgan and Goldman ascendant) and the commercial banking sector (since the crisis, Chase, Wells Fargo, and Bank of America all exceed the legal size limit of 10 percent of all American deposits).

A few years later, a country whose citizens purport to be mad as hell about growing government influence has still said little to nothing about that bizarre sequence of events in which the entire economy was rebuilt via this series of back-alley state-brokered mergers, which left financial power in America in the hands of just a few mostly unaccountable actors on Wall Street. We still know very little about what really went on during this period, who was calling whom, what bank was promised what. We need to see phone records, e-mails, correspondence, the minutes of meetings; we need to know what the likes of Paulson and Geithner and Bernanke were doing during those key stretches of 2008.

But we probably never will, because the country increasingly is forgetting that any of this took place. The ability of its citizens to lose focus so quickly and to be distracted by everything from Lebronamania to the immigration debate is part of what makes America so ripe for this particular type of corporate crime. We have voters who don't pay attention, a news media that either ignores key subjects or willfully misunderstands them, and a regulatory environment that bends easily to lobbying and campaign financing efforts. And we've got a superpower's worth of accumulated wealth that is still there for the taking. You put all that together, and what you get is a thieves' paradise—a Griftopia.

New for the Paperback Edition
The Grift Goes On

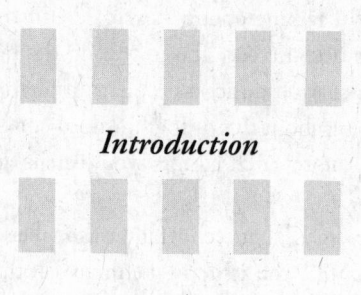

Introduction

EARLY IN FEBRUARY of 2011 I had an interesting experience, one of those revealing behind-the-scenes journalism stories that unfortunately are rarely shared with readers. Just in the course of a few days of trying to do my job, I learned almost as much about how Wall Street works as I had in years of research up to that point.

At the time, I was working on a story that asked a simple question: Why hadn't anyone from Wall Street gone to jail in the wake of the financial crisis? It was a difficult subject to write about from a legal standpoint because the very premise of the story was loaded with uncomfortable implications. Nothing makes your average libel-defense lawyer more nervous than calling a well-represented rich person who has been officially cleared of wrongdoing a criminal who should be in jail.

The story I wrote focused on a number of cases involving prominent Wall Street figures who had been enmeshed in scandal and had whistleblowers and witnesses coming forward against them, but had been let off the hook by the SEC and the Justice Department. These were people like Richard "the Gorilla" Fuld of now-defunct Lehman Brothers, the nebbishy former head of AIG Financial Products Joe Cassano (prominently featured in chapter 3 of this book), and current Morgan Stanley chairman of the board John Mack—among others.

It was a long piece and the fact-checking process was unusually difficult, as we struggled to settle on language that was both accurate and legally defensible in talking about these cases. In the best of circumstances my nerves become very frayed during the fact-checking stage, but in this case I began to notice a peculiar problem with the material. We would be writing about this or that misdeed committed by a certain bank, and one of the research editors would make a superficially very sensible objection.

"But the problem is, that technically wasn't illegal," they'd say.

Take, for example, the issue of Lehman Brothers' use of instruments called "Repo 105s" to hide billions in losses. In that case, the bank took assets on its balance sheet, for instance bundles of securities, and parked them in the hands of certain business partners like UBS. In return, those counterparties would send Lehman billions in cash. This was usually done toward the end of a quarter, and Lehman would record those transactions as "true sales," marking the incoming cash as revenue from honest business transactions. Investors would think the bank had tens of billions of cash revenue from sales of assets.

But as soon as the quarter was over, Lehman would return the money and take back its assets, sending its counterparties a small carrying charge for their trouble. This is like parking your worthless old '83 Grand Am in your neighbor's garage at the end of every month before rent day, borrowing $1,500 to pay the rent from said neighbor, then paying the rent with that cash—then scrambling to repay the money in order to get your car back at the beginning of the next month.

Thus these "repurchase agreements," the Repo 105s, were not in fact sales but loans; Lehman was essentially borrowing tens of billions of dollars at the end of every quarter, using that cash as pancake makeup to gloss over its shaky balance sheet before trotting out its quarterly report for investors to see. Metaphorically speaking, Lehman was claiming that it sold that worthless old car for $1,500, a real sale, when in fact the neighbor was just holding it for collateral.

In the heat of the bubble era, as the bank's insane debt and leverage levels began to overwhelm the company, Lehman repeatedly used these Repo 105 deals to hide the truth about its condition from the outside world. In order to do so, though, it needed accomplices who would sign off on its bad math. The bank shopped these transactions around to various accounting firms and were rejected each time; only Ernst & Young, in the end, agreed to give them an opinion that the transactions were legal (and even then, they had to go overseas to find a law firm that would bless the deals). Thus when Lehman Brothers decided to hide as much as $50 billion in loans each quarter, it had an opinion from both a prominent law firm (the British firm Linklaters) and a major accounting firm (Ernst & Young) that what it was doing was legal, even though executives internally knew they had gone down a very dubious road. Bart McDade, the company's COO at the time, called the Repo 105 transactions "another drug we R on."

By the time I sat down to write about this, the story had been documented quite extensively in public, with a bankruptcy examiner named Anton Valukas explaining everything in a 2,200-page report that was released in March of 2009. But even within the offices of *Rolling Stone* we were having a hard time finding a way to publish the routine assertion that Lehman had done something wrong, because the bank had essentially bought itself an opinion that what it had done was legal.

Within our offices, everyone from the fact-checkers to the editors knew what had gone on here—Lehman Brothers had prettied up its balance sheet using sham transactions—but the issue here was not truth, but legal pull. Absent an SEC case or a successful criminal prosecution against Lehman, there was no easy way to say in print that Lehman and/or Ernst & Young had committed a crime without inviting a potential court case with those parties.

And here we came into conflict with another one of the key points of the story—which was that the lawyers these banks and finance companies hire are not just the best in the country, they also inevitably are all, themselves, former high-ranking prosecutors and regulators. Even thinking about opposing these people is nerve-racking, because they have home-court advantage in the justice system, or what's left of it; everyone from judges to current officials and regulators are former colleagues of theirs.

Anyway, a few days before we went to press with "Why Isn't Wall Street in Jail?" I made a routine call to the attorney for another one of our article subjects, asking if he wanted to comment on what we were writing. Not that we don't always call for comment, but in this case it was sort of a must; given the legal sensitivity of the material, we wanted to make sure we had everything absolutely correct. This was true even though the article was not going to be breaking news; all we were doing was recounting what had already been written about this person in the government's own highly tame official history of the financial crisis, the Financial Crisis Inquiry Commission report.

The attorney in question was, like many of the attorneys in these instances, a former law enforcement official, in this case a former federal prosecutor. When I spoke with him on the phone the first time, he told me that he was going to "insist" that *Rolling Stone* publish, in full, a statement on his client's behalf. Well, okay, we'll take it into consideration, I said.

The attorney instantly became emotional. He told me that if I would not agree to print his statement in full, he *demanded* to speak to my editor—and that if I didn't comply, we would be in a place where "we weren't being helpful to each other." That last phrase instantly sent me hurtling into asshole-pucker mode. One doesn't like to think of a former federal prosecutor drifting into an "unhelpful" frame of mind with regard to your physical person.

In the interest of hearing out all sides and making sure we had our facts right, we eventually had an audience with said lawyer and his assistant at the *Rolling Stone* offices. This was a lot of fuss for a relatively small section of a magazine piece that, again, was not covering any new ground at all. The crux of what we were saying about the attorney's client was simple—we were asserting that the former Wall Street executive had engaged in a certain common financial transaction, then later misled investors about it. For the purposes of this book, let's just say that I was writing that the executive had at one point in a fiscal quarter *sat down* in his living room and later told investors he had been *standing* the entire time.

The attorney took out sheets of paper with all sorts of arguments. You will see in the first tab, he said, that all the relevant parties have agreed that the piece of furniture shown in this photo of the living room is *not a chair*, but in fact *an item for resting continually*. Here in tab 2, he went on, you will see that under section 105-D slash 97 dot X of the federal code, *sitting* is defined as something that "takes place in a chair," and I think you will agree that since the undersigned parties agreed at the outset that the item of furniture pictured was in fact *not* a chair, it cannot be said that my client was ever, in fact, sitting. In tab 3, you will see that an independent auditor asserts that my client is not an expert on sitting, and therefore cannot be held responsible for making statements about sitting in public . . .

This went on for nearly twenty minutes. Almost nothing the attorney said had any relevance at all to what we were writing about, but purely from a spectator's standpoint, it was a mesmerizing performance—bullshit, all of it, but brilliant bullshit, like watching a Kobe or MJ of lawyering go through a layup line. As the meeting went on, it occurred to me that this same attorney had at some point in the last years given the exact same pitch to the government investigators who had targeted his Richie Rich client and apparently had convinced them. This bullshit, in other words, had worked! This surely was an incredible indictment of someone up in the regulatory ranks.

Later, when we pressed him on a certain point, returning to an incontrovertible instance of his client's questionable behavior, he frowned. "Look, you're a magazine committed to social justice," he said. "And that has to apply to everybody, rich and poor." After hearing out the attorney on all his points, we went back over that portion of the story one more time with a fine-toothed comb. Because we had already fact-checked it so carefully, all that was needed was to rework our phraseology in a couple of places. But the point is, even just to repeat what the government itself has already concluded about these Wall Street characters, one has to be incredibly careful.

This whole question of regulation and criminal justice is a matter of who has the best lawyers, and who *are* the lawyers. The simple truth is that Wall Street owns all the best lawyers, and even the ones who aren't in private practice yet soon will be, and they know it. Even if they start out as prosecutors ostensibly representing ordinary people, they will sooner or later become millionaire defense flacks like the one who visited our offices, using their considerable legal skills to throw up thick binders full of fiendish bulwarks to any kind of assertion of wrongdoing.

The reason I tell this story is to explain how it is that so much can have gone wrong, and yet no one has been held responsible. The law is a fungible thing: no matter what is actually written on the books, people in positions of responsibility have to at least generally agree as to what the laws are in order for them to have any practical effect. And if a big enough group of influential people collectively decides that there's nothing illegal per se about hiding billions in debts from investors, or defrauding homeowners with predatory mortgages, or making born-to-lose derivative deals and selling them to foreign banks as AAA-rated investments, then that consensus affects everyone. It seeps into the SEC and the Department of Justice, which is staffed with once and future employees of the big legal defense firms, where this consensus was born in the first place.

And it bleeds far enough into the public consciousness that even within the walls of a magazine like *Rolling Stone*, the mere decision to call these frauds and thefts wrong and illegal and deserving of punishment is highly controversial—even in our own minds, in the minds of politically conscious, liberal-arts-educated lefties, it's hard to take that step. It's not just the threat of a lawsuit you have to overcome, although that's certainly a real enough problem; it's that this consensus has dominated the intellectual atmosphere for so long that you end up double- and triple-checking yourself before leveling any kind of accusation of criminality upward. On the other hand, when you think about the crimes committed by people on the street, about guys selling eight-balls of coke in alleys and ripping stereos out of cars, your mind shifts instantly to punishment and arrest. There's no intellectual obstacle stifling the instinct for punishment and justice.

If I might make a quick digression here, think for instance in comparison about the American attitude toward the sale of drugs. Street dealing is a strictly economic activity voluntarily undertaken by two consenting adults. It's against the law here, but one could make the argument that that's purely an accident of history; it's not illegal everywhere in the world, and selling some of the same drugs one hundred years ago was legal even in this country. But in the last century or so, the sale of narcotics in America has been broadly criminalized and a massive police apparatus has grown up around this now-illegal business, which very conveniently is often the chief commercial activity driving the economies of poor and nonwhite neighborhoods.

That selling drugs and taking drugs is not widely considered inherently *wrong* is proven by the fact that large majorities of the population, including at least a few presidents, have guiltlessly engaged in the activity. If you're white and have money, the chances are very good that you smoked pot from high school on and dabbled at least occasionally in harder stuff somewhere along the line. But do you think of yourself as a criminal? Absolutely not. It just happens to be widely understood that a certain type of nonviolent economic activity is technically illegal in our society and if you want to be sure of avoiding punishment for engaging in it, you can't do it openly if you're on the campus of Harvard or Penn State, and probably not at all if you live on a heavily patrolled street in the Bronx or East St. Louis.

To me this is no different from the laws against selling rabbit hats or blue jeans, or changing money, that I experienced as a college student in the Soviet Union. While the buying and selling of black-market goods was so pervasive and morally accepted that party members and other high-ranking officials didn't worry at all about wearing Western clothes in public (Raisa's furs and Misha's tailored suits come to mind), all the same there was a giant police force ready to jail you if you were caught selling, say, a pair of Dutch dress socks to a tourist in Red Square. While most Russian citizens understood that there wasn't anything morally wrong with these activities, few people questioned it whenever the police hauled away a *farsovshik* (black marketeer) to do time. That's just the way things were. It was just generally understood that when it came to buying and selling black-market consumer goods, what was okay for a party secretary to do in a back room of the Dom

Modelei was not okay for a broke twenty-year-old student to do on the streets of Leningrad.

What does any of this have to do with financial crime in modern America? Well, after the crisis hit, and the whole country was rocked by job losses and foreclosures and soaring commodity prices, the general public was still, overwhelmingly, hesitant to demand punishment for the people responsible. From coast to coast, the mere suggestion that powerful bankers should go to jail for technical infractions like lying to investors and hiding losses and front-running client trades met an immovable wall of public skepticism. "Are those activities really *crimes*?" people continually asked. "Isn't that just being greedy? Can you really put people in jail for *trying to make money*?"

Again, think of the contrast with drug dealing. Man sells bag of dope on the streets of Harlem; an economic transaction between two consenting adults, with no third-party victims involved anywhere. But when a banker sells a million dollars (or ten or a hundred million dollars) of mismarked mortgage bank securities to a pension fund, you don't have two consenting adults. The buyer of the securities is obviously unaware that he's acquiring an essentially counterfeit property, that his fund is going to lose that money. And there are third-party victims galore; all the pensioners or other investors are going to see their savings disappear.

But people still can't wrap their heads around the idea that this highly destructive transaction is a jailable offense. In the extreme form of the argument in defense of the bankers who engaged in that activity, it is said that these deals were legal because it cannot be conclusively proven that the bankers selling this dreck knew that the goods they were trading were worthless and dangerous.

The notion that these bankers didn't know that what they were selling was toxic is, empirically speaking, absurd on its face—there were pools of mortgages that banks like Goldman were selling where more than 50 percent of the borrowers didn't show ID when taking out their loans, and other pools where borrowers had collectively put less than 1 percent cash down on nearly a billion dollars of home loans. Not even the dumbest trader could ever genuinely believe that 60 percent or 70 percent of a pool full of borrowers with no ID buying houses with no money down could be investment-grade securities. But the defenders of these bankers still insist that there can't be a crime without concrete proof of the bankers' mental state when selling those properties.

Again, imagine a drug dealer busted for selling a bag of Drāno instead of heroin arguing, with a straight face, that he *didn't know* that his product was harmful to his buyers. Think that would go over well? And let's say a dozen people end up sick and dying in the hospital because of the stuff he sold: can you imagine anyone arguing that said dealer still can't be prosecuted without proof of his mental state? This is where we are with financial crime. Millions of people around the world lost huge chunks of their life savings to these deals, but still we insist that we cannot punish the dealer without knowing for sure what was in his head when he sold us that financial Drāno.

Well, so be it: let's say now that we have to have proof of their mental state. Here's some proof, right along those lines—the officials from the two Bear Stearns subprime hedge funds that ultimately blew up their company. We know, because we've seen the e-mails that were admitted into evidence at their trials, that Ralph Cioffi and Matthew Tannin knew their fund full of subprime junk was toxic long before they stopped selling it to investors. In April 2007, long before the funds blew up, Tannin wrote an e-mail to Cioffi, saying, "I think we should close the funds now . . . The entire subprime market is toast."

He also wrote this: "The subprime market looks pretty damn ugly . . . If AAA bonds are systematically downgraded then there is simply no way for us to make money—ever." Three days later, he was telling investors that he was "very comfortable with exactly where we are" and "there's no basis for thinking this is one big disaster."

Investors in the Bear hedge funds ended up losing, collectively, $1.6 *billion* dollars. This is exactly what a Wall Street crime looks like: financial players lying to investors, with documentary evidence to prove it. Yet a jury found both Cioffi and Tannin not guilty. This was a rare case of the failure of justice not being the fault of a conspiracy of powerful political interests and captive regulators; this fuckup was on ordinary people in a jury box, who could not bring themselves to see the Bear funds' collapse as a punishable crime.

That the subprime instruments Cioffi and Tannin were selling in the first place were essentially worthless counterfeit marketed as rock-solid, perfectly hedged investments—Drāno sold as dope—never even entered into the equation. The government focused entirely on the "mental state" issue and jurors couldn't see the crime. The state even had the e-mails proving that these rich hustlers knew they were piloting a financial *Titanic* and repeatedly failed to tell their passengers to head for the lifeboats. And it wasn't enough.

After the acquittal in the Bear case there was widespread criticism of the Department of Justice for even subjecting poor Cioffi and Tannin to a trial. Wasn't it enough that they went through the shame of seeing their funds blow up? (A side note: This "on Wall Street, shame is enough" argument is incredibly common. I even had a high-ranking financial regulator tell me privately once that the absurdly small $80,000 and $100,000 fines for two Citigroup officials caught hiding billions in liabilities was appropriate because "just bringing a case against the CFO of a company like Citigroup is a really big deal.")

A law professor at the University of Illinois summed up the consensus on the Bear case nicely. He said the Bear fiasco was about "standard business dealings where the views of the markets were shifting rapidly and these guys were being criminally punished for expressing views on one day and acting differently another day." He added: "This never should have been the subject of a criminal prosecution."

In the end, the only things that made the crimes of these people difficult for the public to see were the identities of the potential defendants. In almost any other arena, fraud is loathed and despised as not merely a technically illegal economic activity like selling rabbit hats in Red Square, or selling weed in Washington Square. Rather, it's understood to be a dangerous and destructive crime with victims who really suffer.

Even when "Crazy" Eddie Antar was caught scamming investors by filling warehouses with empty boxes when auditors inspected his "inventory," there was no call from the public to let good old Crazy Eddie off because he was "just trying to make money" and engaging in "standard business dealings where the views of the markets were shifting rapidly." People understood that Eddie Antar was a rip-off artist, and it came as no surprise when it was learned that he was involved in all sorts of other crimes, from jiggering the digits on his financial reports to putting used merchandise in new boxes.

Yet the remarkable thing about the Wall Street crime wave was the way the public almost unanimously rushed to make excuses for the people who had committed these offenses. There was an almost universal belief that while some of what these bankers did was shady and demonstrated perhaps unhealthy amounts of greed, their transactions were technically legal and certainly not bad enough to make jail time necessary.

This public faith in the essential legality of Wall Street's business model not only allowed bankers to escape scrutiny for the broad fraud scheme of the mortgage bubble. It also somehow shielded these same people from scrutiny when, just like in the Crazy Eddie case, it subsequently came out that most of them were also engaging in all sorts of other crimes, from outright bribery (i.e., in Jefferson County, Alabama; see page 265) to insider trading (countless cases from Galleon on down) to hiding income (i.e., Lehman CEO Dick Fuld, among others) to Enronesque accounting irregularities (the Repo 105 transactions) to systematic front-running (which became epidemic during the bailout period) to the almost comical frauds committed by companies like New Century and Countrywide, where mortgage dealers would literally hold a few sheets of a fixed-rate mortgage contract over a deadly adjustable-rate deal and then tell kindly old black ladies to "sign here" and fork over their life savings.

These guys literally *stole from old ladies* and we couldn't find a way to believe they deserved jail time. This went far beyond the old cliché about the rich having better lawyers and an advantage in court. This was a problem of perception buried deep in the public consciousness. We simply couldn't find a way to view anything these people did as criminal. But if we ourselves had profited from the commission of equivalent offenses in the streets and storefronts of our own communities, few of us would have argued with the logic if and when the state came to take us to jail.

Graham Greene in *Our Man in Havana* wrote about this phenomenon. In describing life in Batista's Cuba, he talked about how there is a "torturable class." In one scene, a corrupt police captain, a torturer who owns a cigarette case made of human skin, explains the distinction to Greene's British antihero, Wormold:

> "Did you torture him?"
>
> Captain Segura laughed. "No. He doesn't belong to the torturable class."
>
> "I didn't know there were class-distinctions in torture."
>
> "Dear Mr. Wormold, surely you realize there are people who expect to be tortured and others who would be outraged by the idea. One never tortures except by a kind of mutual agreement."

We have the same situation here in America now. We have a jailable class and a nonjailable class. The street thieves who go placidly to jail, reporting dutifully to prison after being out on bail, do so by a kind of mutual agreement, implicitly accepting the idea that they deserve jail more than the Dick Fulds of the world. Meanwhile, the high-class thieves on Wall Street who don't go to jail for far worse thefts really are outraged by the very idea that maybe they should. And not only are they outraged—they deploy frightening legal bulldogs to both defend them and to argue furiously as to the inappropriateness of even suggesting that they've done wrong. They are fighting not just to stay out of jail but to preserve this system of mutual consent.

In between are all of us, and the fact that so many of us implicitly accept this bizarre, subterranean, bipolar belief system is a huge part of why nothing was done to change things in the wake of this financial crisis. The vast majority of Americans are, I think, waiting for Wall Street itself to *agree* that it deserves to be punished or reformed, before calling for punishment or reform. But it's never going to happen. I feel strongly that once more people realize this, that they don't have to ask for Wall Street's permission to be angry about what happened to their money and their mortgages and their credit ratings in the last ten years, the politics governing our economy will be altered. And the reason people think they need to ask permission is that they don't understand a lot of what went on, because the details seem complicated and the bankers in charge have great lawyers continually clouding the issue.

The reality, of course, is that this situation is not as complicated as it seems. If you strip away all the verbiage and the long-winded explanations and bought-off legal and accounting opinions, all we're dealing with here is simple stealing and lying and fraud. It's crime and people need to go to jail for it: end of story. The issues in *Griftopia* are really law-enforcement issues, and these stories are cops-and-robbers stories. Describing them as anything else actually clouds the issue.

Anyway, included in this paperback edition are two more of these crime stories I wrote for *Rolling Stone* after *Griftopia* was put to bed. "Looting Main Street" is about the Jefferson County, Alabama, financial disaster, which shows how the same sorts of financial scams that undermined Greece were devised and executed in small-town America. Here we're dealing with crime in the baldest conceivable sense of the word: small-town officials literally bribed with cash and gifts to stick taxpayers with billions in crappy, toxic loans. The theft was so overt that in one case, one bank (JPMorgan Chase) actually paid millions to another bank (Goldman Sachs) to back off the deal—as obvious a case of anticompetitive behavior as you'll find. And again, when disaster strikes, it's not the bankers who suffer, it's the ordinary people who live in the Birmingham, Alabama, area who see their city stripped down and sold for parts.

"Invasion of the Home Snatchers" is another true-crime story, about the foreclosure crisis. Again, this was a story that was sold to America as an "economic disaster," something that happened organically thanks to a poor economy. In fact, it was just criminal fraud on a massive scale. If you peel back the paperwork even a little bit, you see the crime there, bare as can be.

When the financial crisis first struck, it was, for most people, terrifying, depressing, and confusing all at once. Years later it is, at the very least, no longer all that confusing. This material really isn't that hard; these guys aren't nearly as sophisticated as they'd like you to think. It's just stealing, no matter what their lawyers choose to call it. And while there's often despair at the question of what to do about this crisis—the issues seem so staggeringly complex and both the economy and the regulatory system seem so broken—to me the first step is a very simple one. Find the people who are stealing and give them jail time; let's start with that.

You will often hear pundits asking, with straight faces, certain rhetorical questions about the issue of punishment for financial crime. "What good would it do," they ask, to put this or that banker CEO in jail for fraud? After all, they say, giving a Dick Fuld or John Thain jail time "won't change anything."

Which is an interesting point, but consider this: when was the last time anyone stood up at a car thief's trial and argued that jail time wasn't warranted because putting the defendant in jail *wouldn't end car theft*? We don't make that argument because it's absurd; that's not how we measure justice. The chief problem of the financial crisis is that it has made inequality systematic and created two political systems, one for Wall Street and one for everybody else, a financially torturable class. The country has underlying economic problems for sure, and those will be difficult to untangle, but the inequality problem can be fixed relatively quickly. If we force the people on Wall Street to live under our laws and our criminal justice system, who knows—they may even start to see themselves as citizens of the same country. And behave accordingly.

Looting Main Street
How the nation's biggest banks are ripping off American cities with the same predatory deals that brought down Greece

This article originally appeared in the April 15, 2010, issue of Rolling Stone.

IF YOU WANT to know what life in the third world is like, just ask Lisa Pack, an administrative assistant who works in the Roads and Transportation Department in Jefferson County, Alabama. Pack got rudely introduced to life in postcrisis America in August 2009, when word came down that she and one thousand of her fellow public employees would have to take a little unpaid vacation for a while. The county, it turned out, was more than $5 billion in debt—meaning that courthouses, jails, and sheriff's precincts had to be closed so that Wall Street banks could be paid.

As public services in and around Birmingham were stripped to the bone, Pack struggled to support her family on a weekly unemployment check of $260. Nearly a fourth of that went to pay for her health insurance, which the county no longer covered. She also fielded calls from laid-off co-workers who had it even tougher. "I'd be on the phone sometimes until two in the morning," she says. "I had to talk more than one person out of suicide. For some of the men supporting families, it was so hard—foreclosure, bankruptcy. I'd go to bed at night, and I'd be in tears."

Homes stood empty, businesses were boarded up, and parts of already blighted Birmingham began to take on the feel of a ghost town. There were also a few bills that were unique to the area—like the $64 sewer bill that Pack and her family paid each month. "Yeah, it went up about four hundred percent just over the past few years," she says.

The sewer bill, in fact, is what cost Pack and her co-workers their jobs. In 1996, the average monthly sewer bill for a family of four in Birmingham was only $14.71—but that was before the county decided to build an elaborate new sewer system with the help of out-of-state financial wizards with names like Bear Stearns, Lehman Brothers, Goldman Sachs, and JPMorgan Chase. The result was a monstrous pile of borrowed money that the county used to build, in essence, the world's grandest toilet—"the Taj Mahal of sewer-treatment plants" is how one county worker put it. What happened here in Jefferson County would turn out to be the perfect metaphor for the peculiar alchemy of modern oligarchical capitalism: a mob of corrupt local officials and morally absent financiers got together to build a giant device that converted human shit into billions of dollars of profit for Wall Street—and misery for people like Lisa Pack.

And once the giant shit machine was built and the note on all that fancy construction started to come due, Wall Street came back to the local politicians and doubled down on the scam. They showed up in droves to help the poor, broke citizens of Jefferson County cut their toilet finance charges using a blizzard of incomprehensible swaps and refinance schemes—schemes that only served to postpone the repayment date a year or two while sinking the county deeper into debt. In the end, every time Jefferson County so much as breathed near one of the banks, it got charged millions in fees. There was so much money to be made bilking these dizzy southerners that banks like JPMorgan spent millions paying middlemen who bribed—yes, that's right, bribed, criminally *bribed*—the county commissioners and their buddies just to keep their business. Hell, the money was so good, JPMorgan at one point even paid Goldman Sachs $3 million just to back the fuck off, so they could have the rubes of Jefferson County to fleece all for themselves.

Birmingham became the poster child for a new kind of giant-scale financial fraud, one that would threaten the financial stability not only of cities and counties all across America, but even of entire countries like Greece. While for many Americans the financial crisis remains an abstraction, a confusing mess of complex transactions that took place on a cloud high above Manhattan sometime in the mid-2000s, in Jefferson County you can actually see the rank criminality of the crisis economy with your own eyes; the monster sticks his head all the way out of the water. Here you can see a trail that leads directly from a billion-dollar predatory swap deal cooked up at the highest levels of America's biggest banks, across a vast fruited plain of bribes and felonies—"the price of doing business," as one JPMorgan banker says on tape—all the way down to Lisa Pack's sewer bill and the mass layoffs in Birmingham.

Once you follow that trail and understand what took place in Jefferson County, there's really no room left for illusions. We live in a gangster state, and our days of laughing at other countries are over. It's our turn to get laughed at. In Birmingham, lots of people have gone to jail for the crime: more than twenty local officials and businessmen have been convicted of corruption in federal court. Last October, right around the time that Lisa Pack went back to work at reduced hours, Birmingham's mayor was convicted of fraud and money laundering for taking bribes funneled to him by Wall Street bankers—everything from Rolex watches to Ferragamo suits to cash. But those who green-lighted the bribes and profited most from the scam remain largely untouched. "It never gets back to JPMorgan," says Pack.

If you want to get all Glenn Beck about it, you could lay the blame for this entire mess at the feet of weepy, tree-hugging environmentalists. It all started with the Cahaba River, the longest free-flowing river in the state of Alabama. The tributary, which winds its way through Birmingham before turning diagonally to empty out near Selma, is home to more types of fish per mile than any other river in America and shelters sixty-four rare and imperiled species of plants and animals. It's also the source of one of the worst municipal financial disasters in American history.

Back in the early 1990s, the county's sewer system was so anti-quated that it was leaking raw sewage directly into the Cahaba, which also supplies the area with its drinking water. Joined by well-intentioned citizens from the Cahaba River Society, the EPA sued the county to force it to comply with the Clean Water Act. In 1996, county commissioners signed a now-infamous consent decree agreeing not just to fix the leaky pipes but to eliminate *all* sewer overflows—a near-impossible standard that required the county to build the most elabo-rate, ecofriendly, expensive sewer system in the history of the universe. It was like ordering a small town in Florida that gets a snowstorm once every five years to build a billion-dollar fleet of snowplows.

The original cost estimates for the new sewer system were as low as $250 million. But in a wondrous demonstration of the possibilities of small-town graft and contract padding, the price tag quickly swelled to more than $3 billion. County commissioners were literally pocketing wads of cash from builders and engineers and other contractors eager to get in on the project, while the county was forced to borrow obscene sums to pay for the rapidly spiraling costs. Jefferson County, in effect, became one giant, TV-stealing, unemployed drug addict who borrowed a million dollars to buy the mother of all McMansions—and just as it did during the housing bubble, Wall Street made a business of keeping the crook in his house. As one county commissioner put it, "We're like a guy making fifty thousand dollars a year with a million-dollar mort-gage."

To reassure lenders that the county would pay its mortgage, com-missioners gave the finance director—an unelected official appointed by the president of the commission—the power to automatically raise sewer rates to meet payments on the debt. The move brought in billions in financing, but it also painted commissioners into a corner. If costs continued to rise—and with practically every contractor in Alabama sticking his fingers on the scale, they were rising fast—officials would be faced with automatic rate increases that would piss off their voters.

(By 2003, annual interest on the sewer deal had reached $90 million.) So the commission reached out to Wall Street, looking for creative financing tools that would allow it to reduce the county's staggering debt payments.

Wall Street was happy to help. First, it employed the same trick it used to fuel the housing crisis: it switched the county from a fixed rate on the bonds it had issued to finance the sewer deal to an adjustable rate. The refinancing meant lower interest payments for a couple of years—followed by the risk of even larger payments down the road. The move enabled county commissioners to postpone the problem for an election season or two, kicking it to a group of future commissioners who would inevitably have to pay the real freight.

But then Wall Street got really creative. Having switched the county to a variable interest rate, it offered commissioners a crazy deal: For an extra fee, the banks said, we'll allow you to keep paying a fixed rate on your debt to us. In return, we'll give you a variable amount each month that you can use to pay off all that variable-rate interest you owe to bondholders.

In financial terms, this is known as a "synthetic rate swap"—the spidery creature you might have read about playing a role in bringing down places like Greece and Milan. On paper, it made sense: the county got the stability of a fixed rate while paying Wall Street to assume the risk of the variable rates on its bonds. That's the "synthetic" part. The trouble lies in the rate swap. The deal only works if the two variable rates—the one you get from the bank and the one you owe to bondholders—actually match. It's like gambling on the weather. If your bondholders are expecting you to pay an interest rate based on the average temperature in Alabama, you don't do a rate swap with a bank that gives you back a rate pegged to the temperature in Nome, Alaska.

Not unless you're a fucking moron. Or your banker is JPMorgan.

In a small office in a federal building in downtown Birmingham, just blocks from where civil rights demonstrators shut down the city in 1963, Assistant U.S. Attorney George Martin points out the window. He's pointing in the direction of the Tutwiler Hotel, once home to one of the grandest ballrooms in the South but now part of the Hampton Inn chain.

"It was right around the corner here, at the hotel," Martin says. "That's where they met—that's where this all started."

They means Charles LeCroy and Bill Blount, the two principals in what would become the most important of all the corruption cases in Jefferson County. LeCroy was a banker for JPMorgan, serving as managing director of the bank's southeast regional office. Blount was an Alabama wheeler-dealer with close friends on the county commission. For years, when Wall Street banks wanted to do business with municipalities, whether for bond issues or rate swaps, it was standard practice to reach out to a local sleazeball like Blount and pay him a shitload of money to help seal the deal. "Banks would pay some local consultant, and the consultant would then funnel money to the politician making the decision," says Christopher Taylor, the former head of the federal board that regulates municipal borrowing. Back in the 1990s, Taylor pushed through a ban on such backdoor bribery. He also passed a ban on bankers contributing directly to politicians they do business with— a move that sparked a lawsuit by one aggrieved sleazeball, who argued that halting such legalized graft violated his First Amendment rights. The name of that pissed-off banker? "It was the one and only Bill Blount," Taylor says with a laugh.

Blount is a stocky, stubby-fingered southerner with glasses and a pale, pinched face—if Norman Rockwell had ever done a painting titled *Small-Town Accountant Taking Enormous Dump,* it would look just like Blount. LeCroy, his sugar daddy at JPMorgan, is a tall, bloodless, crisply dressed corporate operator with a shiny bald head and silver side patches—a cross between Skeletor and Michael Stipe.

The scheme they operated went something like this: LeCroy paid Blount millions of dollars, and Blount turned around and used the money to buy lavish gifts for his close friend Larry Langford, the now-convicted Birmingham mayor who at the time had just been elected president of the county commission. (At one point Blount took Langford on a shopping spree in New York, putting $3,290 worth of clothes from Zegna on his credit card.) Langford then signed off on one after another of the deadly swap deals being pushed by LeCroy. Every time the county refinanced its sewer debt, JPMorgan made millions of dollars in fees. Even more lucrative, each of the swap contracts contained clauses that mandated all sorts of penalties and payments in the event that something went wrong with the deal. In the mortgage business, this process is known as "churning": you keep coming back over and over to refinance, and they keep "churning" you for more and more fees. "The transactions were complex, but the scheme was simple," said Robert Khuzami, director of enforcement for the SEC. "Senior JPMorgan bankers made unlawful payments to win business and earn fees."

Given the shitload of money to be made on the refinancing deals, JPMorgan was prepared to pay whatever it took to buy off officials in Jefferson County. In 2002, during a conversation recorded in Nixonian fashion by JPMorgan itself, LeCroy bragged that he had agreed to funnel payoff money to a pair of local companies to secure the votes of two county commissioners. "Look," the commissioners told him, "if we support the synthetic refunding, you guys have to take care of our two firms." LeCroy didn't blink. "Whatever you want," he told them. "If that's what you need, that's what you get. Just tell us how much."

Just tell us how much. That sums up the approach that JPMorgan took a few months later, when Langford announced that his good buddy Bill Blount would henceforth be involved with every financing transaction for Jefferson County. From JPMorgan's point of view, the decision to pay off Blount was a no-brainer. But the bank had one small problem: Goldman Sachs had already crawled up Blount's trouser leg, and the broker was advising Langford to pick *them* as Jefferson County's investment bank.

The solution they came up with was an extraordinary one: JPMorgan cut a separate deal with Goldman, paying the bank $3 million to fuck off, with Blount taking a $300,000 cut of the side deal. Suddenly Goldman was out and JPMorgan was sitting in Langford's lap. In another conversation caught on tape, LeCroy joked that the deal was his "philanthropic work," since the payoff amounted to a "charitable donation to Goldman Sachs" in return for "taking no risk."

That such a blatant violation of antitrust laws took place and neither JPMorgan nor Goldman has been prosecuted for it is yet another mystery of the current financial crisis. "This is an open-and-shut case of anticompetitive behavior," says Taylor, the former regulator.

With Goldman out of the way, JPMorgan won the right to do a $1.1 billion bond offering—switching Jefferson County out of fixed-rate debt into variable-rate debt—and also did a corresponding $1.1 billion deal for a synthetic rate swap. The very same day the transaction was concluded, in May 2003, LeCroy had dinner with Langford and struck a deal to do yet *another* bond-and-swap transaction of roughly the same size. This time, the terms of the payoff were spelled out more explicitly. In a hilarious phone call between LeCroy and Douglas MacFaddin, another JPMorgan official, the two bankers groaned aloud about how much it was going to cost to satisfy Blount:

> LECROY: I said, "Commissioner Langford, I'll do that because that's your suggestion, but you gotta help us keep him under control. Because when you give that guy a hand, he takes your arm." You know?
> MACFADDIN: [*Laughing*] Yeah, you end up in the wood chipper.

All told, JPMorgan ended up paying Blount nearly $3 million for "performing no known services," in the words of the SEC. In at least one of the deals, Blount made upward of 15 percent of JPMorgan's entire fee. When I ask Taylor what a legitimate consultant might earn in such a circumstance, he laughs. "What's a 'legitimate consultant' in a case like this? He made this money for doing jack shit."

As the tapes of LeCroy's calls show, even officials at JPMorgan were incredulous at the money being funneled to Blount. "How does he get fifteen percent?" one associate at the bank asks LeCroy. "For doing what? For not messing with us?"

"Not messing with us," LeCroy agrees. "It's a lot of money, but in the end, it's worth it on a billion-dollar deal."

That's putting it mildly: the deals wound up being the largest swap agreements in JPMorgan's history. Making matters worse, the payoffs didn't even wind up costing the bank a dime. As the SEC explained in a statement on the scam, JPMorgan "passed on the cost of the unlawful payments by charging the county higher interest rates on the swap transactions." In other words, not only did the bank bribe local politicians to take the sucky deal, they got local taxpayers to pay for the bribes. And because Jefferson County had no idea what kind of deal it was getting on the swaps, JPMorgan could basically charge whatever it wanted. According to an analysis of the swap deals commissioned by the county in 2007, taxpayers had been overcharged at least $93 million on the transactions.

JPMorgan was far from alone in the scam: virtually everyone doing business in Jefferson County was on the take. Four of the nation's top investment banks, the very cream of American finance, were involved in one way or another with payoffs to Blount in their scramble to do business with the county. In addition to JPMorgan and Goldman Sachs, Bear Stearns paid Langford's bagman $2.4 million, while Lehman Brothers got off cheap with a $35,000 "arranger's fee." At least a dozen of the county's contractors were also cashing in, along with many of the county commissioners. "If you go into the county courthouse," says Michael Morrison, a planner who works for the county, "there's a gallery of past commissioners on the wall. On the top row, every single one of 'em but two has been investigated, indicted, or convicted. It's a joke."

The crazy thing is that such arrangements—where some local scoundrel gets a massive fee for doing nothing but greasing the wheels with elected officials—have been taking place all over the country. In Illinois, during the Upper Volta–esque era of Rod Blagojevich, a Republican political consultant named Robert Kjellander got 10 percent of the entire fee Bear Stearns earned doing a bond sale for the state pension fund. At the start of Obama's term, Bill Richardson's cabinet appointment was derailed for a similar scheme when he was governor of New Mexico. Indeed, one reason that officials in Jefferson County didn't know that the swaps they were signing off on were shitty was because their adviser on the deals was a firm called CDR Financial Products, which is now accused of conspiring to overcharge dozens of cities in swap transactions. According to a federal antitrust lawsuit, CDR is basically a big-league version of Bill Blount—banks tossed money at the firm, which in turn advised local politicians that they were getting a good deal. "It was basically, you pay CDR, and CDR helps push the deal through," says Taylor.

In the end, though, all this bribery and graft was just the table-setter for the real disaster. In taking all those bribes and signing on to all those swaps, the commissioners in Jefferson County had basically started the clock on a financial time bomb that, sooner or later, had to explode. By continually refinancing to keep the county in its giant McMansion, the commission had managed to push into the future that inevitable day when the real bill would arrive in the mail. But that's where the mortgage analogy ends—because in one key area, a swap deal differs from a home mortgage. Imagine a mortgage that you have to keep on paying even *after* you sell your house. That's basically how a swap deal works. And Jefferson County had done twenty-three of them. At one point, they had more outstanding swaps than New York City.

Judgment Day was coming—just like it was for the Delaware River Port Authority, the Pennsylvania school system, the cities of Detroit, Chicago, Oakland, and Los Angeles, the states of Connecticut and Mississippi, the city of Milan and nearly five hundred other municipalities in Italy, the country of Greece, and God knows who else. All of these places are now reeling under the weight of similarly elaborate and ill-advised swaps—and if what happened in Jefferson County is any guide, hoo boy. Because when the shit hit the fan in Birmingham, it *really* hit the fan.

For Jefferson County, the deal blew up in early 2008, when a dizzying array of penalties and other fine-print poison worked into the swap contracts started to kick in. The trouble began with the housing crash, which took down the insurance companies that had underwritten the county's bonds. That rendered the county's insurance worthless, triggering clauses in its swap contracts that required it to pay off more than $800 million of its debt in only *four* years, rather than forty. That, in turn, scared off private lenders, who were no longer interested in bidding on the county's bonds. The banks were forced to make up the difference—a service for which they charged enormous penalties. It was as if the county had missed a payment on its credit card and woke up the next morning to find its annual percentage rate jacked up to a million percent. Between 2008 and 2009, the annual payment on Jefferson County's debt jumped from $53 million to a whopping $636 million.

It gets worse. Remember the swap deal that Jefferson County did with JPMorgan, how the variable rates it got from the bank were supposed to match those it owed its bondholders? Well, they didn't. Most of the payments the county was receiving from JPMorgan were based on one set of interest rates (the London Interbank Offered Rate), while the payments it owed to its bondholders followed a different set of rates (a municipal-bond index). Jefferson County was suddenly getting far less from JPMorgan and owing tons more to bondholders. In other words, the bank and Bill Blount made tens of millions of dollars selling deals to local politicians that were not only completely defective, but blew the entire county to smithereens.

And here's the kicker. In 2009, when Jefferson County, staggered by the weight of its penalties, was unable to make its swap payments to JPMorgan, the bank canceled the deal. That triggered one-time "termination fees" of—yes, you read this right—$647 million. That was money the county would owe no matter what happened with the rest of its debt, even if bondholders decided to forgive and forget every dime the county had borrowed. It was like the herpes simplex of loans—debt that does not go away, ever, for as long as you live. On a sewer project that was originally supposed to cost $250 million, the county now owed a total of $1.28 *billion* just in interest and fees on the debt. Imagine paying $250,000 a year on a car you purchased for $50,000, and that's roughly where Jefferson County stood at the end of 2009.

Last November, the SEC charged JPMorgan with fraud and canceled the $647 million in termination fees. The bank agreed to pay a $25 million fine and fork over $50 million to assist displaced workers in Jefferson County. So far, the county has managed to avoid bankruptcy, but the sewer fiasco has downgraded its credit rating, triggering payments on other outstanding loans and pushing Birmingham toward the status of an African debtor state. For the next generation, the county will be in a constant fight to collect enough taxes just to pay off its debt, which now totals $4,800 per resident.

The city of Birmingham was founded in 1871, at the dawn of the southern industrial boom, for the express purpose of attracting northern capital—it was even named after a famous British steel town to burnish its entrepreneurial cred. There's a gruesome irony in it now lying sacked and looted by financial vandals from the North. The destruction of Jefferson County reveals the basic battle plan of these modern barbarians, the way that banks like JPMorgan and Goldman Sachs have systematically set out to pillage towns and cities from Pittsburgh to Athens. These guys aren't number-crunching whizzes making smart investments; what they do is find suckers in some municipal finance department, corner them in complex lose-lose deals, and flay them alive. In a complete subversion of free-market principles, they take no risk, score deals based on political influence rather than competition, keep consumers in the dark—and walk away with big money. "It's not high finance," says Taylor, the former bond regulator. "It's low finance." And even if the regulators manage to catch up with them billions of dollars later, the banks just pay a small fine and move on to the next scam. This isn't capitalism. It's nomadic thievery.

Invasion of the Home Snatchers
Matt Taibbi on how foreclosure courts are helping big banks screw over homeowners

This article originally appeared in the November 25, 2010, issue of Rolling Stone.

THE FORECLOSURE LAWYERS down in Jacksonville had warned me, but I was skeptical. They told me the state of Florida had created a special super-high-speed housing court with a specific mandate to rubber-stamp the legally dicey foreclosures by corporate mortgage pushers like Deutsche Bank and JPMorgan Chase. This "rocket docket," as it is called in town, is presided over by retired judges who seem to have no clue about the insanely complex financial instruments they are ruling on—securitized mortgages and labyrinthine derivative deals of a type that didn't even exist when most of them were active members of the bench. Their stated mission isn't to decide right and wrong, but to clear cases and blast human beings out of their homes with ultimate velocity. They certainly have no incentive to penetrate the profound criminal mysteries of the great American mortgage bubble of the 2000s, perhaps the most complex Ponzi scheme in human history—an epic mountain range of corporate fraud in which Wall Street megabanks conspired first to collect huge numbers of subprime mortgages, then to unload them on unsuspecting third parties like pension funds, trade unions, and insurance companies (and, ultimately, you and me, as taxpayers) in the guise of AAA-rated investments. Selling lead as gold, shit as Chanel No. 5, was the essence of the booming international fraud scheme that created most all of these now-failing home mortgages.

The rocket docket wasn't created to investigate any of that. It exists to launder the crime and bury the evidence by speeding thousands of fraudulent and predatory loans to the ends of their life cycles, so that the houses attached to them can be sold again with clean paperwork. The judges, in fact, openly admit that their primary mission is not justice but speed. One Jacksonville judge, the Honorable A. C. Soud, even told a local newspaper that his goal is to resolve twenty-five cases per hour. Given the way the system is rigged, that means His Honor could well be throwing one ass on the street every 2.4 minutes.

Foreclosure lawyers told me one other thing about the rocket docket. The hearings, they said, aren't exactly public. "The judges might give you a hard time about watching," one lawyer warned. "They're not exactly anxious for people to know about this stuff." Inwardly, I laughed at this—it sounded like typical activist paranoia. The notion that a judge would try to prevent any citizen, much less a member of the media, from watching an open civil hearing sounded ridiculous. Fucked-up as everyone knows the state of Florida is, it couldn't be that bad. It isn't Indonesia. Right?

Well, not quite. When I went to sit in on Judge Soud's courtroom in downtown Jacksonville, I was treated to an intimate, and at times breathtaking, education in the horror of the foreclosure crisis, which is rapidly emerging as the even scarier sequel to the financial meltdown of 2008: Invasion of the Home Snatchers II. In Las Vegas, one in twenty-five homes is now in foreclosure. In Fort Myers, Florida, one in thirty-five. In September 2010, lenders nationwide took over a record 102,134 properties; that same month, more than a third of all home sales were distressed properties. All told, some 820,000 Americans already lost their homes in the first three months of 2010, and another 1 million faced foreclosure.

Throughout the mounting catastrophe, however, many Americans have been slow to comprehend the true nature of the mortgage disaster. They seem to have grasped just two things about the crisis: One, a lot of people are getting their houses foreclosed on. Two, some of the banks doing the foreclosing seem to have misplaced their paperwork.

For most people, the former bit about homeowners not paying their damn bills is the important part, while the latter, about the sudden and strange inability of the world's biggest and wealthiest banks to keep proper records, is incidental. Just a little office sloppiness, and who cares? Those deadbeat homeowners still owe the money, right? "They had it coming to them," is how a bartender at the Jacksonville airport put it to me.

But in reality, it's the unpaid bills that are incidental and the lost paperwork that matters. It turns out that underneath that little iceberg tip of exposed evidence lies a fraud so gigantic that it literally cannot be contemplated by our leaders, for fear of admitting that our entire financial system is corrupted to its core—with our great banks and even our government coffers backed not by real wealth but by vast landfills of deceptively generated and essentially worthless mortgage-backed assets.

You've heard of Too Big to Fail—the foreclosure crisis is Too Big for Fraud. Think of the Bernie Madoff scam, only replicated tens of thousands of times over, infecting every corner of the financial universe. The underlying crime is so pervasive, we simply can't admit to it—and so we are working feverishly to rubber-stamp the problem away, in sordid little back rooms in cities like Jacksonville, behind doors that shouldn't be, but often are, closed.

And that's just the economic side of the story. The moral angle to the foreclosure crisis—and, of course, in capitalism we're not supposed to be concerned with the moral stuff, but let's mention it anyway— shows a culture that is slowly giving in to a futuristic nightmare ideology of computerized greed and unchecked financial violence. The monster in the foreclosure crisis has no face and no brain. The mortgages that are being foreclosed upon have no real owners. The lawyers bringing the cases to evict the humans have no real clients. It is complete and absolute legal and economic chaos. No single limb of this vast man-eating thing knows what the other is doing, which makes it nearly impossible to combat—and scary as hell to watch.

What follows is an account of a single hour of Judge A. C. Soud's rocket docket in Jacksonville. Like everything else related to the modern economy, these foreclosure hearings are conducted in what is essentially a foreign language, heavy on jargon and impenetrable to the casual observer. It took days of interviews with experts before and after this hearing to make sense of this single hour of courtroom drama. And though the permutations of small-time scammery and grift in the foreclosure world are virtually endless—your average foreclosure case involves homeowners or investors being screwed at least five or six creative ways—a single hour of court and a few cases is enough to tell the main story. Because if you see one of these scams, you see them all.

It's early on a sunny Tuesday morning when I arrive at the chambers of Judge Soud, one of four rotating judges who preside over the local rocket docket. These special foreclosure courts were established in July 2010, after the state of Florida budgeted $9.6 million to create a new court with a specific mandate to clear 62 percent of the foreclosure cases that were clogging up the system. Rather than forcing active judges to hear thousands of individual cases, this strategy relies on retired judges who take turns churning through dozens of cases every morning, with little time to pay much attention to the particulars.

What passes for a foreclosure court in Jacksonville is actually a small conference room at the end of a hall on the fifth floor of the drab brick Duval County Courthouse. The space would just about fit a fridge and a Ping-Pong table. At the head of a modest conference table this morning sits Judge Soud, a small and fussy-looking man who reminds me vaguely of the actor Ben Gazzara.

On one side of the table sits James Kowalski, a former homicide prosecutor who is now defending homeowners. A stern man with a shaved head and a laconic manner of speaking, Kowalski has helped pioneer a whole new approach to the housing mess, slowing down the mindless eviction machine by deposing the scores of "robo-signers" being hired by the banks to sign phony foreclosure affidavits by the thousands. For his work on behalf of the dispossessed, Kowalski was recently profiled in a preposterous *Wall Street Journal* article that blamed attorneys like him for causing the foreclosure mess with their nuisance defense claims. The headline: "Niche Lawyers Spawned Housing Fracas."

On the other side of the table are the plaintiff's attorneys, the guys who represent the banks. On this level of the game, these lawyers refer to themselves as "bench warmers"—volume stand-ins subcontracted by the big, hired-killer law firms that work for the banks. One of the bench warmers present today is Mark Kessler, who works for a number of lenders and giant "foreclosure mills," including the one run by David J. Stern, a gazillionaire attorney and all-Universe asshole who last year tried to foreclose on 70,382 homeowners. Which is a nice way to make a living, considering that Stern and his wife, Jeanine, have bought nearly $60 million in property for themselves in recent years, including a 9,273-square-foot manse in Fort Lauderdale that is part of a Ritz-Carlton complex.

Kessler is a harried, middle-aged man in glasses who spends the morning perpetually fighting to organize a towering stack of folders, each one representing a soon-to-be-homeless human being. It quickly becomes apparent that Kessler is barely acquainted with the names in the files, much less the details of each case. "A lot of these guys won't even get the folders until right before the hearing," says Kowalski.

When I arrive, Judge Soud and the lawyers are already arguing a foreclosure case; at a break in the action, I slip into the chamber with a legal-aid attorney who's accompanying me and sit down. The judge eyes me anxiously, then proceeds. He clears his throat, and then it's ready, set, fraud!

Judge Soud seems to have no clue that the files he is processing at a breakneck pace are stuffed with fraudulent claims and outright lies. "We have not encountered any fraud yet," he recently told a local newspaper. "If we encountered fraud, it would go to [the state attorney], I can tell you that." But the very first case I see in his court is riddled with fraud.

Kowalski has seen hundreds of cases like the one he's presenting this morning. It started back in 2006, when he went to Pennsylvania to conduct what he thought would be a routine deposition of an official at the lending giant GMAC. What he discovered was that the official—who had sworn to having personal knowledge of the case—was, in fact, just a "robo-signer" who had signed off on the file without knowing anything about the actual homeowner or his payment history. (Kowalski's clients, like most of the homeowners he represents, were actually making their payments on time; in this particular case, a check had been mistakenly refused by GMAC.) Following the evidence, Kowalski discovered what has turned out to be a systemwide collapse of the process for documenting mortgages in this country.

If you're foreclosing on somebody's house, you are required by law to have a collection of paperwork showing the journey of that mortgage note from the moment of issuance to the present. You should see the originating lender (a firm like Countrywide) selling the loan to the next entity in the chain (perhaps Goldman Sachs) to the next (maybe JPMorgan), with the actual note being transferred each time. But in fact, almost no bank currently foreclosing on homeowners has a reliable record of who owns the loan; in some cases, they have even intentionally shredded the actual mortgage notes. That's where the robo-signers come in. To create the appearance of paperwork where none exists, the banks drag in these pimply entry-level types—an infamous example is GMAC's notorious robo-signer Jeffrey Stephan, who appears online looking like an age-advanced photo of Beavis or Butt-Head—and get them to sign thousands of documents a month attesting to the banks' proper ownership of the mortgages.

This isn't some rare goof-up by a low-level cubicle slave: virtually every case of foreclosure in this country involves some form of screwed-up paperwork. "I would say it's pretty close to one hundred percent," says Kowalski. An attorney for Jacksonville Area Legal Aid tells me that out of the hundreds of cases she has handled, fewer than five involved no phony paperwork. "The fraud is the norm," she says.

Kowalski's current case before Judge Soud is a perfect example. The Jacksonville couple he represents are being sued for delinquent payments, but the case against them has already been dismissed once before. The first time around, the plaintiff, Bank of New York Mellon, wrote in paragraph 8 that "plaintiff owns and holds the note" on the house belonging to the couple. But in paragraph 3 of the same complaint, the bank reported that the note was "lost or destroyed," while in paragraph 4 it attests that "plaintiff cannot reasonably obtain possession of the promissory note because its whereabouts cannot be determined."

The bank, in other words, tried to claim on paper, in court, that it both lost the note and had it, at the same time. Moreover, it claimed that it had included a copy of the note in the file, which it did—the only problem being that the note (a) was not properly endorsed and (b) was payable not to Bank of New York but to someone else, a company called NovaStar.

Now, months after its first pass at foreclosure was dismissed, the bank has refiled the case—and what do you know, it suddenly found the note. And this time, somehow, the note has the proper stamps. "There's a stamp that did not appear on the note that was originally filed," Kowalski tells the judge. (This business about the stamps is hilarious. "You can get them very cheap online," says Chip Parker, an attorney who defends homeowners in Jacksonville.)

The bank's new set of papers also traces ownership of the loan from the original lender, NovaStar, to JPMorgan and then to Bank of New York. The bank, in other words, is trying to push through a completely new set of documents in its attempts to foreclose on Kowalski's clients.

There's only one problem: the dates of the transfers are completely fucked. According to the documents, JPMorgan transferred the mortgage to Bank of New York on December 9, 2008. But according to the same documents, JPMorgan didn't even receive the mortgage from NovaStar until February 2, 2009—two months after it had supposedly passed the note along to Bank of New York. Such rank incompetence at doctoring legal paperwork is typical of foreclosure actions, where the fraud is laid out in ink in ways that make it impossible for anyone but an overburdened, half-asleep judge to miss. "That's my point about all of this," Kowalski tells me later. "If you're going to lie to me, at least lie well."

The dates aren't the only thing screwy about the new documents submitted by Bank of New York. Having failed in its earlier attempt to claim that it actually had the mortgage note, the bank now tries an all-of-the-above tactic. "Plaintiff owns and holds the note," it claims, "or is a person entitled to enforce the note."

Soud sighs. For Kessler, the plaintiff's lawyer, to come before him with such sloppy documents and make this preposterous argument— that his client either is or is not the note holder—well, that puts His Honor in a tough spot. The entire concept is a legal absurdity, and he can't sign off on it. With an expression of something very like regret, the judge tells Kessler, "I'm going to have to go ahead and accept [Kowalski's] argument."

Now, one might think that after a bank makes multiple attempts to push phony documents through a courtroom, a judge might be pissed off enough to simply rule against that plaintiff for good. As I witness in court all morning, the defense never gets more than one chance to screw up. But the banks get to keep filing their foreclosures over and over again, no matter how atrocious and deceitful their paperwork is.

Thus, when Soud tells Kessler that he's dismissing the case, he hastens to add: "Of course, I'm not going to dismiss with prejudice." With an emphasis on the words "of course."

Instead, Soud gives Kessler twenty-five days to come up with better paperwork. Kowalski fully expects the bank to come back with new documents telling a whole new story of the note's ownership. "What they're going to do, I would predict, is produce a note and say Bank of New York is not the original note holder, but merely the servicer," he says.

This is the dirty secret of the rocket docket: the whole system is set up to enable lenders to commit fraud over and over again, until they figure out a way to reduce the stink enough so some judge like Soud can sign off on the scam. "If the court finds for the defendant, the plaintiffs just refile," says Parker, the local attorney. "The only way for the caseload to get reduced is to give it to the plaintiff. The entire process is designed with that result in mind."

Now, all of this—the obviously cooked-up documents, the magically appearing stamp, and the rest of it—may just seem like nothing more than sloppy paperwork. After all, what does it matter if the bank has lost a few forms or mixed up the dates? The homeowners still owe what they owe, and the deadbeats have no right to keep living in a house they haven't paid for.

But what's going on at the Jacksonville rocket docket, and in foreclosure courts all across the country, has nothing to do with sloppiness. All this phony paperwork was actually an essential part of the mortgage bubble, an integral element of what has enabled the nation's biggest lenders to pass off all that subprime lead as AAA gold.

In the old days, when you took out a mortgage, it was probably through a local bank or a credit union, and whoever gave you your loan held on to it for life. If you lost your job or got too sick to work and suddenly had trouble making your payments, you could call a human being and work things out. It was in the banker's interest, as well as yours, to make a modified payment schedule. From his point of view, it was better that you pay something than nothing at all.

But that all changed about a decade ago, thanks to the invention of new financial instruments that magically turned all these mortgages into high-grade investments. Now when you took out a mortgage, your original lender—which might well have been a big mortgage mill like Countrywide or New Century—immediately sold off your loan to big banks like Deutsche and Goldman and JPMorgan. The banks then dumped hundreds or thousands of home loans at a time into tax-exempt real estate trusts, where the loans were diced up into securities, examined and graded by the ratings agencies, and sold off to big pension funds and other institutional suckers.

Even at this stage of the game, the banks generally knew that the loans they were buying and reselling to investors were shady. A company called Clayton Holdings, which analyzed nearly 1 million loans being prepared for sale in 2006 and 2007 by twenty-three banks, found that nearly half of the mortgages failed to meet the underwriting standards being promised to investors. Citigroup, for instance, had 29 percent of its loans come up short, but it still sold a third of those mortgages to investors. Goldman Sachs had 19 percent of its mortgages flunk the test, yet it knowingly hawked 34 percent of the risky deals to investors.

D. Keith Johnson, the head of Clayton Holdings, was so alarmed by the findings that he went to officials at three of the main ratings agencies—Moody's, Standard and Poor's, and Fitch—and tried to get them to properly evaluate the loans. "Wouldn't this information be great for you to have as you assign risk levels?" he asked them. (Translation: Don't you ratings agencies want to know that half these loans are crap before you give them a thumbs-up?) But all three agencies rejected his advice, fearing they would lose business if they adopted tougher standards. In the end, the agencies gave large chunks of these mortgage-backed securities AAA ratings—which means "credit risk almost zero."

Since these mortgage-backed securities paid much higher returns than other AAA investments like Treasury notes or corporate bonds, the banks had no trouble attracting investors, foreign and domestic, from pension funds to insurance companies to trade unions. The demand was so great, in fact, that they often sold mortgages they didn't even have yet, prompting big warehouse lenders like Countrywide and New Century to rush out into the world to find more warm bodies to lend to.

In their extreme haste to get thousands and thousands of mortgages they could resell to the banks, the lenders committed an astonishing variety of fraud, from falsifying income statements to making grossly inflated appraisals to misrepresenting properties to home buyers. Most crucially, they gave tons and tons of credit to people who probably didn't deserve it, and why not? These fly-by-night mortgage companies weren't going to hold on to these loans, not even for ten minutes. They were issuing this credit specifically to sell the loans off to the big banks right away, in furtherance of the larger scheme to dump fraudulent AAA-rated mortgage-backed securities on investors. If you had a pulse, they had a house to sell you.

As bad as Countrywide and all those lenders were, the banks that had sent them out to collect these crap loans were a hundred times worse. To sell the loans, the banks often dumped them into big tax-exempt buckets called REMICs, or real estate mortgage investment conduits. Each one of these Enron-ish, offshore-like real estate trusts spelled out exactly what kinds of loans were supposed to be in the pool, when they were to be collected, and how they were to be managed. In order to both preserve their tax-exempt status and deserve their AAA ratings, each of the loans in the pool had to have certain characteristics. The loans couldn't already be in default or foreclosure at the time they were sold to investors. If they were advertised as nice, safe, fixed-rate mortgages, they couldn't turn out to be high-interest junk loans. And, on the most basic level, the loans had to actually exist. In other words, if the trust stipulated that all the loans had to be collected by August 2005, the bank couldn't still be sticking in mortgages months later.

Yet that's exactly what the banks did. In one case handled by Jacksonville Area Legal Aid, a homeowner refinanced her house in 2005 but almost immediately got into trouble, going into default in December of that year. Yet somehow, this woman's loan was placed into a trust called Home Equity Loan Trust Series AE 2005-HE5 in January 2006—five months after the deadline for that particular trust. The loan was not only late, it was already in foreclosure—which means that, by definition, whoever the investors were in AE 2005-HE5 were getting shafted.

Why does stuff like this matter? Because when the banks put these pools together, they were telling their investors that they were putting their money into tidy collections of real, performing home loans. But frequently, the loans in the trust were complete shit. Or sometimes, the banks didn't even have all the loans they said they had. But the banks sold the securities based on these pools of mortgages as AAA-rated gold anyway.

In short, all of this was a scam—and that's why so many of these mortgages lack a true paper trail. Had these transfers been done legally, the actual mortgage note and detailed information about all of these transactions would have been passed from entity to entity each time the mortgage was sold. But in actual practice, the banks were often committing securities fraud (because many of the mortgages did not match the information in the prospectuses given to investors) and tax fraud (because the way the mortgages were collected and serviced often violated the strict procedures governing such investments). Having unloaded this diseased cargo onto their unsuspecting customers, the banks had no incentive to waste money keeping "proper" documentation of all these dubious transactions.

"You've already committed fraud once," says April Charney, an attorney with Jacksonville Area Legal Aid. "What do you have to lose?"

Sitting in the rocket docket, James Kowalski considers himself lucky to have won his first motion of the morning. To get the usually intractable Judge Soud to forestall a foreclosure is considered a real victory, and I later hear Kowalski getting props and attaboys from other foreclosure lawyers. In a great deal of these cases, in fact, the homeowners would have a pretty good chance of beating the rap, at least temporarily, if only they had lawyers fighting for them in court. But most of them don't. In fact, more than 90 percent of the cases that go through Florida foreclosure courts are unopposed. Either homeowners don't know they can fight their foreclosures, or they simply can't afford an attorney. These unopposed cases are the ones the banks know they'll win—which is why they don't sweat it if they take the occasional whipping.

That's why all these colorful descriptions of cases where foreclosure lawyers like Kowalski score in court are really just that—a little color. The meat of the foreclosure crisis is the unopposed cases; that's where the banks make their money. They almost always win those cases, no matter what's in the files.

This becomes evident after Kowalski leaves the room.

"Who's next?" Judge Soud says. He turns to Mark Kessler, the counsel for the big foreclosure mills. "Mark, you still got some?"

"I've got about three more, Judge," says Kessler.

Kessler then drops three greenish-brown files in front of Judge Soud, who spends no more than a minute or two glancing through each one. Then he closes the files and puts an end to the process by putting his official stamp on each foreclosure with an authoritative finality:

Kerchunk!

Kerchunk!

Kerchunk!

Each one of those kerchunks means another family on the street. There are no faces involved here, just beat-the-clock legal machinery. Watching Judge Soud plow through each foreclosure reminds me of the scene in *Fargo* where the villain played by Swedish character actor Peter Stormare pushes his victim's leg through a wood chipper with that trademark bored look on his face. Mechanized misery and brainless bureaucracy on the one hand, cash for the banks on the other.

What's sad is that most Americans who have an opinion about the foreclosure crisis don't give a damn about all the fraud involved. They don't care that these mortgages wouldn't have been available in the first place if the banks hadn't found a way to sell oregano as weed to pension funds and insurance companies. They don't care that the Countrywides of the world pushed borrowers who qualified for safer fixed-rate loans into far more dangerous adjustable-rate loans, because their brokers got bigger commissions for doing so. They don't care that in the rush to produce loans, people were sold houses that turned out to have flood damage or worse, and they certainly don't care that people were sold houses with inflated appraisals, which left them almost immediately underwater once housing prices started falling.

The way the banks tell it, it doesn't matter if they defrauded homeowners and investors and taxpayers alike to get these loans. All that matters is that a bunch of deadbeats aren't paying their fucking bills. "If you didn't pay your mortgage, you shouldn't be in your house—period," is how Walter Todd, portfolio manager at Greenwood Capital Associates, puts it. "People are getting upset about something that's just procedural."

Jamie Dimon, the CEO of JPMorgan, is even more succinct in dismissing the struggling homeowners that he and the other megabanks scammed before tossing them out into the street. "We're not evicting people who deserve to stay in their house," Dimon says.

There are two things wrong with this argument. (Well, more than two, actually, but let's just stick to the two big ones.)

The first reason is it simply isn't true. Many people who are being foreclosed on have actually paid their bills and followed all the instructions laid down by their banks. In some cases, a homeowner contacts the bank to say that he's having trouble paying his bill, and the bank offers him loan modification. But the bank tells him that in order to qualify for modification, he must first be delinquent on his mortgage. "They actually tell people to stop paying their bills for three months," says Parker.

The authorization gets recorded in what's known as the bank's

"contact database," which records every phone call or other commu-
nication with a homeowner. But no mention of it is entered into the
bank's "number history," which records only the payment record. When
the number history notes that the homeowner has missed three payments in a row, it has no way of knowing that the homeowner was given
permission to stop making payments. "One computer generates a default letter," says Kowalski. "Another computer contacts the credit bu-
reaus." At no time is there a human being looking at the entire picture.

Which means that homeowners can be foreclosed on for all sorts of
faulty reasons: misplaced checks, address errors, you name it. This inability of one limb of the foreclosure beast to know what the other limb
is doing is responsible for many of the horrific stories befalling homeowners across the country. Patti Parker, a local attorney in Jacksonville,
tells of a woman whose home was seized by Deutsche Bank two days
before Christmas. Months later, Deutsche came back and admitted that
they had made a mistake: they had repossessed the wrong property. In
another case that made headlines in Orlando, an agent for JPMorgan
mistakenly broke into a woman's house that wasn't even in foreclosure
and tried to change the locks. Terrified, the woman locked herself in her
bathroom and called 911. But in a profound expression of the state's re-
flexive willingness to side with the bad guys, the police made no arrest
in the case. Breaking and entering is not a crime, apparently, when it's
authorized by a bank.

The second reason the whole "they still owe the fucking money"
thing is bogus has to do with the changed incentives in the mortgage
game. In many cases, banks like JPMorgan are merely the servicers of
all these home loans, charged with collecting your money every month
and paying every penny of it into the trust, which is the real owner of
your mortgage. If you pay less than the whole amount, JPMorgan is
now obligated to pay the trust the remainder out of its own pocket.
When you fall behind, your bank falls behind, too. The only way it gets
off the hook is if the house is foreclosed on and sold.

That's what this foreclosure crisis is all about: fleeing the scene of
the crime. Add into the equation the fact that some of these big banks
were simultaneously betting big money against these mortgages—
Goldman Sachs being the prime example—and you can see that there

were heavy incentives across the board to push anyone in trouble over the cliff.

Things used to be different. Asked what percentage of struggling homeowners she used to be able to save from foreclosure in the days before securitization, Charney is quick to answer. "Most of them," she says. "I seldom came across a mortgage I couldn't work out."

In Judge Soud's court, I come across a shining example of this mindless rush to foreclosure when I meet Natasha Leonard, a single mother who bought a house in 2004 for $97,500. Right after closing on the home, Leonard lost her job. But when she tried to get a modification on the loan, the bank's offer was not helpful. "They wanted me to pay $1,000," she says. Which wasn't exactly the kind of modification she was hoping for, given that her original monthly payment was $840.

"You're paying $840, you ask for a break, and they ask you to pay $1,000?" I ask.

"Right," she says.

Leonard now has a job and could make some kind of reduced payment. But instead of offering loan modification, the bank's lawyers are in their fourth year of doggedly beating her brains out over minor technicalities in the foreclosure process. That's fine by the lawyers, who are collecting big fees. And there appears to be no human being at the bank who's involved enough to issue a sane decision to end the costly battle. "If there was a real client on the other side, maybe they could work something out," says Charney, who is representing Leonard. In this lunatic bureaucratic jungle of securitized home loans issued by transnational behemoths, the borrower-lender relationship can only go one of two ways: full payment or total war.

The extreme randomness of the system is exemplified by the last case I see in the rocket docket. While most foreclosures are unopposed, with homeowners not even bothering to show up in court to defend themselves, a few pro se defendants—people representing themselves—occasionally trickle in. At one point during Judge Soud's proceeding, a tallish blond woman named Shawnetta Cooper walks in with a confused look on her face. A recent divorcee delinquent in her payments, she has come to court today fully expecting to be foreclosed on by Wells Fargo. She sits down and takes a quick look around at the lawyers who are here to kick her out of her home. "The land has been in my family for four generations," she tells me later. "I don't want to be the one to lose it."

Judge Soud pipes up and inquires if there's a plaintiff's lawyer present; someone has to lop off this woman's head so the court can move on to the next case. But then something unexpected happens: it turns out that Kessler is supposed to be foreclosing on her today, but he doesn't have her folder. The plaintiff, technically, has forgotten to show up to court.

Just minutes before, I had watched what happens when defendants don't show up in court: kerchunk! The judge more or less automatically rules for the plaintiffs when the homeowner is a no-show. But when the plaintiff doesn't show, the judge is suddenly all mercy and forgiveness. Soud simply continues Cooper's case, telling Kessler to get his shit together and come back for another whack at her in a few weeks. Having done this, he dismisses everyone.

Stunned, Cooper wanders out of the courtroom looking like a person who has stepped up to the gallows expecting to be hanged, but has instead been handed a fruit basket and a new set of golf clubs.

I follow her out of the court, hoping to ask her about her case. But the sight of a journalist getting up to talk to a defendant in his kangaroo court clearly puts a charge into His Honor, and he immediately calls Cooper back into the conference room. Then, to the amazement of everyone present, he issues the following speech:

"This young man," he says, pointing at me, "is a reporter for *Rolling Stone*. It is your privilege to talk to him if you want." He pauses. "It is also your privilege to not talk to him if you want."

I stare at the judge, openmouthed. Here's a woman who still has to come back to this guy's court to find out if she can keep her home, and the judge's admonition suggests that she may run the risk of pissing him off if she talks to a reporter. Worse, about an hour later, April Charney, the lawyer who accompanied me to court, receives an e-mail from the judge actually threatening her with contempt for bringing a stranger to his court. Noting that "we ask that anyone other than a lawyer remain in the lobby," Judge Soud admonishes Charney that "your unprofessional conduct and apparent authorization that the reporter could pursue a property owner immediately out of Chambers into the hallway for an interview, may very well be sited [*sic*] for possible contempt in the future."

Let's leave aside for a moment that Charney never said a word to me about speaking to Cooper. And let's overlook entirely the fact that the judge can't spell the word "cited." The key here isn't this individual judge—it's the notion that these hearings are not and should not be entirely public. Quite clearly, foreclosure is meant to be neither seen nor heard.*

After Soud's outburst, Cooper quietly leaves the court. Once out of sight of the judge, she shows me her file. It's not hard to find the fraud in the case. For starters, the assignment of mortgage is autographed by a notorious robo-signer—John Kennerty, who gave a deposition this summer admitting that he signed as many as 150 documents a day for Wells Fargo. In Cooper's case, the document with Kennerty's signature on it places the date on which Wells Fargo obtained the mortgage as May 5, 2010. The trouble is, the bank bought the loan from Wachovia—a bank that went out of business in 2008. All of which is interesting, because in her file, it states that Wells Fargo sued Cooper for foreclosure on February 22, 2010. In other words, the bank foreclosed on Cooper three months before it obtained her mortgage from a nonexistent company.

There are other types of grift and outright theft in the file. As is typical in many foreclosure cases, Cooper is being charged by the bank for numerous attempts to serve her with papers. But a booming industry has grown up around fraudulent process servers; companies will claim they made dozens of attempts to serve homeowners, when in fact they made just one or none at all. Who's going to check? The process servers

---

*This ridiculous incident resulted in action by the ACLU and a number of other groups, including the Florida Association of Broadcasters, the Florida Society of News Editors, the Florida Press Association, the *Florida Times-Union* newspaper, and the First Amendment Foundation. On November 15, 2010, the group sent a letter to Florida Supreme Court judge Charles Canady to complain about rocket docket judges restricting access to their courts. Judge Canady responded two days later with an order directing judges across the state to make all courtrooms open to the public. "Today I have sent to the chief judges of Florida's twenty judicial circuits a supervisory memorandum . . . setting forth my administrative directive on this matter. Under that directive, the chief judges shall ensure that the judges they supervise and the staff who report to those judges, as well as bailiffs and employees of the clerks of court, are not violating the rights of Floridians by improperly closing judicial proceedings to the public."

cover up the crime using the same tactic as the lenders, saying they lost the original summons. From 2000 to 2006, there were a total of 1,031 "affidavits of lost summons" here in Duval County; in the past two years, by contrast, more than 4,000 have been filed.

Cooper's file contains a total of $371 in fees for process service, including one charge of $55 for an attempt to serve process on an "unknown tenant." But Cooper's house is owner occupied—she doesn't even have a tenant, she tells me with a shrug. If Mark Kessler had had his shit together in court today, Cooper would not only be out on the street, she'd be paying for that attempt to serve papers to her nonexistent tenant.

Cooper's case perfectly summarizes what the foreclosure crisis is all about. Her original loan was made by Wachovia, a bank that blew itself up in 2008 speculating in the mortgage market. It was then transferred to Wells Fargo, a megabank that was handed some $50 billion in public assistance to help it acquire the corpse of Wachovia. And who else benefited from that $50 billion in bailout money? Billionaire Warren Buffett and his Berkshire Hathaway fund, which happens to be a major shareholder in Wells Fargo. It was Buffett's vice chairman, Charles Munger, who recently told America that it should "thank God" that the government bailed out banks like the one he invests in, while people who have fallen on hard times—that is, homeowners like Shawnetta Cooper—should "suck it in and cope."

Look: it's undeniable that many of the people facing foreclosure bear some responsibility for the crisis. Some borrowed beyond their means. Some even borrowed knowing they would never be able to pay off their debt, either hoping to flip their houses right away or taking on mortgages with low initial teaser rates without bothering to think of the future. The culture of take-for-yourself-now, let-someone-else-pay-later wasn't completely restricted to Wall Street. It penetrated all the way down to the individual consumer, who in some cases was a knowing accomplice in the bubble mess.

But many of these homeowners are just ordinary Joes who had no idea what they were getting into. Some were pushed into dangerous loans when they qualified for safe ones. Others were told not to worry about future jumps in interest rates because they could just refinance down the road, or discovered that the value of their homes had been overinflated by brokers looking to pad their commissions. And that's not even accounting for the fact that most of this credit wouldn't have been available in the first place without the Ponzi-like bubble scheme cooked up by Wall Street, about which the average homeowner knew nothing—hell, even the average U.S. senator didn't know about it.

At worst, these ordinary homeowners were stupid or uninformed—while the banks that lent them the money are guilty of committing a bald-faced crime on a grand scale. These banks robbed investors and conned homeowners, blew themselves up chasing the fraud, then begged the taxpayers to bail them out. And bail them out we did: we ponied up billions to help Wells Fargo buy Wachovia, paid Bank of America to buy Merrill Lynch, and watched as the Fed opened up special facilities to buy up the assets in defective mortgage trusts at inflated prices. And after all that effort by the state to buy back these phony assets so the thieves could all stay in business and keep their bonuses, what did the banks do? They put their foot on the foreclosure gas pedal and stepped up the effort to kick people out of their homes as fast as possible, before the world caught on to how these loans were made in the first place.

Why don't the banks want us to see the paperwork on all these mortgages? Because the documents represent a death sentence for them. According to the rules of the mortgage trusts, a lender like Bank of America, which controls all the Countrywide loans, is required by law to buy back from investors every faulty loan the crooks at Countrywide ever issued. Think about what that would do to Bank of America's bottom line the next time you wonder why they're trying so hard to rush these loans into someone else's hands.

When you meet people who are losing their homes in this foreclosure crisis, they almost all have the same look of deep shame and anguish. Nowhere else on the planet is it such a crime to be down on your luck, even if you were put there by some of the world's richest banks, which continue to rake in record profits purely because they got a big fat handout from the government. That's why one banker

CEO after another keeps going on TV to explain that despite their own deceptive loans and fraudulent paperwork, the real problem is these deadbeat homeowners who won't pay their fucking bills. And that's why most people in this country are so ready to buy that explanation. Because in America, it's far more shameful to owe money than it is to steal it.

NOTE ON SOURCES

Much of the information in this book relies upon interviews with industry professionals, government regulators, and members of Congress and their staff. Most of those people are named in the text, but a few are not. In most instances the use of anonymous sources is incidental—in the "Hot Potato" chapter, for instance, the characters "Andy" and "Miklos" are describing general industry practices and the decision to keep their identities anonymous was made strictly with the aim of protecting them from future professional difficulties. Similarly, there were sources in the chapter "The Outsourced Highway" whose employers would certainly be unhappy if they were aware that one of their own was talking to me, despite the fact that most of the information I got from those sources was very general in nature and not terribly sensitive.

Because information is so valuable in the financial services industry, being known as someone who talks to reporters can be fatal to the career of a young banker or trader; therefore, there were a number of occasions in the book when I kept identities secret solely to allow those sources to feel comfortable being candid in their explanations of how their businesses work. In almost every circumstance, from the commodities chapter where I spoke with commodities traders, to the mortgage chapter where I spoke to people like Andy and Miklos who worked on billion-dollar mortgage deals, to the Goldman Sachs chapter where I spoke with hedge fund managers and traders who had done business with that bank, the information I was after was about general processes, i.e., how things work in these businesses on a day-to-day basis. In only one part of the book, at the end of the "Hot Potato" chapter, where I talk about AIG, did I rely upon anonymous sources to provide new information about previously unreported material.

In that section, my sources were people who were involved, at a high level, with the negotiations to keep AIG's subsidiary insurance companies solvent and prevent their seizure by state insurance departments. In the text I tried to emphasize that what I'm reporting in the book is the point of view of these particular actors in the story, who perceived that some of the counterparties to AIG's CDS business may have been using the threat of massive collateral calls to AIG's securities-lending business (which might have caused a widespread "Main Street" disaster involving thousands of personal insurance policies) as a lever to force AIG, and later on the Federal Reserve, to pay up. One of those sources, Eric Dinallo, the former head of the New York State Insurance Department, is named. But I had other high-ranking sources telling me a similar story. There are doubtless others who were involved in the AIG bailout who perceived things differently. But it is a fact that key actors in those events *did* perceive things in the way they are reported here, and I believe that is significant because it gets to the larger point in the book—that the responsibility for maintaining order and financial stability in our society has at times been transferred into the hands of private financial interests whom even top government officials believe to be capable of holding ordinary taxpayers hostage for profit.

Additionally, I relied in certain chapters on a number of excellent books. In "The Biggest Asshole in the Universe," for instance, I drew from some key sources, including William Fleckenstein's dark and funny *Greenspan's Bubbles,* Frederick Sheehan's *Panderer to Power,* and of course Greenspan's own unintentionally hilarious auto-hagiography, *The Age of Turbulence.* In "The Great American Bubble Machine" I appealed to John Kenneth Galbraith's *The Great Crash 1929*, while in the "Hot Potato" chapter I drew from books like Robert Shiller's *The Subprime Solution* and Bill Bamber and Andrew Spencer's *Bear Trap*. And a dog-eared galley of my good friend Nomi Prins's book *It Takes a Pillage* has been an important source for me throughout.

The sourcing for the rest of the book is mostly self-explanatory, relying upon interviews with named sources or publicly reported material.

PHOTO: ROBIN HOLLAND

MATT TAIBBI is a contributing editor for *Rolling Stone* and the author of four previous books, including the *New York Times* bestseller *The Great Derangement*. He lives in Jersey City, New Jersey.